Houghton Mifflin Reading

Practice Book

Level 5

Practice Book

Illustration:
Tony Caldwell 28, 33-34, 85, 115, 119, 121, 139, 162-163, 165-166, 199, 202, 213, 215, 224, 230, 232-236, 244, 245; Moffitt Cecil 5, 25, 35, 90, 116-117, 120, 280, 291, 292, 330, 337; Dan Clifford 66, 73, 145, 149, 164, 193, 220, 232, 241, 276-277, 289-290, 311-313, 320; Sue Dahl 10, 21-22, 29, 45, 48-49, 91, 124-125, 136, 203, 204, 207, 208; Michael DiGiorgio 12, 26-27, 38, 51, 349, 360, 374-375, 379, 381-383, 397, 400; Leslie Evans 1-2, 8, 13, 20, 61-62, 75-77, 97-98, 101-102, 104, 127, 132, 137-138, 140-141, 153, 160-161, 168-169, 179, 182, 185, 218-219, 226, 233, 350-351, 369-371, 373, 377-378, 387, 389, 391; Alexander Farquharson 9, 14, 44, 63, 69, 72, 74, 81, 86-87, 103, 106-107, 147-148, 167, 170, 183, 188, 282, 293, 302, 308, 310, 318-319, 321, 323, 367, 385-386, 388, 392-394; Simon Galkin 68, 83, 88, 94, 105, 150, 177-178, 186, 197, 206, 217, 221, 237, 258; Doug Knutson 65, 93, 142-143; Dan Krovatin 6-7, 41, 108-109, 113-114, 123, 159, 174, 176, 180, 184, 283-285, 294-295, 298, 314, 328; Katie Lee 345-347, 352, 356-357, 359, 363; Kristina Rodanas 36, 43, 52, 55, 67, 155, 192, 223, 227, 228, 231, 238, 242, 246, 249, 253-254, 261, 269-273, 275, 278, 286-287, 306-307, 326-327, 329, 353, 355, 364-366, 372; Nancy Rodden 40, 42, 59-60, 70, 89, 158, 172-173, 200-201, 251, 256-257, 299, 303-305, 315, 322, 333-334, 336. Dictionary art by Michael DiGiorgio. Notebooks and paper by Nathan Jarvis.

Photography:
Photographs by Ralph J. Brunke Photography

Printed in the U.S.A.

ISBN: 978-0-547-19543-8

15 16 17 0928 17 16 15 14
4500465679

Contents

Contents

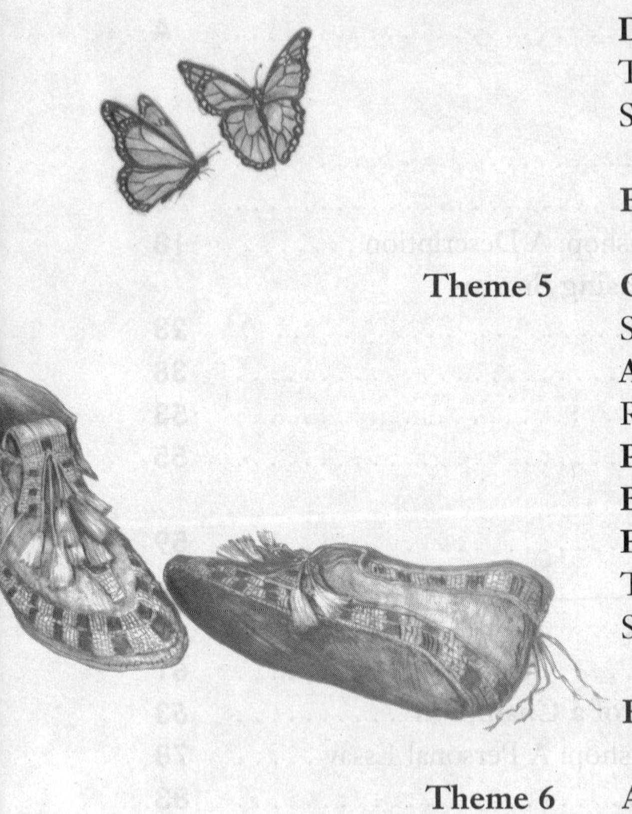

Name ______________________________

Strategy Workshop

As you listen to the story "The Pumpkin Box," by Angela Johnson, you will stop from time to time to do some activities on these practice pages. These activities will help you think about different strategies that can help you read better. After completing each activity, you will discuss what you've written with your classmates and talk about how to use these strategies.

Remember, strategies can help you become a better reader. Good readers

- use strategies whenever they read
- use different strategies before, during, and after reading
- think about how strategies will help them

Name ______________________________

Strategy 1: Predict/Infer

Use this strategy before and during reading to help make predictions about what happens next or what you're going to learn.

Here's how to use the Predict/Infer Strategy:

1. Think about the title, the illustrations, and what you have read so far.
2. Tell what you think will happen next—or what you will learn. Thinking about what you already know on the topic may help.
3. Try to figure out things the author does not say directly.

Listen as your teacher begins "The Pumpkin Box." When your teacher stops, complete the activity to show that you understand how to predict what the pumpkin box is.

Think about the story and respond to the question below.

What do you think the pumpkin box is?

____

____

____

____

As you continue listening to the story, think about whether your prediction was right. You might want to change your prediction or write a new one below.

____

____

____

____

____

Name ______________________________

Strategy 2: Phonics/Decoding

Use this strategy during reading when you come across a word you don't know.

Here's how to use the Phonics/Decoding Strategy:

1. Look carefully at the word.
2. Look for word parts you know and think about the sounds for the letters.
3. Blend the sounds to read the words.
4. Ask yourself: Is this a word I know? Does it make sense in what I am reading?
5. If not, ask yourself: What else can I try? Should I look in a dictionary?

Listen as your teacher continues the story. When your teacher stops, use the Phonics/Decoding Strategy.

Now write down the steps you used to decode the word *munching*.

____

____

____

____

____

____

____

____

____

____

____

Remember to use this strategy whenever you are reading and come across a word that you don't know.

Name ______________________________

Strategy 3: Monitor/Clarify

Use this strategy during reading whenever you're confused about what you are reading.

Here's how to use the Monitor/Clarify Strategy:

- Ask yourself if what you're reading makes sense—or if you are learning what you need to learn.
- If you don't understand something, reread, use the illustrations, or read ahead to see if that helps.

Listen as your teacher continues the story. When your teacher stops, complete the activity to show that you understand how to figure out how the pumpkin box got underground.

Think about the pumpkin box and respond below.

1. Describe the pumpkin box.

____

____

____

2. Can you tell from listening to the story how the pumpkin box got there? Why or why not?

____

____

____

____

3. How can you find out why the pumpkin box was buried in the ground?

____

____

____

____

Name ______________________________

Strategy 4: Question

Use this strategy during and after reading to ask questions about important ideas in the story.

Here's how to use the Question Strategy:

- Ask yourself questions about important ideas in the story.
- Ask yourself if you can answer these questions.
- If you can't answer the questions, reread and look for answers in the text. Thinking about what you already know and what you've read in the story may help you.

Listen as your teacher continues the story. Then complete the activity to show that you understand how to ask yourself questions about important ideas in the story.

Think about the story and respond below.

Write a question you might ask yourself at this point in the story.

____

____

____

____

____

____

____

____

____

____

____

If you can't answer your question now, think about it while you listen to the rest of the story.

Name ______________________________

Strategy 5: Evaluate

Use this strategy during and after reading to help you form an opinion about what you read.

Here's how to use the Evaluate Strategy:

- Tell whether or not you think this story is entertaining and why.
- Is the writing clear and easy to understand?
- This is a realistic fiction story. Did the author make the characters believable and interesting?

Listen as your teacher continues the story. When your teacher stops, complete the activity to show that you are thinking of how you feel about what you are reading and why you feel that way.

Think about the story and respond below.

1. Tell whether or not you think this story is entertaining and why.

____

____

____

____

2. Is the writing clear and easy to understand?

____

____

____

____

3. This is a realistic fiction story. Did the author make the characters interesting and believable?

____

____

____

____

Name ______________________________

Strategy 6: Summarize

Use this strategy after reading to summarize what you read.

Here's how to use the Summarize Strategy:

- Think about the characters.
- Think about where the story takes place.
- Think about the problem in the story and how the characters solve it.
- Think about what happens in the beginning, middle, and end of the story.

Think about the story you just listened to. Complete the activity to show that you understand how to identify important story parts that will help you summarize the story.

Think about the story and respond to the questions below:

1. Who is the main character?

____

____

____

2. Where does the story take place?

____

____

____

3. What is the problem and how is it resolved?

____

____

____

Now use this information to summarize the story for a partner.

Name ______________________________

Nature's Fury

After reading each selection, complete the chart below and on the next page to show what you discovered.

	What is the setting or settings for the action or descriptions in the selection?	What dangers do people face in the selection?
Earthquake Terror		
Eye of the Storm		
Volcanoes		

Name ______________________________

Nature's Fury

After reading each selection, complete the chart to show what you discovered.

	What warnings or events happen before nature's fury occurs in the selection?	What did you learn about an example of nature's fury in the selection?
Earthquake Terror		
Eye of the Storm		
Volcanoes		

What advice would you give others about the different kinds of nature's fury featured in this theme?

____

____

Name ______________________

A Scientist's Report

Use the words in the box to complete the scientist's report on the Magpie Island earthquake.

Vocabulary

- shuddered
- debris
- undulating
- fault
- jolt

Earthquake Report

Magpie Island lies near the San Andreas ______________________, so it was susceptible to the recent earthquake. On a cloudless day, witnesses reported hearing a sound like thunder and feeling a ______________________ as the earth started to shake. Next, the ground below their feet ______________________ and heaved. Trees began to fall with a forceful impact. As the earthquake reached its peak, the ground began ______________________ in a continuous motion.

After the shaking stopped, people examined the devastation that the earthquake had caused. ______________________ lay everywhere. The upheaval had struck a great blow to the island.

Name ______________________________

Event Map

Record in this Event Map the main story events in the order in which they occurred.

Page 30

At first Moose listens. Then he barks and paces back and forth as if he senses ______________________________

Pages 30–31

After Jonathan puts the leash on Moose, they all slowly start to ______________________________.

Pages 32–33

Jonathan and Abby hear a strange noise. At first Jonathan thinks it is thunder or hunters. Then suddenly he realizes they are ______________________________

Page 35

Abby screams and falls. As Jonathan lunges forward, he tries to catch Abby. Then he shouts, ______________________________

Pages 36–37

Jonathan sees the huge redwood tree sway back and forth. Then ______________________________

Name ______________________________

True or False?

Read each sentence. Write T if the sentence is true, or F if the sentence is false. If a sentence is false, correct it to make it true.

1. _____ Jonathan and Abby's parents had left the island to go grocery shopping.

   ____

2. _____ Moose became restless because he could feel the earthquake coming.

   ____

3. _____ Jonathan thought the first rumblings of the earthquake were distant thunder.

   ____

4. _____ Jonathan knew what to do because he had been in an earthquake before.

   ____

5. _____ When the giant redwood began to fall, Moose dragged Jonathan to safety.

   ____

6. _____ Jonathan and Abby found shelter in a large ditch.

   ____

7. _____ In a panic, Moose ran off and didn't come back.

   ____

8. _____ As quickly as it had begun, the earthquake stopped and the woods were silent.

   ____

Name ______________________________

Mapping the Sequence

Read this passage. Then complete the activity on page 7.

Rapids Ahead!

Alison scanned the river nervously. She had already endured two sets of violent rapids. Each time, she had grasped the ropes of the raft so hard that her knuckles turned white. Luckily, the guide on her raft was strong and skilled. "Relax, Alison," Anushka had smiled when the trip had begun three hours earlier. "Rafting is a blast, once you get the hang of it."

During the first hour on the river, Anushka had taught Alison how to paddle on one side to make the raft go in the opposite direction. She had instructed Alison on what to do if the raft flipped or if she were tossed out. "Don't fight the current," Anushka had said. "Let it carry you downstream as you swim for the shore."

Six months earlier, when Alison's parents had proposed a whitewater rafting trip down the Snake River, Alison said, "No way." Her brother Zack was thrilled, though, so Alison's parents signed all four of them up for a seven-day run. So far, the trip was as bad as Alison had expected.

"Rapids ahead. Hold on!" Anushka said. Alison's stomach knotted as the raft pitched forward with the current. "Paddle left!" Anushka shouted. As Alison's paddle hit the water, the bow of the raft hit a boulder and shot into the air. Alison shut her eyes as icy water drenched her.

When she opened her eyes, Anushka was gone. In a panic, Alison scanned the rapids. "Anushka!" she screamed. Then she saw her. Anushka was making her way to shore, feet first, letting the current do the work. "It's up to me now," Alison said to herself. She paddled left, then right, steering between the rocks. She was amazed that she could control it. Left. Right. Left again. Now Anushka was on the bank, shouting directions over the roar of the river. Alison managed to nose the raft into an eddy and a moment later, onto the shore.

"Great job, Alison!" Anushka grinned. "You really kept your head out there!" Alison beamed. Maybe this trip would be all right after all.

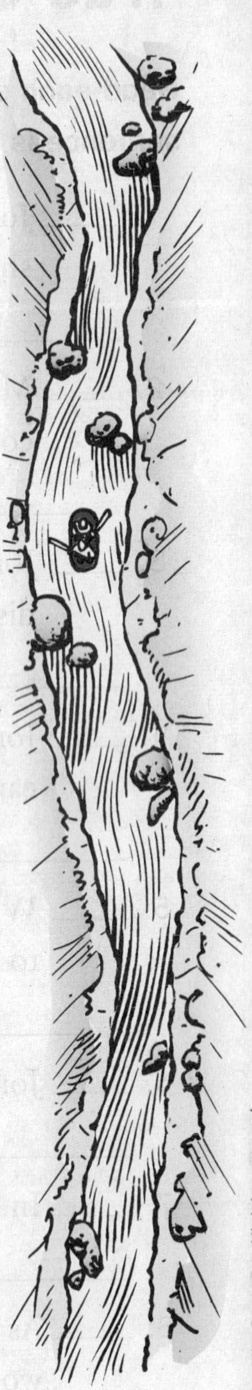

Name ______________________________

Mapping the Sequence continued

Write each story event from page 6 in the sequence map below. Put the events in order.

- Alison successfully guides the raft to shore.
- Anushka tells Alison to relax.
- The raft hits a boulder and Anushka falls overboard.
- Anushka teaches Alison how to steer the raft.
- Alison's parents suggest a raft trip on the Snake River.

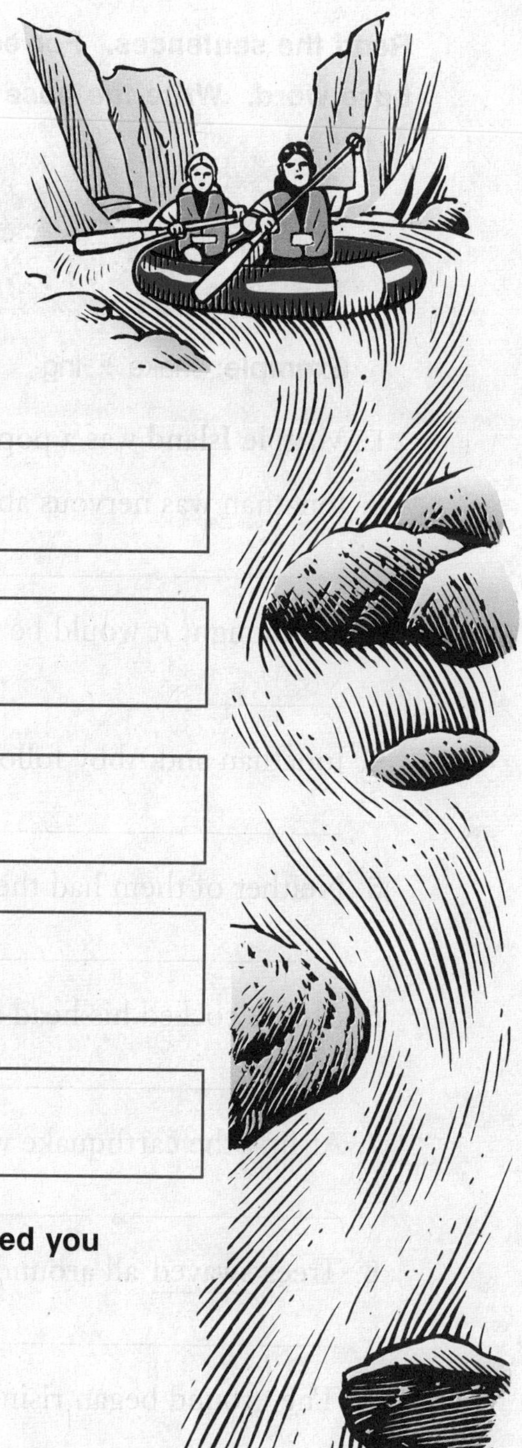

Now go back to the passage. Circle the words that helped you understand the following:

- when the family plans the trip
- when Anushka tells Alison that rafting is fun
- when Anushka teaches Alison some basic rafting techniques
- whether Anushka's spill occurs during the first, second, or third set of rapids that she and Alison encounter

Name ______________________

Getting to Base

Read the sentences. For each underlined word, identify the base word. Write the base word and the ending.

Example: shake + -ing

1. Magpie Island was a popular place for hiking.
2. Jonathan was nervous about staying in such an isolated place.
   ____
3. He thought it would be safer to go back to their trailer.
   ____
4. Jonathan and Abby followed the trail past blackberry bushes.
   ____
5. Neither of them had the slightest idea how the day would end.
   ____
6. Moose cocked his head and began sniffing the ground.
   ____
7. At first the earthquake was a thunderous noise in the distance.
   ____
8. Trees swayed all around Jonathan and Abby.
   ____
9. The ground began rising and falling like ocean waves.
   ____
10. Abby cried for Jonathan to come help her. ______________________

Name ________________________________

Short Vowels

Remember that a short vowel sound is usually spelled by one vowel and followed by a consonant sound. This is the **short vowel pattern.** These vowels usually spell short vowel sounds:

/ă/ *a* /ĕ/ *e* /ĭ/ *i* /ŏ/ *o* /ŭ/ *u*

► The short vowel sounds in the starred words do not have the usual short vowel spelling patterns. The /ĕ/ sound is spelled *ea* in *breath* and *deaf.* The /ŭ/ sound is spelled *ou* in *tough* and *rough.*

Write each Spelling Word under its vowel sound.

/ă/ Sound

____
____

/ĕ/ Sound

____
____
____
____
____

/ĭ/ Sound

____
____
____
____

/ŏ/ Sound

____
____

/ŭ/ Sound

____
____
____
____
____
____
____

Spelling Words

1. bunk
2. staff
3. dock
4. slept
5. mist
6. bunch
7. swift
8. stuck
9. breath*
10. tough*
11. fond
12. crush
13. grasp
14. dwell
15. fund
16. ditch
17. split
18. swept
19. deaf*
20. rough*

Name ______________________

Spelling Spree

Letter Math Add and subtract letters from the words below to make Spelling Words. Write the new words.

1. b + dunk – d = ____________
2. sl + kept – k = ____________
3. f + pond – p = ____________
4. burn – r + ch = ____________
5. st + duck – d = ____________
6. dw + shell – sh = ____________
7. cr + mush – m = ____________
8. d + rock – r = ____________
9. m + wrist – wr = ____________
10. sw + lift – l = ____________
11. spl + bit – b = ____________
12. t + cough – c = ____________
13. d + leaf – l = ____________
14. gr + clasp – cl = ____________

Spelling Words

1. bunk
2. staff
3. dock
4. slept
5. mist
6. bunch
7. swift
8. stuck
9. breath*
10. tough*
11. fond
12. crush
13. grasp
14. dwell
15. fund
16. ditch
17. split
18. swept
19. deaf*
20. rough*

Phrase Fillers Write the Spelling Word that best completes each phrase.

15. to take a deep ____________
16. as ____________ as sandpaper
17. to put money into a ____________
18. to dig a ____________
19. ____________ with a broom
20. to join a company's ____________

Name ______________________________

Proofreading and Writing

Proofreading **Circle the five misspelled Spelling Words in this newspaper article. Then write each word correctly.**

MAGPIE ISLAND — An earthquake struck yesterday, and children are reported to be stranded in the island campground. No one on the campground's staf was there at the time. An early report said that "a bunch of kids" were stouk on the island. However, it turns out that only two children are there. Rescuers in a boat are reported to be nearing the island's dok. A heavy missed has slowed the rescue effort. One rescuer said, "It's been touph going so far, but we'll get them off the island safely."

1. ______________ 4. ______________
2. ______________ 5. ______________
3. ______________

Spelling Words

1. bunk
2. staff
3. dock
4. slept
5. mist
6. bunch
7. swift
8. stuck
9. breath*
10. tough*
11. fond
12. crush
13. grasp
14. dwell
15. fund
16. ditch
17. split
18. swept
19. deaf*
20. rough*

Write a Description If you were to go to the scene of an earthquake right after it happened, what do you think you would find? What would you see? Whom would you meet?

On a separate piece of paper, write a description of the scene you might encounter. Use Spelling Words from the list.

Name ______________________________

Synonym Shakeup

Read the definition of each thesaurus word and its synonyms. Then rewrite the numbered sentences using a different synonym for each underlined word.

shake *verb* To move to and fro with short, quick movements. *The branch shook as the eagle flew off.*

quake To shake or vibrate, as from shock or lack of balance. *With all the students stamping their feet, the gym floor quaked.*

shiver To shake or tremble without control. *She was shivering when she came out of the swimming pool.*

quiver To shake with a slight vibrating motion. *I felt the horse quiver as I patted its leg.*

noise *noun* A sound that is loud, unpleasant, or unexpected. *I was awakened by a noise in the alley.*

crash A loud noise, as of a sudden impact or collapse. *They heard a crash of thunder.*

racket A loud, unpleasant noise. *The students made a racket while tuning their instruments.*

thud A heavy, dull sound. *Jeff dropped his books with a thud.*

1. Soon after the ground began to shake, the children heard the noise of a deer leaping from the bushes.

____

____

2. Jonathan began to shake from cold and fear, listening to the noise of the crows.

____

____

3. Abby's lip began to shake as she heard the noise of running footsteps.

____

Name ______________________________

Sensing Danger

Kinds of Sentences There are four kinds of sentences:

1. A declarative sentence tells something and ends with a period.
   Earthquakes occur along fault lines in the earth.
2. An interrogative sentence asks a question and ends with a question mark.
   Can earthquakes be predicted?
3. An imperative sentence gives a request or an order and usually ends with a period.
   Protect your head in an earthquake.
4. An exclamatory sentence expresses strong feeling and ends with an exclamation mark.
   How frightening an earthquake is!

Add the correct punctuation mark to each sentence below. Then write what kind of sentence each one is.

1. Why is the dog barking_____
   ____
2. Put him on his leash_____
   ____
3. Some animals can sense a coming earthquake_____
   ____
4. How frightened I am_____
   ____
5. The earth has stopped shaking at last_____
   ____

Name ______________________________

On Vacation

Subjects and Predicates Every sentence has a subject. It tells whom or what the sentence is about. The complete subject includes all the words in the subject, and the simple subject is the main word or words in the complete subject.

Every sentence has a predicate too. It tells what the subject is or does. The complete predicate includes all the words in the predicate, and the simple predicate is the main word or words in the complete predicate.

Draw a slash mark (/) between the complete subject and the complete predicate in the sentences below. Then circle the simple subject and underline the simple predicate.

1. The whole family travels in our new camper.
2. Everybody helps to pitch the tent under a tree.
3. They will use a compass on their hike.
4. A good fire is difficult to build.
5. The smell of cooking is delicious to the hungry campers.

Name ______________________________

Sentence Combining

A **compound subject** is made up of two or more simple subjects that have the same predicate. Use a connecting word such as ***and*** or ***or*** to join the simple subjects.

Jonathan yelled. **Abby** yelled. **Jonathan and Abby** yelled.

Combine two simple subjects into one compound subject, as shown above, to make your writing clearer and less choppy.

A **compound predicate** is made up of two or more simple predicates that have the same subject. Use a connecting word such as ***and*** or ***or*** to join the simple predicates.

Moose **barked**. Moose **howled**. Moose **barked and howled**.

Combine simple predicates into compound predicates, as shown above, to make your writing smoother.

Suppose Jonathan wrote a draft of a letter to his aunt about his vacation. Revise his letter by combining sentences. Each new sentence will have either a compound subject or a compound predicate. Only Jonathan's first sentence will remain the same.

What an exciting vacation we had! Mom broke her ankle. Mom had to go to the hospital. Abby stayed on the island. I stayed on the island during an earthquake. Moose barked. Moose warned us. The ground shook. The ground rolled. Have you ever been in an earthquake? Has Uncle Adam ever been in an earthquake?

____

____

____

____

____

Name ______________________________

Writing an Article

Jonathan and Abby Palmer experience firsthand an unforgettable event — the terror of an earthquake. Imagine you are a writer for your local newspaper. Use the chart below to gather details for an article about an interesting or unusual event at your school, in your neighborhood, or in your town. Answer these questions: What happened? Who was involved? When, where, and why did this event occur? How did it happen?

Who?
What?
When?
Where?
Why?
How?

Name ______________________________

Adding Details

A good writer uses details to explain what happened and to bring an event to life. Read the following article that might have been written about the earthquake. Then rewrite it on the lines below, adding details from the list to improve the article.

Details

- twelve-year-old
- in the woods
- giant redwood
- one-hundred-year-old
- for several weeks
- under a fallen redwood
- afternoon
- to the mainland
- on Magpie Island
- his six-year-old sister

Quake Rocks Campground

A powerful earthquake rocked an isolated campground in California yesterday. No serious injuries were reported. Some trees were uprooted, and a bridge was destroyed. Two members of the Palmer family, Jonathan and his sister Abby, were trapped during the quake.

"I was very scared," said Jonathan Palmer. "I'm just glad no one got hurt. My sister only had a minor cut."

The campground will be closed to visitors until the debris is cleared and the bridge is repaired.

____

____

____

____

____

____

____

____

____

____

Name ____________________________________

Revising Your Description

Reread your description. What do you need to make it better? Use this page to help you decide. Put a checkmark in the box for each sentence that describes what you have written.

Rings the Bell!

- ☐ My description is well organized and easy to follow.
- ☐ All the details are important and in order.
- ☐ My description has a lively style.
- ☐ My description has a strong ending.
- ☐ There are almost no mistakes.

Getting Stronger

- ☐ My description could be easier to follow.
- ☐ Some details are not important to the description.
- ☐ My word choices could be more lively.
- ☐ The ending doesn't make the description feel finished.
- ☐ There are a few mistakes.

Try Harder

- ☐ My description is not easy to follow.
- ☐ Many details are not important.
- ☐ My word choices are not interesting.
- ☐ There are a lot of mistakes.

Name ______________________

Writing Complete Sentences

Make each incomplete sentence complete. Change words or add extra words if you need to.

1. Being a photographer
2. Photographing nature
3. Lightning flashing in the sky
4. Chasing storms
5. Tornadoes in the distance
6. The black funnel is impressive, even far away.
7. Planes in storms
8. A bumpy ride
9. Dangerous to be out in some storms
10. Don't stand under a tree when there's lightning.

Name ______________________________

Spelling Words

Words Often Misspelled Look for familiar spelling patterns to help you remember how to spell the Spelling Words on this page. Think carefully about the parts that you find hard to spell in each word.

Write the missing letters and apostrophes in the Spelling Words below.

1. en ____ ____ ____ ____
2. c ____ ____ ____ ____ t
3. br ____ ____ ____ ____ t
4. th ____ ____ ____ ____ t
5. ev ____ ry
6. nin ____ ty
7. th ____ ____ r
8. th ____ ____ ____ re
9. th ____ r ____
10. th ____ ____ ____ ____ s
11. ____ ____ ow
12. ____ ____ ew
13. ____ ____ ____ lock
14. w ____ ____ ____ e
15. p ____ ____ ple

Study List **On a separate piece of paper, write each Spelling Word. Check your spelling against the words on the list.**

Spelling Words

1. enough
2. caught
3. brought
4. thought
5. every
6. ninety
7. their
8. they're
9. there
10. there's
11. know
12. knew
13. o'clock
14. we're
15. people

Name ______________________________

Spelling Spree

Word Clues **Write the Spelling Word that best fits each clue.**

1. the sum of eighty-nine and one
2. a contraction for describing what other people are doing
3. to be aware of a fact
4. a time-telling word
5. as much as is needed
6. a word for other people's belongings
7. took along
8. a contraction for "there is"

1. ______________ 5. ______________
2. ______________ 6. ______________
3. ______________ 7. ______________
4. ______________ 8. ______________

Spelling Words

1. enough
2. caught
3. brought
4. thought
5. every
6. ninety
7. their
8. they're
9. there
10. there's
11. know
12. knew
13. o'clock
14. we're
15. people

Word Addition **Write a Spelling Word by adding the beginning of the first word to the end of the second word.**

9. caution + fight — 9. ______________
10. we'll + more — 10. ______________
11. knight + flew — 11. ______________
12. peony + steeple — 12. ______________
13. even + wary — 13. ______________
14. them + cure — 14. ______________
15. think + bought — 15. ______________

Name ______________________________

Proofreading and Writing

Proofreading **Circle the five misspelled Spelling Words in this announcement. Then write each word correctly.**

The staff of the Science Museum is pleased to announce that our new Natural Disasters Hall will open to the public next Monday at nine oclock in the morning. We've put a lot of thaught into this exhibit, and we're sure that you'll enjoy it. Just about evry form of nature's fury is represented, from lightning to earthquakes to volcanoes. Even if you already kno a lot about the topic, we think you'll learn something new. We hope to see you their.

Spelling Words

1. enough
2. caught
3. brought
4. thought
5. every
6. ninety
7. their
8. they're
9. there
10. there's
11. know
12. knew
13. o'clock
14. we're
15. people

1. ____________ 4. ____________

2. ____________ 5. ____________

3. ____________

Write Song Titles **Pick five Spelling Words from the list. Then, for each one, make up a song title that includes the word and mentions some form of Nature's Fury.**

Name ______________________

Stormy Weather

Use words from the box to complete the diary entry below.

Vocabulary

- sizzling
- collide
- funnel clouds
- tornadoes
- lightning
- rotate
- jagged
- prairie
- severe

May 10, 2000
Dear Diary,

Today was by far the scariest day of my trip. Everything was fine as I crossed the border into Oklahoma. The highway stretched out over a ______________ that seemed to go on forever. As I looked into my rear-view mirror, I spotted some dense clouds forming behind me. "I hope they aren't ______________," I thought. Then I spotted a flash of ______________. The clouds started to ______________, slowly at first, and then faster and faster. A couple of ______________ were forming right before my eyes! I realized that a ______________ storm had formed behind me, and it was moving fast in my direction. The ______________ bolts of lightning were getting closer. One of the tornadoes lifted a tractor into the air, spun it around, and dropped it. I watched it ______________ with a shed on the ground. Lightning struck a dry bush behind me. It turned into a ______________ ball of flames.

Write a sentence to end the diary entry.

____

____

Name ______________________________

Selection Map

Fill in this selection map.

Pages 59–68

Page 59 Storm Chasing ______________________________

Page 60 Warren Faidley: Storm Chaser ______________________________

____

Page 64 What Happens to Warren's Photos After He Takes Them?

____

____

Page 65 Storm Seasons and Chasing ______________________________

____

Page 67 Chasing Tornadoes ______________________________

____

Pages 69–75

One Day in the Life of a Storm Chaser

Morning ______________________________

____

Afternoon ______________________________

____

Evening ______________________________

____

____

Name ______________________________

An Interview with Warren Faidley

The questions below can be used to interview Warren Faidley about his life and work. Write the answer Warren might give to each question.

What is your occupation? ______________________________

____

When did you first become interested in storms? Describe one of your early experiences with storms. ______________________________

____

What led you to become a professional storm chaser? ______________________________

____

____

____

____

How important is it for someone in your line of work to have a good knowledge of weather patterns? Why? ______________________________

____

____

____

What advice would you give a young person who wants to become a storm chaser? ______________________________

Name ______________________________

Eye of the Storm

Comprehension Skill Text Organization

Text Tracking

Read the article below. Then complete the activity on page 27.

Hurricane Basics

A hurricane is a powerful storm with swirling winds. Hurricanes form over water in tropical parts of the North Atlantic and North Pacific Oceans. Most hurricanes in these regions occur between June and November.

Rise of a Hurricane

A hurricane does not form all at once. First, areas of low pressure develop in ocean winds. These areas, called easterly waves, then grow into a tropical depression, where winds blow at up to 31 miles per hour. As the winds pick up speed, they become a tropical storm. Finally, when the winds reach 74 miles per hour or more, and the storm is 200 to 300 miles wide, it is considered a hurricane.

Path of Destruction

The great speed of a hurricane's winds can cause severe damage. A hurricane can destroy buildings and other property when it reaches land. The force of these winds can also create huge waves. The waves along with the heavy rains may cause flooding in rivers and low-lying coastal lands. Many hurricane deaths are the result of flooding. Because of the devastating power of hurricanes, meteorologists keep a close watch on the Pacific and Atlantic Oceans during hurricane season.

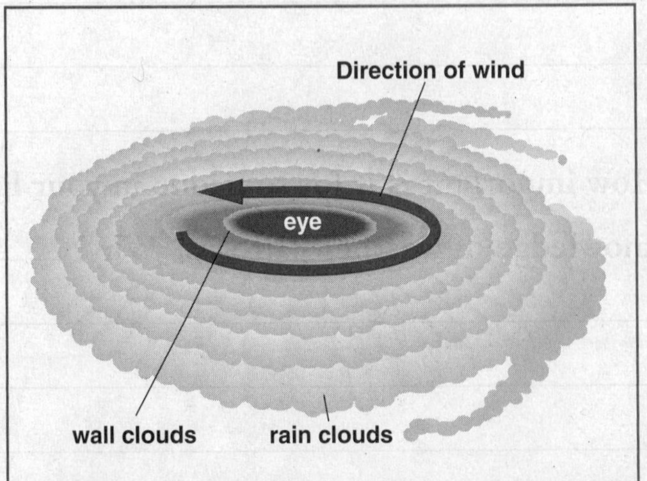

The winds of a hurricane rotate around the eye, which is an area of calm in the storm's center. Wall clouds surround the eye.

Name ______________________________

Text Tracking continued

Write words from the box to indicate the order in which these parts appear in the article on page 26. Then answer the questions.

caption graphic aid headings introduction

1. ______________________________
2. ______________________________
3. ______________________________
4. ______________________________
5. What is each paragraph about?
   Paragraph 1: ______________________________
   Paragraph 2: ______________________________
   Paragraph 3: ______________________________
6. Is the information in paragraph 2 organized by main idea and details, or by sequence of events? ______________________________
7. How is the information in paragraph 3 organized? ______________________________

Name ______________________________

Stormy Syllables

Write the underlined word using slash marks (/) between its syllables. Then write a new sentence that uses the underlined word.

1. The photographer changed her position to get a better shot of the storm.

   ____

2. A good photographer tries to capture the excitement of the moment.

   ____

3. Warren showed exciting videos of tornadoes. ______________

   ____

4. I wonder how she was able to get so close to the lightning bolt.

   ____

5. By rotating his body, he could follow the circular path of the tornado.

   ____

Name ______________________________

The /ā/, /ē/, and /ī/ Sounds

When you hear the /ā/ sound, think of the patterns *a*-consonant-*e*, *ai*, and *ay*. When you hear the /ē/ sound, think of the patterns *ea* and *ee*. When you hear the /ī/ sound, think of the patterns i-consonant-*e*, *igh*, and *i*.

/ā/	**fade claim stray**
/ē/	**leaf speech**
/ī/	**strike thigh sign**

► The long vowel sounds in the starred words have different spelling patterns. The /ē/ sound in *thief* and in *niece* is spelled *ie*. The /ī/ sound in *height* is spelled *eigh*.

Write each Spelling Word under its vowel sound.

/ā/	/ē/	/ī/
______	______	______
______	______	______
______	______	______
______	______	______
______	______	______
______	______	______
______		______

Spelling Words

1. speech
2. claim
3. strike
4. stray
5. fade
6. sign
7. leaf
8. thigh
9. thief*
10. height*
11. mild
12. waist
13. sway
14. beast
15. stain
16. fleet
17. stride
18. praise
19. slight
20. niece*

Name ______________________

Spelling Spree

Find a Rhyme For each sentence write a Spelling Word that rhymes with the underlined word and makes sense in the sentence.

1. On what day did you last see the ___________ cat?
2. It looks like the ___________ got washed out by the rain.
3. She liked to ___________ down the beach at low tide.
4. They swam out to meet the ___________ of ships.
5. How high on the ___________ did the ball hit you?
6. His ___________ asked for another piece of pie.
7. The police chief took credit for catching the ___________.
8. The young child liked ___________ food better than spicy food.

Spelling Words

1. speech
2. claim
3. strike
4. stray
5. fade
6. sign
7. leaf
8. thigh
9. thief*
10. height*
11. mild
12. waist
13. sway
14. beast
15. stain
16. fleet
17. stride
18. praise
19. slight
20. niece*

Crack the Code **Some Spelling Words have been written in the code below. Use the code to figure out each word. Then write the word correctly.**

CODE:	R	V	L	O	C	A	D	X	P	T	Y	Q	J	N	E	I	M
LETTER:	a	b	c	e	f	g	h	i	l	m	n	p	r	s	t	w	y

9. LPRXT ___________
10. IRXNE ___________
11. VORNE ___________
12. NQOOLD ___________
13. NXAY ___________
14. DOXADE ___________
15. NPXADE ___________
16. NIRM ___________
17. QJRXNO ___________
18. PORC ___________

Name ______________________________

Eye of the Storm

Spelling The /ā/, /ē/, and /ī/ Sounds

Proofreading and Writing

Proofreading Circle the five misspelled Spelling Words in this weather log entry. Then write each word correctly.

May 20 — There was a report today of a lightning streik at the shopping mall outside town. The same storm passed over our house, with heavy winds. It made the trees sweigh so much that I was sure at least one would fall. The winds started to faide before that happened, though. On the news, the reporter said that the base of the storm clouds was actually at a hight of over 5,000 feet. The weather tomorrow is supposed to be mild, with a slite chance of rain.

1. ______________________
2. ______________________
3. ______________________
4. ______________________
5. ______________________

Spelling Words

1. speech
2. claim
3. strike
4. stray
5. fade
6. sign
7. leaf
8. thigh
9. thief*
10. height*
11. mild
12. waist
13. sway
14. beast
15. stain
16. fleet
17. stride
18. praise
19. slight
20. niece*

Write a Storm Warning Storm chasers are able to provide firsthand, "you are there" reports of storms because they chase the storms.

On a separate sheet of paper, write the script of a storm warning that a storm chaser might issue by radio. Use Spelling Words from the list.

Name ______________________________

Words in Their Places

Read each set of words, and decide which two could be the guide words and which one the entry word on a dictionary page. Then in the columns below, write the guide words under the correct heading, and the entry word beside them.

trout	weather	prance	durable	chase
trust	wayward	practice	dust	charter
tropical	weave	prairie	dusky	chatterbox

Guide Words		Entry Word
________	________	________
________	________	________
________	________	________
________	________	________
________	________	________

Name ______________________________

It's a Twister!

Conjunctions The words *and*, *or*, and *but* are **conjunctions**. A conjunction may be used to join words in a sentence or to join sentences. Use *and* to add information. Use *or* to give a choice. Use *but* to show contrast.

- Clouds **and** wind signal a coming storm.
  This conjunction joins words.
- I saw lightning, **and** I heard thunder.
  This conjunction joins sentences.

Write the conjunction *and*, *or*, or *but* to best complete each sentence. Then decide whether each conjunction you wrote joins words or joins sentences. Write W after a sentence in which words are joined. Write S after a sentence in which sentences are joined.

1. Kansas ________ Oklahoma have many tornadoes. ___
2. Warren Faidley chases tornadoes ________ thunderstorms. ___
3. Warren has special equipment, ________ he has a special vehicle to carry it. ___
4. I have never seen a tornado, ________ I have seen lightning many times. ___
5. Go into a cellar ________ another low place if you see a funnel cloud. ___

Name ______________________________

In Focus

Compound Sentences A **compound sentence** is made by joining two closely related simple sentences with a comma and a conjunction.

I like to read.
You like to write. } I like to read, but you like to write.

Draw a line from each simple sentence in column A to the most closely related sentence in column B. Read all the choices before you decide.

A	B
1. Zoe takes photos for the school paper	Zoe took pictures of the musicians.
2. Should Zoe use color film	Tom writes stories for the paper.
3. Color photos are nice	the photos in our newspaper are black and white.
4. Tom wrote about the school concert	should she use black and white film?

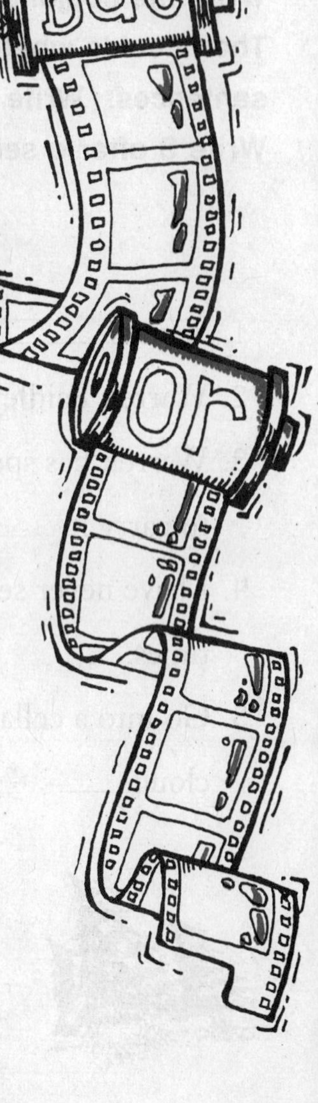

Now, write the sentences above and join them by using conjunctions instead of lines. Don't forget to put a comma before each conjunction!

1. ______________________________
____

2. ______________________________
____

3. ______________________________
____

4. ______________________________
____

Name ______________________________

Lightning Strikes!

Correcting Run-on Sentences A **run-on sentence** occurs when a writer runs one simple sentence into another without using a comma and a conjunction between them. The sentence below is a run-on sentence.

Marco lives on a farm his cousin likes to visit him there.

Correct run-on sentences in your writing by inserting a comma and conjunction to make a compound sentence:

Marco lives on a farm, and his cousin likes to visit him there.

Marco is excited and has quickly typed an e-mail message to his cousin Jamie. Revise Marco's message by adding missing commas and conjunctions.

Lightning struck near our farm I saw it happen. The bolt hit an old tree on top of a hill, the tree split in half. There was a loud boom the air crackled. It was scary I was safe in our house at the bottom of the hill. Should I send you a picture of the tree do you want to visit to see it for yourself?

Name ______________________________

Response to Literature

Prompt Explain why photographing tornadoes is difficult. Use information and details from *Eye of the Storm* to support your answer.

Use the chart below to help you write a response. First, jot down main ideas and details you might include. Then number your main ideas beginning with *1,* from most to least important.

Main Ideas	Details

Name ________________________________

Capitalizing and Punctuating Sentences

A fifth-grade class was given this writing prompt: **Warren Faidley is a storm chaser. Summarize what he does for a living.** One fifth grader wrote the response below but forgot to check for capitalization and punctuation errors.

Use these proofreading marks to add the necessary capital letters and end punctuation.

⊙	Add a period.	^!	Add an exclamation point.
≡	Make a capital letter.	^?	Add a question mark.

what does Warren Faidley do for a living He follows dangerous storms for example, he tracks down tornadoes and hurricanes then he photographs lightning striking the earth and funnel clouds whirling in the sky. if he has been successful, he can sell his dramatic photos to magazines, newspapers, and other publications What a risky but exciting job storm chasers have

Name ______________________

Volcanic Activity

Write each word from the box under the correct category below.

Vocabulary

molten
lava
crater
crust
cinders
eruption
magma
summit

Description of Hot Lava

____

Earth Layer

____

Materials in a Volcano

____

____

____

Volcano Parts

____

____

Event

____

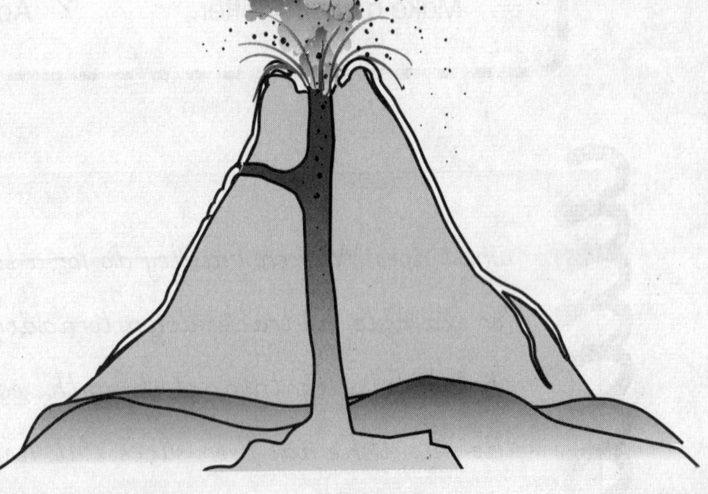

Now choose at least four words from the box. Use them to write a short paragraph describing an exploding volcano.

____

____

____

____

____

Name ______________________________

Category Chart

Fill in the boxes in each category.

How Volcanoes Form

Two Types of Volcanic Vents

Where Volcanoes Form

Types of Volcanoes

examples

examples

examples

examples

Name ______________________________

Show What You Know!

The following questions ask about volcanoes. Answer each question by writing the letter of the correct answer in the space provided.

_____ 1. Where does the word *volcano* come from?
A. the Hawaiian name for the goddess of fire, Pele
B. the name for the Roman god of fire, Vulcan
C. the scientific name for mountains that spout fire and ash
D. the name for a race of mythological creatures called Vulcans

_____ 2. How are volcanoes formed?
A. Hot magma beneath the earth's crust pushes up through cracks or holes.
B. The earth's crust melts and forms rivers of hot lava.
C. Wood and other materials catch fire and cause explosions that melt mountaintops.
D. Glaciers melt, leaving craters through which magma can escape.

_____ 3. What happened when Mt. St. Helens erupted in 1980?
A. The first of the Hawaiian islands was formed in the Pacific Ocean.
B. Homes, roads, and forests were destroyed, and 60 people were killed.
C. Ash spewed into the air, but no real damage was done.
D. A new volcanic island appeared in the North Atlantic Ocean.

_____ 4. Where in the earth's crust do most volcanoes erupt?
A. in the weakest parts of the earth's plates, near the center
B. in the Atlantic Ocean
C. wherever mountains or mountain ranges are found
D. in places where two of the earth's plates meet

_____ 5. How have volcanoes helped to create the Hawaiian Islands?
A. Eruptions destroyed much of the land area, leaving only islands.
B. Eruptions caught the attention of explorers, who settled there.
C. Eruptions built up the islands, and new eruptions add lava to the shoreline.
D. Ash and cinders from thousands of eruptions have mixed with seawater to help form new land.

Name ______________________________

Classifying Clouds

Read the article. Then complete the activity on page 42.

Clouds

Clouds come in a variety of forms and colors. They occur at different heights. Some are made of water and some of ice. With all these differences, a good way to identify clouds is by their groups.

Clouds are grouped by how high above the earth they are found. Low clouds are usually not more than 6,000 feet above sea level. They include stratus and stratocumulus clouds. A stratus cloud looks like a smooth sheet, while stratocumulus clouds are lumpy. They look like fluffy gray piles of cotton.

Middle clouds form between 6,000 and 20,000 feet. They include altostratus, altocumulus, and nimbostratus clouds. An altostratus cloud forms a white or gray sheet. Altocumulus clouds appear as fluffy piles that may be separated or connected in a lumpy mass. Nimbostratus clouds look like a smooth, gray layer. Rain or snow often falls from them, making them hard to see.

High clouds form above 20,000 feet. Unlike other kinds of clouds, which are made of water droplets, these clouds consist of ice crystals. Cirrus, cirrostratus, and cirrocumulus are types of high clouds. Cirrus clouds are very high in the sky and have a feathery appearance. A cirrostratus cloud is a very thin cloud layer. Cirrocumulus clouds look like millions of bits of fluff high in the sky.

Name ______________________

Classifying Clouds continued

Follow the directions or answer the questions based on the

1. Add the names of any cloud types mentioned in the article that are missing from this chart.

low	middle	high
stratus	altostratus	cirrus
______	______	______
	______	______

2. How are the clouds in this chart classified? ______________________
   Write the correct category for each list of clouds in this chart.

______	______
stratus altostratus nimbostratus cirrostratus	stratocumulus altocumulus cirrocumulus

3. How are the clouds in this chart classified? ______________________
   Add the names of cloud types not listed to the correct column.

water	ice
stratus altostratus nimbostratus ______ ______	cirrus cirrostratus ______

Name ______________________________

Construct a Word

Read each sentence. Then, using two or three columns in the chart, build a word containing the root *-struct* or *-rupt* that completes the sentence. Write the word on the line.

de	rupt	ive
dis	struct	or
con		ion
e		ure
inter		
in		

1. Sam's swimming ______________________ taught him how to do the backstroke.
2. I watched the ______________________ of the volcano from my window.
3. We helped our cousin ______________________ a tree house in the backyard.
4. The hurricane left a path of ______________________ along the coast.
5. Please don't ______________________ me when I'm talking!
6. The noise in the hall was very ______________________ during our rehearsal.
7. The leak was caused by a ______________________ in the pipeline.
8. The children sat on top of the climbing ______________________ in the playground.

Volcanoes

Spelling The /ō/, /o͞o/, and /yo͞o/ Sounds

Name ______________________

The /ō/, /o͞o/, and /yo͞o/ Sounds

When you hear the /ō/ sound, think of the patterns *o*-consonant-*e*, *oa*, *ow*, and *o*. When you hear the /o͞o/ and the /yo͞o/ sounds, think of the patterns *u*-consonant-*e*, *ue*, *ew*, *oo*, *ui*, and *ou*.

/ō/ **slope, boast, thrown, stroll**

/o͞o/ or /yo͞o/ **rule, clue, dew, choose, cruise, route**

Write each Spelling Word under its vowel sound.

/ō/ Sound

______________________ ______________________

______________________ ______________________

______________________ ______________________

______________________ ______________________

/o͞o/ or /yo͞o/ Sounds

______________________ ______________________

______________________ ______________________

______________________ ______________________

______________________ ______________________

______________________ ______________________

______________________ ______________________

Spelling Words

1. thrown
2. stole
3. clue
4. dew
5. choose
6. rule
7. boast
8. cruise
9. stroll
10. route
11. mood
12. loaf
13. growth
14. youth
15. slope
16. bruise
17. loose
18. rude
19. flow
20. flute

Name ____________________

Spelling Spree

Letter Swap Write a Spelling Word by changing the underlined letter to a different letter.

1. stale ____________
2. louse ____________
3. club ____________
4. load ____________
5. role ____________
6. toast ____________
7. moon ____________
8. den ____________

1. thrown
2. stole
3. clue
4. dew
5. choose
6. rule
7. boast
8. cruise
9. stroll
10. route
11. mood
12. loaf
13. growth
14. youth
15. slope
16. bruise
17. loose
18. rude
19. flow
20. flute

Word Switch Write a Spelling Word to replace each underlined definition in the sentences. Write your words on the lines.

9. My parents are taking a sea voyage for pleasure on that ship.
10. Which item did you pick out from the catalog?
11. Many people are active in sports in their time of life before adulthood.
12. You can use a ruler to measure the increase in size of the plant.
13. I play the woodwind instrument shaped like a tube in the band.
14. A clerk should never be lacking in courtesy to a shopper.
15. Would you care to walk slowly down the beach with me?

9. ____________
10. ____________
11. ____________
12. ____________
13. ____________
14. ____________
15. ____________

Name ______________________________

Proofreading and Writing

Proofreading Circle the five misspelled Spelling Words in this paragraph from a personal narrative. Then write each word correctly.

Our roote led us up the side of the volcano. We had just reached an old area of lava flo when we heard a rumbling noise from above. Hikers ahead of us on the trail had knocked some rocks loose! The avalanche was heading down the sloap of the mountain, straight for us. In the rush to reach safety, I tripped and was thron off the trail. Luckily, the mass of rocks passed me by, and all I got was a briuse on my leg.

1. ______________
2. ______________
3. ______________
4. ______________
5. ______________

Spelling Words

1. thrown
2. stole
3. clue
4. dew
5. choose
6. rule
7. boast
8. cruise
9. stroll
10. route
11. mood
12. loaf
13. growth
14. youth
15. slope
16. bruise
17. loose
18. rude
19. flow
20. flute

Write a List of Safety Tips What safety tips would it be good to keep in mind when exploring a volcano?

On a separate sheet of paper, list some tips for volcano explorers. Use Spelling Words from the list.

Name ______________________________

Missing Definitions

The dictionary entries below include an entry word and a sample sentence, but they are missing the definition. Read each sample sentence and use it to help you fill in the definition.

1. ancient (**ān′** shənt) ______________________

   The dinosaur tracks in the rocks show how ancient they are.

2. astonishing (ə **stŏn′** ĭ shĭng) ______________________

   It was astonishing to see it snowing in the middle of July.

3. awaken (ə **wā′** kən) ______________________

   The campers awaken at the first light of dawn.

4. damage (**dăm′** ĭj) ______________________

   Using too much water can damage the plants.

5. extinct (ĭk **stĭngkt′**) ______________________

   Since its last eruption a thousand years ago, the volcano has been extinct.

6. fiery (**fīr′** ē) ______________________

   The flames made a fiery glow in the sky.

7. spout (spout) ______________________

   Water from the fountain spouts into the air.

8. summit (**sŭm′** ĭt) ______________________

   After a long hard climb, we reached the summit of the mountain.

Name ______________________________

Finding Your Way

Singular and Plural Nouns A **singular noun** names one person, one place, one thing, or one idea. A **plural noun** names more than one person, place, thing, or idea. To decide how to form a plural, look at the end of the singular noun. Here are four rules to study:

1. To most singular nouns, add *-s* to form the plural.
2. If a singular noun ends in *s*, *ss*, *x*, *ch*, or *sh*, add *-es* to form the plural.
3. For singular nouns ending with a vowel plus *y*, add *-s* to form the plural.
4. If a singular noun ends in a consonant plus *y*, change the *y* to *i* and add *-es*.

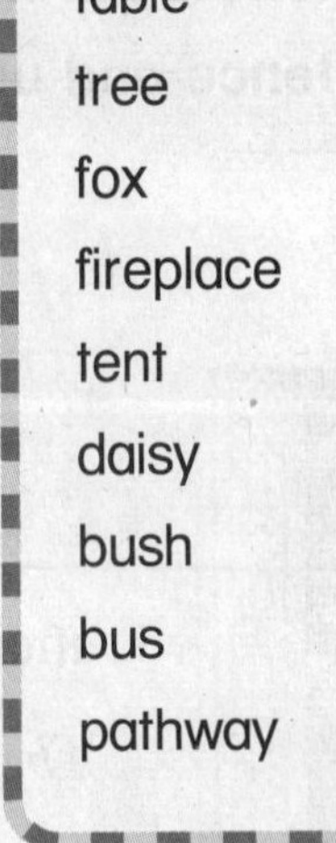

Conrad and Carmen have drawn a map of a campground they are visiting. Label each landmark on the map with a plural noun. Use nouns from the list.

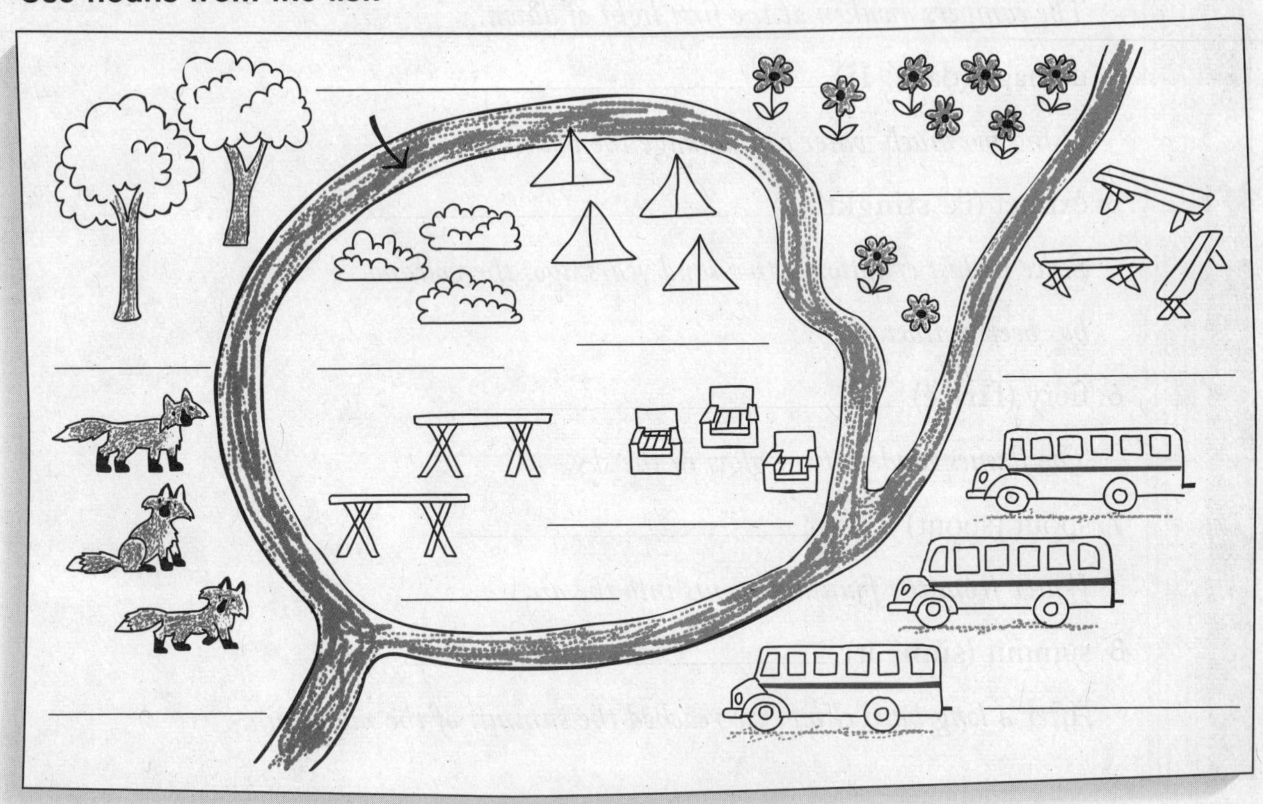

Name ______________________________

Science Fair

More Plural Nouns Here are a few more rules for forming plurals:

1. To form the plural of some nouns ending in *f* or *fe*, change the *f* to *v* and add *-es.* For others ending in *f*, simply add *-s.*
2. To form the plural of nouns ending with a vowel plus *o*, add *-s.*
3. To form the plural of nouns ending with a consonant plus *o*, add *-s* or *-es.*
4. Some nouns have special plural forms.
5. Some nouns are the same in the singular and the plural.

For the science fair, Jody made a model of the volcano Mount Saint Helens and wrote a report about it. Jody isn't sure how to form the plural of some words in her report. She made a list of these words.

Write the plural next to each word on Jody's list. Check your dictionary if you are unsure of a plural.

leaf ______________________

child ______________________

volcano ______________________

man ______________________

ash ______________________

home ______________________

deer ______________________

woman ______________________

plant ______________________

mouse ______________________

Name ______________________________

Roaming Through the Woods

Using Exact Nouns You can make your writing more lively and interesting by replacing general nouns with more specific ones. Here is an example of writing with a general noun:

For my birthday, I received **several things**.

A reader does not know what the person received. Here is the same sentence revised to use more specific nouns:

For my birthday, I received **a book about sports legends, a basketball, and basketball shoes.**

Read the following paragraph. Revise the general nouns in bold type by replacing them with a more specific noun from the box.

a rabbit
dragonfly
maples and oaks
Duck Pond
minnows
peanut butter
sandwiches
my ankles
mint
bark
sneakers

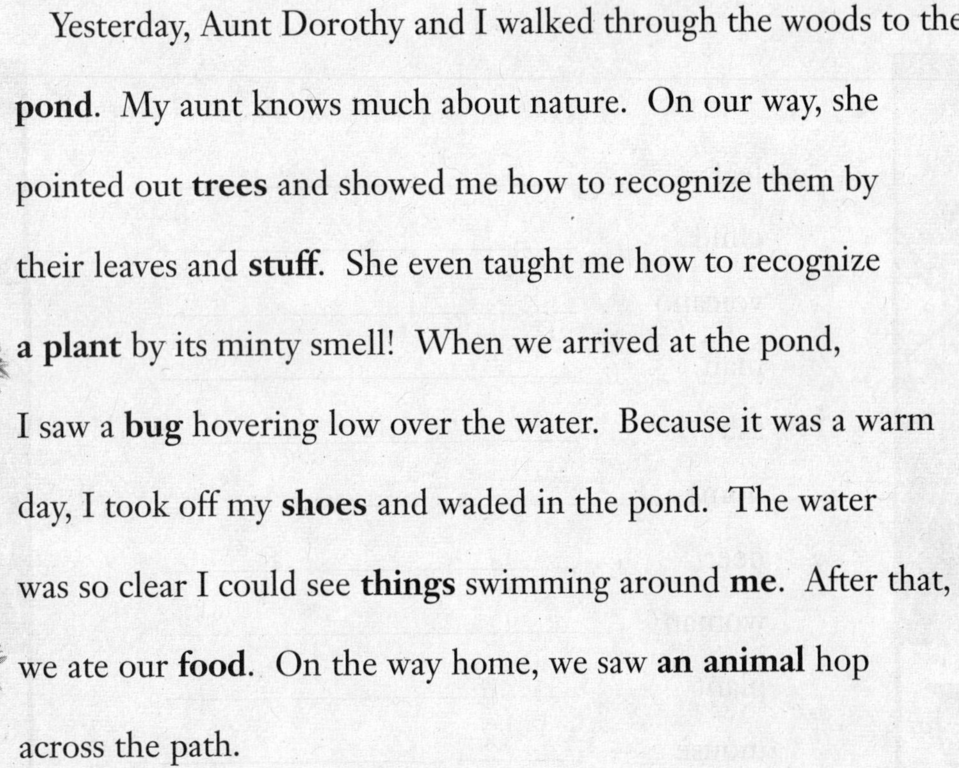

Yesterday, Aunt Dorothy and I walked through the woods to the **pond**. My aunt knows much about nature. On our way, she pointed out **trees** and showed me how to recognize them by their leaves and **stuff**. She even taught me how to recognize **a plant** by its minty smell! When we arrived at the pond, I saw a **bug** hovering low over the water. Because it was a warm day, I took off my **shoes** and waded in the pond. The water was so clear I could see **things** swimming around **me**. After that, we ate our **food**. On the way home, we saw **an animal** hop across the path.

Name ______________________________

Writing a Report

Read the following example of a main idea and details from page 87 of *Volcanoes.*

Volcanoes are formed by cracks or holes that poke through the earth's crust. Magma pushes its way up through the cracks. This is called a volcanic eruption. When magma pours onto the surface it is called lava. . . . As lava cools, it hardens to form rock.

Now get ready to write a report on a topic that interests you. Use the following graphic organizer to help you organize your writing.

Topic:

Main Idea:

Details:

Main Idea:

Details:

Main Idea:

Details:

Name ______________________________

Correcting Sentence Fragments

A sentence fragment is a group of words that is missing either a subject or a predicate. The following groups of words are sentence fragments. Turn them into complete sentences by adding either a subject or a predicate. Write the complete sentence on the lines.

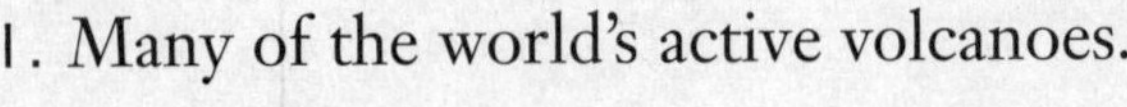

1. Many of the world's active volcanoes.

____

____

2. Clouds of hot ash.

____

____

3. Buries plants and animals.

____

____

4. The blast of an eruption.

____

____

5. Are seriously injured or killed.

____

____

Name ______________________________

Choosing the Best Answer

Use the test-taking strategies and tips you have learned to help you answer multiple-choice questions. This practice will help you when you take this kind of test.

Read each question. Choose the best answer. Fill in the circle in the answer row.

1 At the beginning of the story, why did Jonathan think that Moose was acting strangely?

A He thought Moose knew that Jonathan was worried about his mother.
B He thought Moose was looking for Mrs. Smith, who lived next door.
C He thought Moose knew there was going to be an earthquake.
D He thought Moose saw the children's father driving into the campground.

2 When did Jonathan plan to listen to the baseball game on the radio?

F After he hitched the car to the trailer
G After he found out how his mother was
H After he took Moose for a walk
J After Abby was in bed

3 When Jonathan and Abby first heard the rumbling noise, what did they think it was?

A An earthquake
B Thunder
C A bomb
D Rifles

4 Why couldn't Jonathan get to Abby during the earthquake?

F He couldn't see where she was.
G Birch trees fell on top of him.
H He couldn't keep his balance.
J He fell into the river.

ANSWER ROWS 1 Ⓐ Ⓑ Ⓒ Ⓓ 3 Ⓐ Ⓑ Ⓒ Ⓓ
2 Ⓕ Ⓖ Ⓗ Ⓙ 4 Ⓕ Ⓖ Ⓗ Ⓙ

Name ______________________________

Choosing the Best Answer

continued

5 What did Jonathan see right before the redwood almost fell on him?

A He saw the trunk tremble.

B He saw the roots rip loose from the ground.

C He saw the tree sway back and forth.

D He saw the trunk tilt toward him.

6 What did Jonathan do when he reached Abby?

F He helped her walk toward their trailer.

G He helped her look for their dog Moose.

H He helped her take shelter under a fallen tree.

J He helped her understand why earthquakes occur.

7 What did Jonathan think about as he hugged Moose after the earthquake?

A When he chose the dog

B The last earthquake his family had experienced

C His mother's broken ankle

D Bandaging his sister's cut knee

8 When did Abby realize that she and her brother could have been killed during the earthquake?

F When she saw the destruction around her

G When Jonathan told her

H When her parents got home

J When Grandma Whitney called from Iowa

ANSWER ROWS	5 Ⓐ Ⓑ Ⓒ Ⓓ	7 Ⓐ Ⓑ Ⓒ Ⓓ
	6 Ⓕ Ⓖ Ⓗ Ⓙ	8 Ⓕ Ⓖ Ⓗ Ⓙ

Name ______________________________

Spelling Review

Write Spelling Words from the list on this page to answer the questions.

1–9. Which nine words have a short vowel sound?

1. ______________ 6. ______________
2. ______________ 7. ______________
3. ______________ 8. ______________
4. ______________ 9. ______________
5. ______________

10–19. Which ten words have the /ā/, /ē/, or /ī/ sound?

10. ______________ 15. ______________
11. ______________ 16. ______________
12. ______________ 17. ______________
13. ______________ 18. ______________
14. ______________ 19. ______________

20–30. Which eleven words have the /ō/, /yo͞o/, or /o͞o/

20. ______________ 26. ______________
21. ______________ 27. ______________
22. ______________ 28. ______________
23. ______________ 29. ______________
24. ______________ 30. ______________
25. ______________

Spelling Words

1. fond
2. swift
3. beast
4. slept
5. fleet
6. staff
7. flute
8. grasp
9. thigh
10. dew
11. bunk
12. fade
13. dwell
14. strike
15. praise
16. slight
17. split
18. claim
19. sway
20. mild
21. clue
22. slope
23. boast
24. stole
25. stroll
26. cruise
27. mood
28. crush
29. youth
30. thrown

Name ______________________________

Spelling Spree

Spelling Words

1. crush
2. mood
3. swift
4. dwell
5. fade
6. strike
7. cruise
8. sway
9. beast
10. thrown
11. slope
12. stole
13. flute
14. dew
15. youth

Puzzle Power Use the Spelling Words to complete the sentences. Write the words in the puzzle.

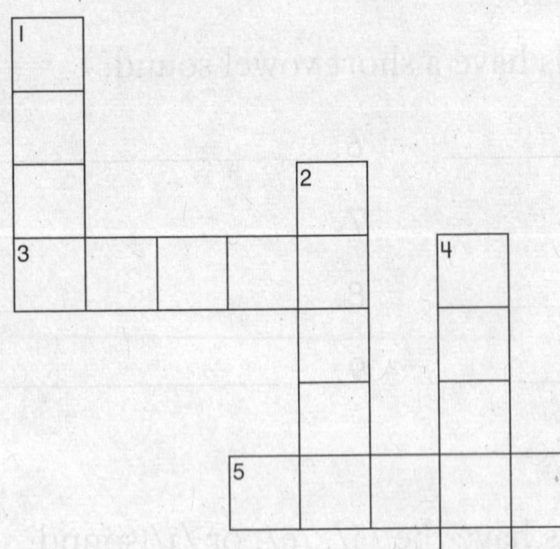

Across

3. The animals ______ in the forest.
5. A lion is a large ______.

Down

1. I am in a good ______ today.
2. The ______ is very steep.
4. Don't ______ that flower with your foot!

Book Titles Write the Spelling Word to complete each book title. Remember to use capital letters.

6. *My* ______________ *Down the River,* by C. Mann
7. *The Thief Who* ______________ *the Diamonds,* by Tay Kitaway
8. *The* ______________ *and Dangerous River,* by Can O. Tripp
9. *Earthquake:* ______________ *to the Ground!* by Shay Keeg Round
10. *Why Do Colors* ______________ *in the Sun and Other Science Questions,* by Sy N. Tist
11. *Adventures of My Childhood and* ______________, by A. Jing X. Plorer
12. *Flowers* ______________ *in the Breeze* by Heather Rose Marigold
13. *Mist in the Air,* ______________ *on the Grass* by I. M. Dampp
14. ______________ *Music for Beginners,* by Mary Days
15. *The Clock Will* ______________ *at Midnight,* by Miss Stear E. Yuss

Name ______________________________

Proofreading and Writing

Proofreading **Circle the six misspelled Spelling Words in this newspaper article. Then write each word correctly.**

At 11:30 last night, a milde earthquake gently rocked the city. Little damage was reported, and some people sleept right through it. This morning Helen and Joe Dalton boste that they were not afraid. There was only slite damage downtown. With prayse for his workers, the mayor said, "My staf responded quickly to all questions."

1. ______________ 4. ______________
2. ______________ 5. ______________
3. ______________ 6. ______________

Spelling Words

1. slept
2. praise
3. fond
4. clue
5. staff
6. thigh
7. stroll
8. slight
9. claim
10. fleet
11. mild
12. grasp
13. split
14. bunk
15. boast

In the News **A reporter takes notes after an earthquake. Complete his ideas by writing Spelling Words in the blanks.**

- No one is ______________ of surprises like this.
- Scientists have no ______________ about why this quake occurred at night.
- It is a strange time to ______________ through town!
- I'd rather be in my ______________ sleeping.
- A man has cuts on his ______________ and ankle.
- A large ______________ of fire trucks roars by.
- Large crevice in ground. Oak street is ______________ in two!
- It's hard to fully ______________ the power of a quake.
- Some people ______________ that animals can predict earthquakes.

Write a Safety Plan **On a separate sheet of paper, write about what you should do in an earthquake. Use the Spelling Review Words.**

Name ______________________________

You'll Never Believe Who I Just Met

Think about characters you might find in a tall tale. Describe five tall tale characters by completing each sentence with an exaggeration.

1. This character is so tall that
____
____

2. This character is so loud that
____
____

3. This character is so old that
____
____

4. This character is so fast that
____
____
____

5. This character is so strong that
____
____

Name ______________________________

That Could Never Happen!

Each of the four selections in *Focus on Tall Tales* contains at least one exaggerated event. Write the event after each story title.

Paul Bunyan, the Mightiest Logger of Them All

____

____

John Henry Races the Steam Drill

____

____

Sally Ann Thunder Ann Whirlwind

____

____

February

____

____

Name ______________________

Give It All You've Got

How do the characters in this theme "give their all"? After reading each selection, answer the questions to complete the chart.

	Michelle Kwan: Heart of a Champion	La Bamba
What kind of writing is the selection an example of?		
What traits does the main character have? What actions or achievements help reveal those traits?		
Why does this selection belong in a theme called *Give It All You've Got*?		
What advice might the main character give to others?		

Name ______________________

Give It All You've Got

	Mae Jemison: Space Scientist	The Fear Place
What kind of writing is the selection an example of?		
What traits does the main character have? What actions or achievements help reveal those traits?		
Why does this selection belong in a theme called *Give It All You've Got*?		
What advice might the main character give to others?		

What have you learned in this theme about facing challenges?

____

____

Name ______________________

Top Marks

Read the word in each box from *Michelle Kwan: Heart of a Champion.* Write a word from the list that is related in meaning. Then use a dictionary to check if you were right.

Vocabulary

- demonstrations
- officials
- perform
- components
- stress
- elegant
- nonprofessional
- skilled
- specified
- spectators

pressure ______________	required ______________
presentations ______________	audience ______________
elements ______________	artistic ______________
judges ______________	amateur ______________
technical ______________	compete ______________

Name ______________________________

Is That a Fact?

Passage	Fact or Opinion?	How I Can Tell
Page 139, paragraph 1: "I thought I was ready to become a Senior skater, at the age of twelve."		
Page 140, paragraph 5: "Frank is one of the greatest coaches in the world."		
Page 144, paragraph 6: "The judges look for many required elements in a program."		
Page 146, paragraph 3: "Elvis Stojko...does quadruple/triple combinations."		
Page 147, paragraph 1: "Most elite skaters have three forty-five-minute-long practice sessions on the ice every day . . ."		
Page 150, paragraph 4: "And you can never forget how important school is."		

Name ______________________________

A Figure Skater's Trading Card

What if figure skaters were featured on trading cards as baseball players are? Complete the fact sheet so it gives vital information about Michelle Kwan. Then use the facts to write a paragraph that might appear on the back of a Michelle Kwan trading card.

FACT SHEET

Who Michelle Kwan is:

____

Who her coach was:

____

What she was especially good at when she was young:

____

Age at which she became a Senior skater:

____

How she had to improve in order to compete as a Senior skater:

____

____

____

Her world records (see page 153):

____

Two pieces of advice she might give other young athletes:

1. ______________________________
2. ______________________________

Name ______________________________

Is That a Fact?

Read the following passage. Then answer the questions on page 67.

A Track Legend

Wilma Rudolph was perhaps the greatest female track athlete of her time. She was the first American woman to win three gold medals in a single Olympics. She also received many honors, including the Sullivan Award as the country's top amateur athlete, and a place in the Women's Sports Hall of Fame, the Black Sports Hall of Fame, and the United States Olympic Hall of Fame.

Rudolph achieved success despite great personal obstacles. As a child, she was stricken with polio, pneumonia, and scarlet fever. Some doctors said she would never walk. Yet no one could have been more determined to beat the odds. After years of physical therapy, Rudolph put aside her leg brace at age eleven and went on to become a great athlete in high school and college.

At the 1960 Olympic Games, Rudolph was the star of the American team. She won gold medals and set world records in the 100-meter dash, the 200-meter dash, and the 400-meter relay.

Rudolph later became a coach and a teacher. She also wrote a book about her life that was made into a movie. There has never been an American athlete who overcame more obstacles in life than Wilma Rudolph. She should be an inspiration to all Americans, and to athletes everywhere.

Name ______________________________

Is That a Fact? continued

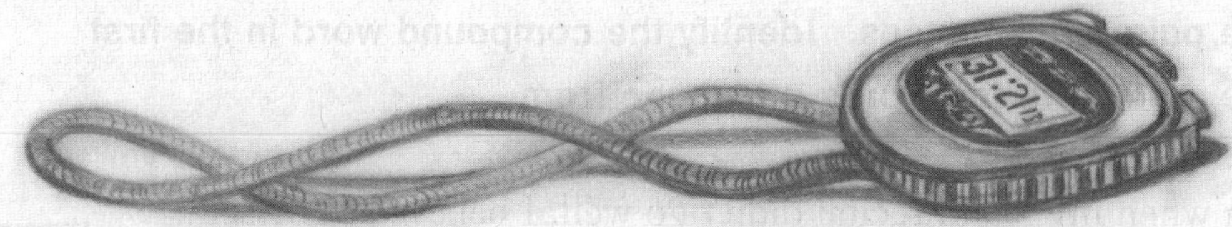

Answer these questions about the passage on page 66.

1. What opinion about Wilma Rudolph does the author give in the first paragraph? Write the sentence that states the opinion.

   ____

   ____

2. Which words in this sentence show that the statement is an opinion and not a fact?

   ____

3. Which sentence from the second paragraph contains no opinions?

   ____

   ____

4. The third paragraph contains one opinion and several facts. Write them here.

   Opinion: ______________________________

   ____

   Facts: ______________________________

   ____

5. Reread the last paragraph to find two facts and two opinions. Write them here.

   Opinion: ______________________________

   ____

   Facts: ______________________________

   ____

Name ______________________

Compound Creativity

Read the pairs of sentences. Identify the compound word in the first sentence, and write the words it is made from.

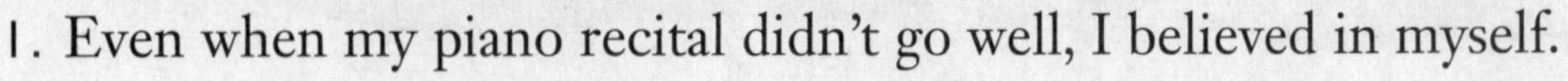

1. Even when my piano recital didn't go well, I believed in myself.

   ______________ + ______________

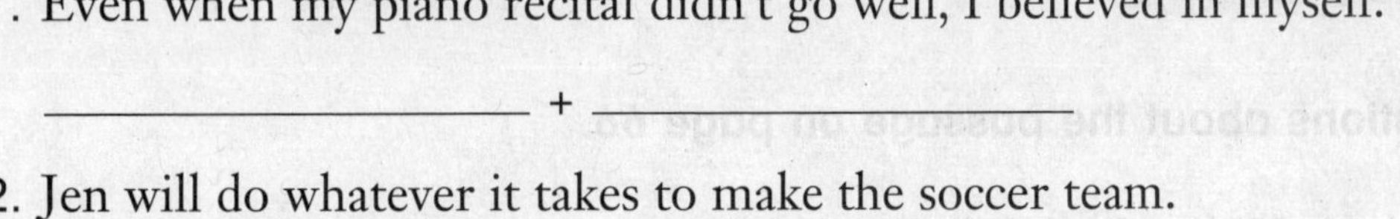

2. Jen will do whatever it takes to make the soccer team.

   ______________ + ______________

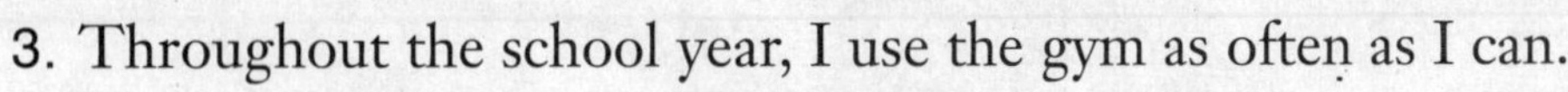

3. Throughout the school year, I use the gym as often as I can.

   ______________ + ______________

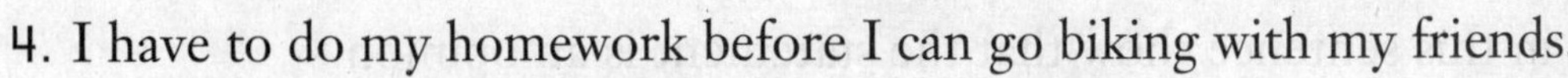

4. I have to do my homework before I can go biking with my friends.

   ______________ + ______________

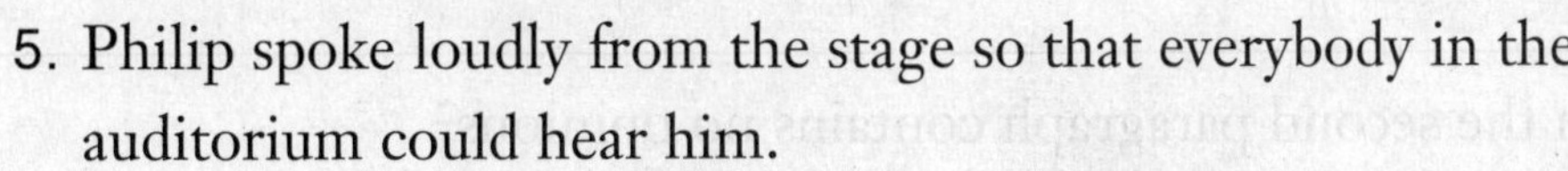

5. Philip spoke loudly from the stage so that everybody in the auditorium could hear him.

   ______________ + ______________

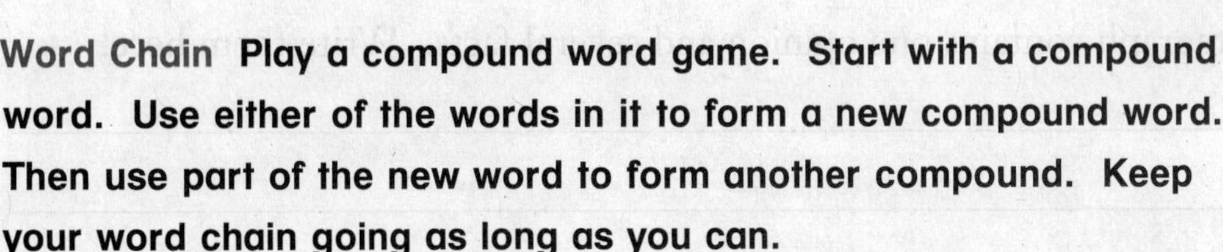

Word Chain Play a compound word game. Start with a compound word. Use either of the words in it to form a new compound word. Then use part of the new word to form another compound. Keep your word chain going as long as you can.

Example: anymore ⟶ anyway ⟶ freeway ⟶ wayside ⟶ ?

Name ______________________________

Compound Words

A **compound word** is made up of two or more smaller words. To spell a compound word correctly, you must remember if it is written as one word, as a hyphenated word, or as separate words.

wheel + chair = wheelchair **up + to + date** = up-to-date
first + aid = first aid

Write each Spelling Word under the heading that tells how the compound word is written.

Spelling Words

1. basketball
2. wheelchair
3. cheerleader
4. newscast
5. weekend
6. everybody
7. up-to-date
8. grandparent
9. first aid
10. wildlife
11. highway
12. daytime
13. whoever
14. test tube
15. turnpike
16. shipyard
17. homemade
18. household
19. salesperson
20. brother-in-law

One Word

________________ ________________
________________ ________________
________________ ________________
________________ ________________
________________ ________________
________________ ________________
________________ ________________
________________ ________________

With a Hyphen

____
____

Separate Words

____
____

Name ______________________

Spelling Spree

Exchanging Word Parts Write the Spelling Word that has one of the parts in each compound word below.

1. wildfire ______________
2. dateline ______________
3. grandstand ______________
4. sales tax ______________
5. evergreen ______________
6. wayside ______________
7. turnover ______________
8. holdup ______________

Clue Addition Add the clues to create a Spelling Word.

9. large boat + play area =
10. comes before second + assist =
11. "Hooray!" + person in charge =
12. try out + hollow cylinder =
13. container made of twigs + sphere =
14. not night + what a watch measures =
15. circular frame with spokes + piece of furniture =

9. ______________
10. ______________
11. ______________
12. ______________
13. ______________
14. ______________
15. ______________

Spelling Words

1. basketball
2. wheelchair
3. cheerleader
4. newscast
5. weekend
6. everybody
7. up-to-date
8. grandparent
9. first aid
10. wildlife
11. highway
12. daytime
13. whoever
14. test tube
15. turnpike
16. shipyard
17. homemade
18. household
19. salesperson
20. brother-in-law

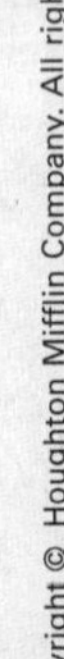

Name ____________________

Proofreading and Writing

Proofreading Circle the five misspelled Spelling Words in this transcript of a television news report. Then write each word correctly.

To end tonight's newskast, we have a story about a local girl who made good. Debbie Martin, who started skating years ago on a pair of homemad skates, is going to the Junior Nationals. Debbie's parents, older sister, and brother-in-lor will accompany her to Seattle. For years, they have watched Debbie practice on the family's basketball court, which her father flooded in winter and allowed to freeze over. This week-end they will watch her in a world-class arena. We know that everbody in town will be rooting for Debbie!

1. ____________________
2. ____________________
3. ____________________
4. ____________________
5. ____________________

Spelling Words

1. basketball
2. wheelchair
3. cheerleader
4. newscast
5. weekend
6. everybody
7. up-to-date
8. grandparent
9. first aid
10. wildlife
11. highway
12. daytime
13. whoever
14. test tube
15. turnpike
16. shipyard
17. homemade
18. household
19. salesperson
20. brother-in-law

Write a Comparison and Contrast Think of a sport you enjoy playing or watching. Does it have anything in common with figure skating? How is it different from figure skating?

On a separate piece of paper, write a paragraph in which you compare and contrast two sports. Use Spelling Words from the list.

Name ______________________________

Word Family Matters

Decide which word best completes each sentence. Write the word in the blank.

1. When he realized that he had missed the team tryouts, Todd turned red with ______________________.

furious fury infuriate

2. Twenty school bands besides ours were entered in this year's state ______________________.

compete competition competitive

3. Vanilla ice cream with fudge sauce is a dessert I find ______________________.

irresistible resistance resist

4. Because the top math student receives a prize, my sister is ______________________ to get a good grade on her next test.

move motion motivated

5. Please wait ______________________ until it is your turn to play the computer game.

impatient patience patiently

Now write two sentences, using two words you have not used yet.

6. ____

____

7. ____

____

Name ______________________________

Champion Michelle

Common and Proper Nouns A **common noun** names any person, place, or thing. A **proper noun** names a particular person, place, or thing. Each important word in a proper noun begins with a capital letter.

We met at the **statue**. *statue:* common noun
We met at the **Statue of Liberty.** *Statue of Liberty:* proper noun
Coach Boe taught me how to skate. *Coach Boe:* proper noun
A **coach** taught me how to skate. *coach:* common noun
She is from another **state.** *state:* common noun
She is from **California.** *California:* proper noun

Copy the nouns from the following sentences into the proper columns below. When you rewrite a proper noun, be sure to capitalize correctly.

1. debbie went to the skating rink on saturday.
2. In the winter, the pond is frozen.
3. miguel is fast when he puts on his skates.
4. I competed in the race at valley middle school.
5. Have you ever skated at rockefeller center?

Common Nouns	Proper Nouns
______________	______________
______________	______________
______________	______________
______________	______________
______________	______________

Name ___________________________

The People's Favorite

Singular and Possessive Nouns A **possessive noun** shows ownership or possession. To form a singular possessive noun, add an apostrophe and *-s* ('s). To form a plural possessive noun, add an apostrophe (') if the noun ends with *s*. Otherwise, add an apostrophe and *-s* ('s).

Singular	Singular Possessive	Plural	Plural Possessive
cat	cat's	cats	cats'
country	country's	countries	countries'
Jones	Jones's	Joneses	Joneses'
woman	woman's	women	women's
mouse	mouse's	mice	mice's

Fill in the blank in each sentence below with the possessive form of the noun in parentheses. Write an S on the line at the end of the sentence if you wrote a singular possessive noun. Write a P on the line if you wrote a plural possessive noun.

1. Our (school) ____________________ skating club sponsored a citywide competition. ___
2. The fifth grade (classes) ____________________ skaters were great. ___
3. The first event was the (seniors) ____________________ short program. ___
4. The (competition) ____________________ rules were strict. ___
5. The audience's favorite event was the (children) ____________________ competition. ___

Name ____

My Friend's Skating Pond

Writing Possessive Phrases It is easy to make a mistake when forming the possessive of a plural or a singular noun. Therefore, when you proofread, pay special attention to possessive nouns.

Chris in Maine wants to send this e-mail message to Joann in Florida. Proofread the message for errors in possessive nouns. Write the correct possessive forms above the line, as shown.

friends'

Example: My two friend's reports are about hockey.
^

To: joann@tropics.net
From: cwm@frozennorth.com
Re: Ice and Snow

Hi Joann!

I have been ice-skating on my familys pond. The pond froze solid last week. It is safe to skate on it now. Last evening, Toms family and my family skated on the pond. Our families dogs played in the snow. The dogs tails never stopped wagging. They enjoyed this winters snow as much as we did!

Chris

Name ______________________________

Autobiography

An **autobiography** is a writer's narrative about his or her own life. It includes the most important and interesting events, usually in time order.

Use this flow chart to organize your episode for an autobiography. First, identify your topic or title. Next, write the main events in time order, one in each box. Finally, write details about each event.

Topic or Title: ______________________________

Event:

Details:

↓

Event:

Details:

↓

Event:

Details:

Name ______________________________

Ordering Important Information

A careful writer makes sure that the events and details in an autobiography are presented in a clear order. Time-order words, such as *first*, *next*, and *last*, help clarify the order of events and call attention to what is most important.

This part of an autobiography is scrambled. Reorder the sentences to follow the sequence of events. Time-order words give clues to the sequence. Then write the revised autobiography on the lines below.

Now I am in fifth grade, and I speak both English and Spanish. Over the next few weeks, he taught me new words and phrases. Some of the kids in my class are now learning to speak Spanish. It is my turn to be the translator! When I was seven, my family moved to California from Ecuador. I did not speak any English, so I was very scared to start school. Then I met Paulo, who would become my best friend. Paulo spoke English and Spanish. That first day, at recess, groups of children played and talked together. I felt very alone. He became my translator. Soon, I was talking with other children in my class.

Name ______________________________

Revising Your Personal Essay

Reread your personal essay. What do you need to make it better? Use this page to help you decide. Put a checkmark in the box for each sentence that describes your personal essay.

Rings the Bell!

- ☐ My introduction catches the reader's attention.
- ☐ My main focus is clear throughout the essay.
- ☐ I wrote the essay in my own voice from my own point of view.
- ☐ The ending sums up the main focus of my essay.
- ☐ There are almost no mistakes.

Getting Stronger

- ☐ My introduction could be more interesting.
- ☐ My main focus is not always clear.
- ☐ The point of view is sometimes unclear.
- ☐ The ending doesn't make the essay feel finished.
- ☐ There are a few mistakes.

Try Harder

- ☐ My introduction is boring.
- ☐ The main focus is not clear.
- ☐ The point of view is unclear.
- ☐ There are a lot of mistakes.

Name ____________________

Using Possessive Nouns

- Possessive nouns show ownership.
- To form the possessive of a singular noun add an apostrophe and *s*.
- To form the possessive case of a plural noun ending in *s*, add just an apostrophe.

Rewrite each phrase, using a possessive noun. Then use the new phrase in a sentence of your own.

1. the music of the composer ____________________
____
2. the skill of the musicians ____________________
____
3. the authority of the conductor ____________________
____
4. the hush of the spectators ____________________
____
5. the sore throat of the actress ____________________
____
6. the big chance for the understudy ____________________
____
7. the groan of the audience ____________________
____
8. the surprise of the critics ____________________
____

Name ______________________________

Spelling Words

Look for familiar spelling patterns to help you remember how to spell the Spelling Words on this page. Think carefully about the parts that you find hard to spell in each word.

Write the missing letters in the Spelling Words below.

1. w ___ ___ ___ d
2. w ___ ___ ___ dn't
3. clo ___ ___ ___ ___
4. happ ___ ___ ___ ___
5. som ___ one
6. sometim ___ ___
7. diff ___ r ___ nt
8. an ___ ther
9. w ___ ___ ___ d
10. eig ___ ___ ___
11. c ___ ___ ing
12. g ___ ___ ___ ing
13. g ___ ing
14. st ___ ___ ___ ed
15. h ___ ___ ___

Spelling Words

1. would
2. wouldn't
3. clothes
4. happened
5. someone
6. sometimes
7. different
8. another
9. weird
10. eighth
11. coming
12. getting
13. going
14. stopped
15. here

Study List **On a separate piece of paper, write each Spelling Word. Check your spelling against the words on the list.**

Name ______________________________

Spelling Spree

Find a Rhyme For each sentence write a Spelling Word that rhymes with the underlined word and makes sense in the sentence.

1. The band _____ playing when the singer dropped his microphone.
2. When Alison peered out the window, she saw a _____ looking bird.
3. If my sweatshirt had a hood, I _____ definitely wear it on a day like this.
4. A humming sound was _____ from the car's engine.
5. We're _____ to the store after you finish mowing the lawn.
6. You shouldn't treat anyone in a way you _____ want to be treated yourself.
7. You have nothing to fear _____.

1. ____________________
2. ____________________
3. ____________________
4. ____________________
5. ____________________
6. ____________________
7. ____________________

Spelling Words

1. would
2. wouldn't
3. clothes
4. happened
5. someone
6. sometimes
7. different
8. another
9. weird
10. eighth
11. coming
12. getting
13. going
14. stopped
15. here

Finding Words Each word below is hidden in a Spelling Word. Write the Spelling Word.

8. pen
9. on
10. eight
11. tin
12. cloth
13. not
14. met
15. rent

8. ____________________
9. ____________________
10. ____________________
11. ____________________
12. ____________________
13. ____________________
14. ____________________
15. ____________________

Name ______________________________

Proofreading and Writing

Proofreading **Circle the five misspelled Spelling Words in this certificate. Then write each word correctly.**

Certificate of Effort

This is to certify that Eduardo Díaz gave it all he had in the four hundred meter race held on the eighthth day of May of this year. Just as the runners were geting to the first turn, Eduardo fell. (No one is sure just how it happenned.) He could easily have stoped running there. Instead, he got back up, kept goeing, and finished the race. We are proud to recognize him here for his extraordinary effort.

Spelling Words

1. would
2. wouldn't
3. clothes
4. happened
5. someone
6. sometimes
7. different
8. another
9. weird
10. eighth
11. coming
12. getting
13. going
14. stopped
15. here

1. ______________ 4. ______________

2. ______________ 5. ______________

3. ______________

Writing Headlines **Write four headlines for newspaper stories about people who gave it all they had. The headlines can be about people in the theme's selections, can be about people you know of from somewhere else, or can be completely made up. Include a Spelling Word in each headline.**

Name ______________________________

What a Performance!

Words are missing in the sentences. Fill each blank with a word or words from the box.

Vocabulary

- talent
- pantomime
- forty-five record
- limelight
- applause
- volunteered
- rehearsal
- embarrassed
- duo
- debut

1. If you are the only one on stage, you are in the ______________________________.
2. If you are good at something, you have ______________________________.
3. If you buy an old record with one song on each side, you become the owner of a ______________________________.
4. If you have agreed to help, you have ______________________________.
5. If you act without speaking, you ______________________________.
6. If you perform for the first time, you make your ______________________________.
7. If you go to practice a play, you attend a ______________________________.
8. If you forget your lines during a play, you may feel ______________________________.
9. If you please the audience, you may hear ______________________________.
10. If you perform with a partner, you are part of a ______________________________.

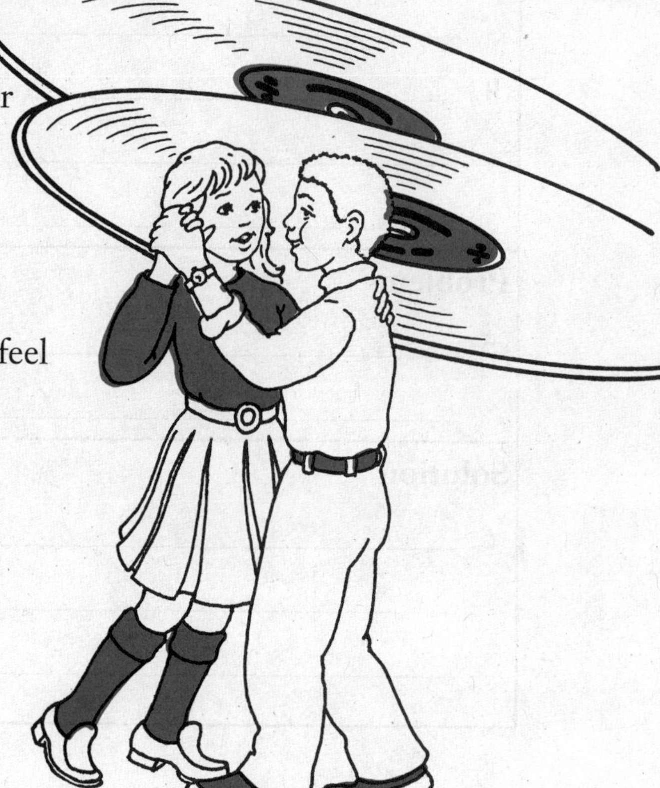

Name ______________________

Talent Report

Fill in the story map with information from the selection.

Characters	**Setting**
______________________	______________________
______________________	______________________

Plot

Events

1. ______________________

2. ______________________
____

3. ______________________
____

4. ______________________
____
____

Problem

5. ______________________
____

Solution

6. ______________________
____
____

Name ________________________________

Manuel's Journal

Suppose Manuel wrote about the talent show in his journal. Finish each sentence to show what he might have said about his performance.

September ____________, ____________
(today's date) (year)

I can't believe I survived the talent show. Here's how it happened. I'd volunteered to ________________________ ________________________. Two things happened at rehearsal that should have made me nervous. First, Mr. Roybal's record player speed ________________________. Then, when Benny blew his trumpet, I ________________________.

On the night of the show, I had to wait for my turn onstage. A lot of other kids performed before me. As I watched them, I ________________________. Finally it was my turn. At first, ________________________.

Then, suddenly, something awful happened: ________________________ ________________________.

I didn't know what to do, so I ________________________ ________________________. As I left the stage, I ________________________.

Here's the funny thing. After the performance ________________________ ________________________.

I couldn't believe that ________________________.

Name ______________________________

A Class Act

Read the story. Then complete the activity on page 87.

Horsing Around

Every year, the fifth grade classes held a big softball game and talent show. This year, Amy and Carmen decided to enter the talent show. Since their team was the Mustangs, the girls decided to dance in a horse costume. Amy would be the front half and Carmen the back half.

They spent an entire weekend making a papier-mâché horse's head. Carmen's dad sewed the body from fleecy brown cloth. The girls made the mane and tail out of thick black yarn. Amy's mom helped them learn a dance to a song called "Plains Pony."

At last it was the day of the show. But as the girls nervously galloped onto the softball diamond, they heard giggling from the audience. Someone called, "Hey, Horsey! You forgot something!" Carmen gasped, "Oh, no!" Peeking out from the horse's head, Amy saw something black near home plate. Their tail!

"What will we do?" Carmen whispered. Amy replied, "We'll pretend we planned it this way!" The next time they passed home plate, they danced around the tail and Amy snatched it up. Then she and Carmen danced backwards off the field, shaking their hooves to the music as Amy waved goodbye with the tail. The audience applauded noisily, screaming with laughter.

Name ______________________________

A Class Act continued

Fill in the story map so it sums up the story on page 86. Write the characters' names, the setting, and the events that make up the plot.

Main Characters	Setting (time and place)
______________________	______________________

Plot

____

____

____

____

____

Problem

____

____

____

Solution

____

____

____

Name ___________________________

Record Roots

Some words in the box contain the word root *spec*. Others contain the root *opt*. Write the words that match each clue. Then write each numbered letter in the space with the matching number to find a message.

inspector
optician
optometry
respect
spectacle
suspect

1. a person who makes or sells eyeglasses

___ ___ ___ ___ ___ ___ ___ ___
(9 under the 3rd blank, 6 under the 7th blank)

2. to look up to or regard highly

___ ___ ___ ___ ___ ___ ___
(7 under the 1st blank)

3. a remarkable or impressive sight

___ ___ ___ ___ ___ ___ ___ ___ ___
(3 under the 2nd blank, 5 under the 8th blank)

4. the profession of examining a person's vision

___ ___ ___ ___ ___ ___ ___ ___ ___
(10 under the 9th blank)

5. to look upon someone as guilty without proof

___ ___ ___ ___ ___ ___ ___
(4 under the 2nd blank, 1 under the 4th blank)

6. a person who examines something closely and carefully

___ ___ ___ ___ ___ ___ ___ ___ ___
(8 under the 1st blank, 2 under the 8th blank)

Manuel gained a lot of ___ ___ ___ ___ ___ ___ ___ ___ ___ ___ after his performance.
1 2 3 4 5 6 7 8 9 10

Name ____________________

La Bamba

Spelling The /ou/, /ô/, and /oi/ Sounds

The /ou/, /ô/, and /oi/ Sounds

When you hear the /ou/, the /ô/, and the /oi/ sounds, think of these patterns:

/ou/ *ou, ow* **ou**nce, t**ow**er

/ô/ *aw, au, a* before *l* cl**aw**, p**au**se, b**a**ld

/oi/ *oi, oy* m**oi**st, l**oy**al

Remember that the patterns *ou, au,* and *oi* are usually followed by a consonant sound.

Write each Spelling Word under its vowel sound.

/ou/ Sound

______
______
______
______
______
______
______

/ô/ Sound

______
______
______
______
______
______
______
______
______

/oi/ Sound

______
______
______
______

Spelling Words

1. hawk
2. claw
3. bald
4. tower
5. halt
6. prowl
7. loyal
8. pause
9. moist
10. ounce
11. launch
12. royal
13. scowl
14. haunt
15. noisy
16. coward
17. fawn
18. thousand
19. drown
20. fault

Name ______________________________

Spelling Spree

Contrast Clues The second part of each clue contrasts with the first part. Write a Spelling Word after each clue.

1. not hairy, but ______________
2. not a traitor, but ______________
3. not a smile, but a ______________
4. not to dock, but to ______________
5. not an adult deer, but a ______________
6. not a pound, but an ______________
7. not a sparrow, but a ______________
8. not lowly or common, but ______________
9. not quiet, but ______________
10. not to move about openly, but to ______________

Finding Words Each word below is hidden in a Spelling Word. Write the Spelling Words that contain these words.

11. aunt ______________
12. tow ______________
13. sand ______________
14. law ______________
15. use ______________

Spelling Words

1. hawk
2. claw
3. bald
4. tower
5. halt
6. prowl
7. loyal
8. pause
9. moist
10. ounce
11. launch
12. royal
13. scowl
14. haunt
15. noisy
16. coward
17. fawn
18. thousand
19. drown
20. fault

Name ___________________________

La Bamba

Spelling The /ou/, /ô/, and /oi/ Sounds

Proofreading and Writing

Circle the five misspelled Spelling Words in this e-mail that Manuel might have sent. Then write each word correctly.

File Edit View Toolbox Help

To: Grandma
From: Manuel
Subject: Talent Show

The show turned out okay, but I was pretty nervous beforehand. My hands were moyst with sweat. I'm no cowerd, though. I went out and started my act. Then the record stuck, and I had to sing the same words over and over. It was Benny's falt for making me scratch the record. When the music finally came to a hault, I ran offstage. I felt awful! At the end of the show, though, I got a round of applause noisy enough to droun out the names of the other acts. Nobody was more surprised than I was!

1. ___________________
2. ___________________
3. ___________________
4. ___________________
5. ___________________

Spelling Words

1. hawk
2. claw
3. bald
4. tower
5. halt
6. prowl
7. loyal
8. pause
9. moist
10. ounce
11. launch
12. royal
13. scowl
14. haunt
15. noisy
16. coward
17. fawn
18. thousand
19. drown
20. fault

Write an Announcement Suppose that Manuel decided to give another performance of "La Bamba." How would you go about advertising it? What information would you need to include? How would you describe his act?

On a separate piece of paper, write an announcement for this repeat performance. Use Spelling Words from the list.

Name ______________________________

Mixed Meanings

Read the definitions of each word. Then write one or two sentences that use different meanings of each word.

fall (fôl) *v.* **fell, fallen, falling, falls. 1.** To drop or come down. **2.** To suffer defeat or capture. **3.** *n.* The season of the year occurring between summer and winter.

1. ______________________________

____

hand (hănd) *n.* **1.** The part of the arm below the wrist. **2.** A round of applause. *v.* To give or pass with the hands; transmit.

2. ______________________________

____

stage (stāj) *n.* **1.** A raised platform, especially one in a theater on which entertainers perform. **2.** A level or step in a process. *v.* To produce or direct a performance.

3. ______________________________

____

step (stĕp) *n.* **1.** The movement of raising one foot and putting it down. **2.** An action taken to achieve a goal. *v.* To press the foot down or against.

4. ______________________________

____

stick (stĭk) *n.* A long slender piece of wood. *v.* **1.** To fasten or attach, as with a pin or nail. **2.** To become fixed and unable to move.

5. ______________________________

____

Name ______________________________

Mary Sings and Puppets Move

Action Verbs An **action verb** tells what the subject does or did. It is the main word in the complete predicate.

The performers **bowed** to the audience.

action verb

Underline the action verb in each of the following sentences.

1. Martin and Mary built a small theater for their puppet show.
2. Martin's father cut the wood for them.
3. Martin painted designs on the wooden theater.
4. Mary picked a song for their show.
5. On the night of the show, Martin watches the audience.
6. The audience claps for the tap dancer.
7. Martin and Mary carry their puppets on stage.
8. The puppets dance to the music.
9. The puppeteers wait for applause.
10. The crowd cheers!

Name ______________________________

He Gave a Speech

Direct Objects A **direct object** is a noun or pronoun in a predicate that receives the action of the verb. It answers the question *What?* or *Whom?*

The dancer tied his **shoes.**

The dancer tied *what?* His shoes. Therefore, *shoes* is the direct object.

Underline the action verb and circle the direct object in each sentence below.

1. Mr. Bruno needed a volunteer to give a speech.
2. Sydney raised his hand.
3. Mr. Bruno thanked him for volunteering.
4. Sydney nervously shuffled his notes.
5. Then he cleared his throat.
6. He projected his voice throughout the room.
7. Susan heard his words in the back of the classroom.
8. After the speech, Mario asked a question of Sydney.
9. Sydney answered the query politely.
10. Then Sydney set his notes down.

La Bamba

Grammar Skill Using Exact Verbs

Name ______________________________

She Wrote and I Scribbled

Using Exact Verbs Your writing will be more vivid if you use action verbs that tell exactly what the subject of the sentence is doing. Look at the two sentences below. Which verb gives you a better idea of how Sandy made her way across the stage?

Sandy **moved** across the stage.

Sandy **twirled** across the stage.

stomped
stumbled
shouted
fumbled
scribbled

Pat is writing a review of the class play for the school newspaper. Replace each underlined verb with a more exact one. Choose from among the verbs in the box.

Last night I saw the class play *Ramshackle Inn.* There were five main characters. The innkeeper was a loud man with a beard. When he said his lines, others onstage covered their ears. The brother was clumsy. He walked back and forth across the stage. His rude and angry sister walked up and down the stairs. The reporter wrote constantly in his pad. The inept police officer was the funniest character of all. She played with her radio, trying to get it to work. The plot of this play was silly, but the actors were fun to watch.

Name ______________________________

Writing a Summary

If you were asked to summarize "La Bamba," you would probably tell who performed in the talent show and what happened during the performances. A **summary** is a brief account of a story or selection. Writing a summary is a good way to share what a story is about and to recall main events and characters.

Fill in the graphic organizer below with the most important events in *Earthquake Terror*.

Selection: Earthquake Terror

Idea/ Event	Idea/ Event	Idea/ Event	Idea/ Event

Name ______________________________

Paraphrasing

When you **paraphrase** a passage from a book, article, or story, you put it into your own words without changing the author's meaning. A careful writer makes sure to paraphrase without copying any passages word-for-word from the work of other writers.

Read the following passage from "La Bamba."

But when Manuel did a fancy dance step, there was a burst of applause and some girls screamed. Manuel tried another dance step. He heard more applause and screams and started getting into the groove as he shivered and snaked around the stage. But the record got stuck, and he had to sing

Para bailar la bamba
Para bailar la bamba
Para bailar la bamba
Para bailar la bamba

again and again.

Now read one fifth grader's paraphrase of the passage.

Paraphrase

Manuel did one fancy dance step and then another. The audience applauded and screamed when he shivered and snaked across the stage. Then the record got stuck, and he sang one line of "La Bamba" again and again.

Improve the student's paraphrase by reducing it to a single sentence that tells what happened in the passage. You may want to reorder the information and reduce the number of details. Be sure to avoid repetition of whole phrases that appeared in the original passage. Write your improved version on the lines below.

____

____

Name ___________________________

Have No Fear

Read the words in the chart. Then look in the word box to find a synonym and an antonym for each, and write these in the chart. Use a dictionary if you need help.

Vocabulary

monotony
stationary
reckless
pain
disregard
strength
unafraid
uncertain
comfort
bewildered
mobile
untroubled
careful
focus
weakness
agitation
sure
frightened

	synonym	antonym
terrified		
dismayed		
excitement		
stamina		
concentrate		
discomfort		
unsure		
cautious		
immobile		

Choose a word from the word box and write your own sentence.

____

____

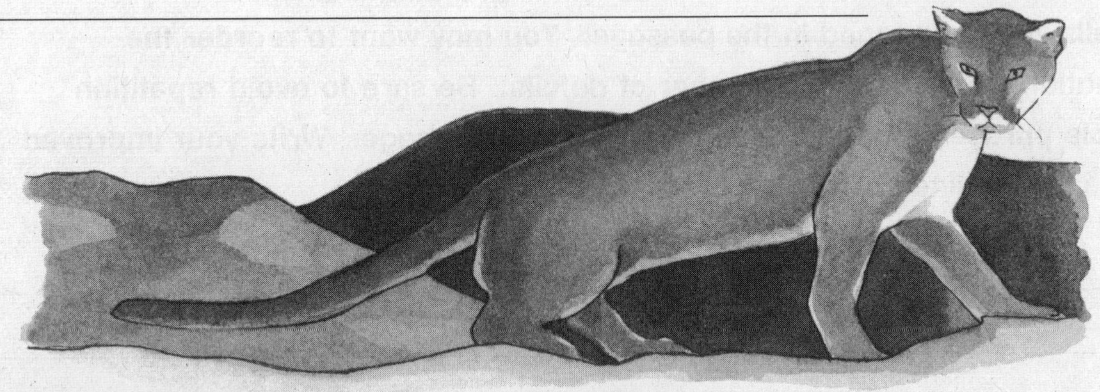

Name ______________________________

I Predict . . .

Fill in the chart with your predictions, based on details from the selection and on what you know from personal experience.

Predicting Outcomes	
selection details + personal knowledge + THINKING = prediction	
Selection Details ► Doug needs to get past a narrow ledge. ► The journey seems futile. ► Doug has made it to the narrow ledge before.	**Personal Knowledge** ► People who have done something before, even if it was difficult, know that they can do it again.
Prediction: Doug will make it back to the ledge.	

Selection Details	**Personal Knowledge**
______________________	______________________
______________________	______________________
Prediction: ______________________	

Selection Details	**Personal Knowledge**
______________________	______________________
______________________	______________________
Prediction: ______________________	

Name ______________________________

Events Leading to the Climax

The events in *The Fear Place* lead to a climax when Doug must face his fear. Fill in the event map with sentences that describe the events that lead up to and come after the climax. Start at the bottom of the page.

7. Doug knows he is past the "fear place" when ______________________________
____

↑

6. When Doug reaches the narrowest part of the ledge, he ______________________________
____

↑

5. Doug reaches the "fear place" and ______________________________

↑

4. Doug watches where Charlie goes and ______________________________
____

↑

3. Charlie ______________________________

↑

2. Doug reaches the first ridge. He ______________________________
____

↑

1. Doug begins to climb, but ______________________________

Name ______________________________

Looking Forward

Read the passage. Then complete the activity on page 102.

The Apology

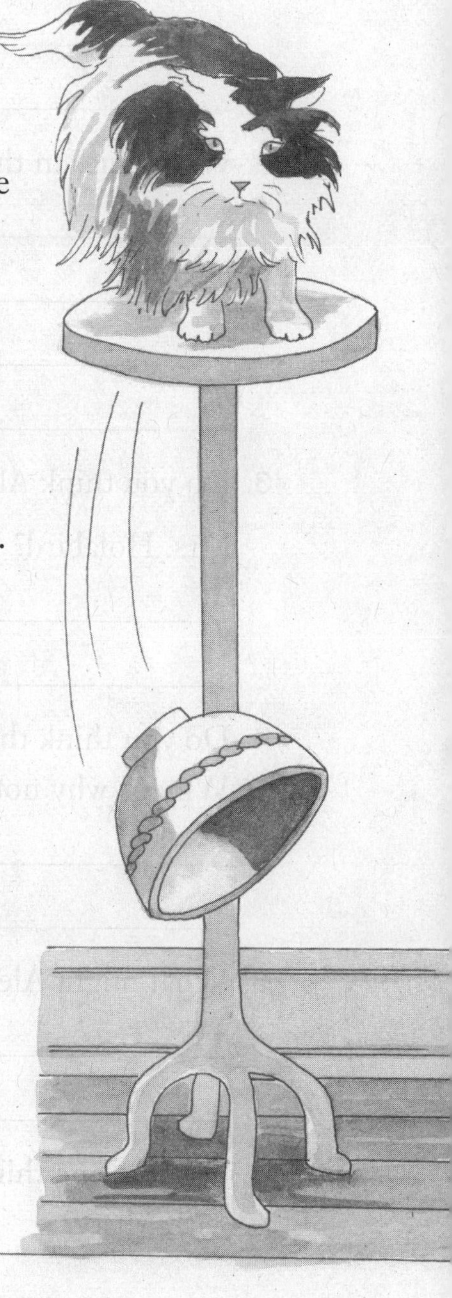

Alexa hadn't meant to break the bowl. In fact, she'd always loved that china bowl and its pretty blue pattern. But she had broken it, and all week she'd listened with dread for the phone call she knew would come. It would be Mrs. Holabird, their neighbor, calling to tell her mother about the accident.

The Holabirds had no children of their own, so they were especially fond of Alexa. She had been helping Mrs. Holabird with chores for about two years. When they went out of town, the Holabirds always paid Alexa to cat-sit for Misty. Alexa would come twice a day and refill Misty's food and water bowls. She usually stayed for a while, holding the big, silky cat on her lap and scratching her behind the ears. Sometimes she helped Misty exercise. It was fun to toss a ball or a catnip mouse into the air and watch the fat, fluffy cat leap and grab for it with her paws. How was she to know that Misty would crash into the bowl and knock it off its stand?

Alexa had been so horrified that she had hidden the broken pieces under the sideboard. She went home and fearfully awaited the phone call. But three days later it still had not come, even though the Holabirds had returned two days ago.

On the fourth morning, Alexa awoke with her mind made up. She put on her coat and walked to the front door, calling, "Mom, I need to go see Mr. and Mrs. Holabird."

Name ______________________________

Looking Forward continued

Answer these questions about the passage on page 101.

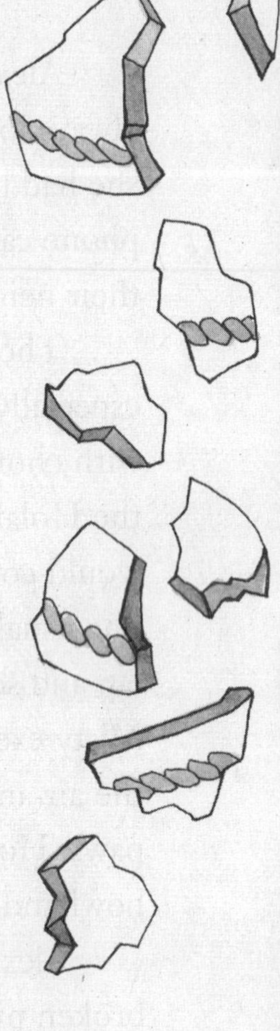

1. What do you think Alexa will do next?

2. What clues in the passage helped you make this prediction?

3. Do you think Alexa's mother will be glad that Alexa apologized to Mrs. Holabird? Why or why not?

4. Do you think the Holabirds will ask Alexa to care for Misty again? Why or why not?

5. What might Alexa do to make up for breaking the bowl?

6. What is one thing Alexa might do differently the next time she plays with Misty?

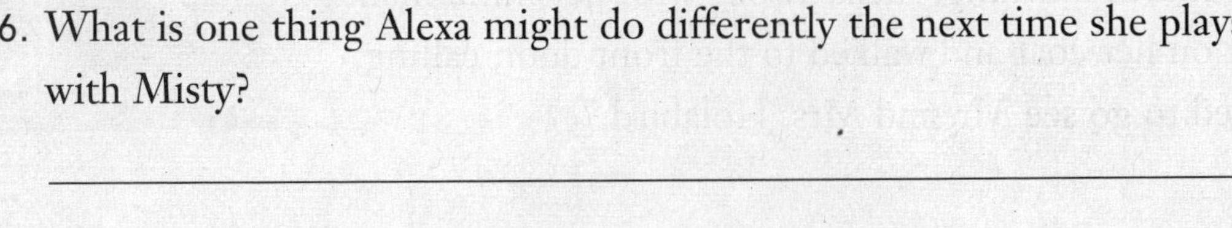

The Fear Place

Structural Analysis Suffixes *-ward* and *-ous*

Name ______________________________

Nervous? No, Onward!

Read this diary page. Underline each word with the suffix *-ward* or *-ous*.

The Hike

Climbing to the mountaintop was a frightening experience. At first, it didn't seem so bad. The path upward was wide, even spacious. After a while, though, I began to be nervous. The rise was continuous, and the path began to narrow. When I looked over the edge, I saw a monstrous gap between me and the canyon bottom far below. Still, I made my way toward the top, pausing only now and then. I knew that if I glanced backward, I would be in trouble. Instead, I gazed outward to the golden plain in the distance. It was a marvelous sight. I knew I would head homeward in less than an hour.

Now write each word you underlined next to its meaning.

1. ______________________: in a direction nearer
2. ______________________: uncomfortable
3. ______________________: in a direction away from
4. ______________________: huge
5. ______________________: toward where one lives
6. ______________________: heading above
7. ______________________: to the rear
8. ______________________: roomy
9. ______________________: ongoing, with no break
10. ______________________: wonderful

Name ______________________________

The /ôr/, /âr/, and /är/ Sounds

When you hear the /ôr/ sound, think of the patterns *or*, *oar*, and *ore*. When you hear the /âr/ sound, think of the patterns *are* and *air*. When you hear the /är/ sound, think of the pattern *ar*.

/ôr/ **torch, soar, sore** /âr/ **hare, flair** /är/ **scar**

► The vowel sound + *r* spellings of the starred words differ from the usual spelling patterns. The /ôr/ sound is spelled *ar* in *warn* and *oor* in *floor*.

Write each Spelling Word under its vowel + *r* sound.

/ôr/ Sound

____
____
____
____
____
____
____
____
____

/âr/ Sound

____
____
____
____
____
____
____

/är/ Sound

____
____
____
____

Spelling Words

1. hare
2. scar
3. torch
4. soar
5. harsh
6. sore
7. lord
8. flair
9. warn*
10. floor*
11. tore
12. lair
13. snare
14. carve
15. bore
16. fare
17. gorge
18. barge
19. flare
20. rare

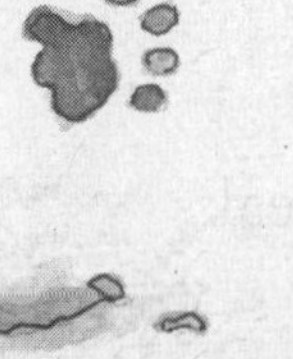
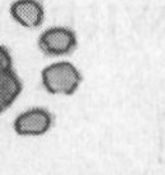

Name ______________________________

Spelling Spree

Word Hunt Write the Spelling Word that you find in each of the longer words below.

Example: snowboarder *board*

1. torchlight ____________
2. harebrained ____________
3. warlord ____________
4. scarcely ____________
5. welfare ____________
6. restored ____________
7. floorshow ____________

Alphabet Puzzler Write the Spelling Word that fits alphabetically between the two words in each group.

8. apple, ____________, bicycle
9. butter, ____________, dinner
10. ladder, ____________, loan
11. sock, ____________, stomach
12. father, ____________, flame
13. harmful, ____________, kitchen
14. sneeze, ____________, solid
15. secret, ____________, snow

Spelling Words

1. hare
2. scar
3. torch
4. soar
5. harsh
6. sore
7. lord
8. flair
9. warn*
10. floor*
11. tore
12. lair
13. snare
14. carve
15. bore
16. fare
17. gorge
18. barge
19. flare
20. rare

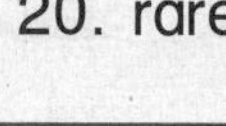

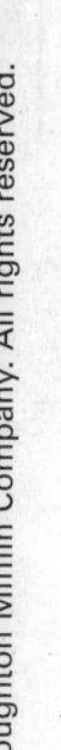

The Fear Place

Spelling The /ôr/, /âr/, and /är/ Sounds

Name ____________________________________

Proofreading and Writing

Proofreading Circle the five misspelled Spelling Words in this part of a note. Then write each word correctly.

To the Park Rangers:

I have to leave unexpectedly for a day. Will you keep an eye on my two boys, who are camping on the north ledge? They are experienced climbers, but their tempers sometimes flar when they're alone with each other. For that matter, it's rair for them to get along anytime! The younger one has a sore knee from sliding down a gorg. I won't boar you with the details, but I would appreciate it if you could check on them during the day. I'll woarn them to behave themselves.

1. ____________________
2. ____________________
3. ____________________
4. ____________________
5. ____________________

Spelling Words

1. hare
2. scar
3. torch
4. soar
5. harsh
6. sore
7. lord
8. flair
9. warn*
10. floor*
11. tore
12. lair
13. snare
14. carve
15. bore
16. fare
17. gorge
18. barge
19. flare
20. rare

Write a Prediction Now that Doug has made it past the Fear Place, what do you think will happen next? Will he find his brother safe or in danger? Will Charlie continue to help him?

On a separate piece of paper, write a paragraph giving your prediction of what will happen next in the story. Use Spelling Words from the list.

Name ______________________________

Homophone Echoes

Match the letter of the correct definition to the underlined word. Then write the homophone pairs at the bottom of the page.

1. The hiker makes her way <u>through</u> a narrow canyon. _____
2. As she climbs, objects below <u>seem</u> to get smaller _____
3. She kneels beside the <u>burrow</u> of a ground squirrel. _____
4. In the distance she can see a snow-capped <u>peak</u>. _____
5. Will she <u>freeze</u> when she gets to the top? _____
6. She takes a quick <u>peek</u> into the canyon. _____
7. The <u>seam</u> in her boot rubs her heel. _____
8. She's a long way from the <u>borough</u> of Brooklyn! _____
9. If she <u>threw</u> a stone, it might cause a rockslide below. _____
10. Watching an eagle fly <u>frees</u> her from her fear. _____

a. in and out of
b. tossed
c. glance
d. stitch
e. appear
f. tunnel
g. liberates
h. summit
i. be cold
j. city section

11. __________ __________
12. __________ __________
13. __________ __________
14. __________ __________
15. __________ __________

Name ______________________

We Are Diving

Main Verbs and Helping Verbs A simple predicate can be more than one word. The **main verb** is the most important word in the predicate. The **helping verb** comes before the **main verb**.

I have climbed the rope. main verb: *climbed* helping verb: *have*

Write the main verb and the helping verb in each of the following sentences.

1. This summer camp program has challenged me.

Main verb: ______________________

Helping verb: ______________________

2. I am facing my fear of water in the swimming classes.

Main verb: ______________________

Helping verb: ______________________

3. The swimming teacher has given me much encouragement.

Main verb: ______________________

Helping verb: ______________________

4. I have swum two laps so far this morning.

Main verb: ______________________

Helping verb: ______________________

5. Next summer, I will learn to dive!

Main verb: ______________________

Helping verb: ______________________

Name ______________________________

Jellyfish Are Nasty

Linking Verbs A **linking verb** links the subject to a word in the predicate that names or describes the subject. It does not show action. A **predicate noun** following a linking verb names the subject. A **predicate adjective** following a linking verb describes the subject.

Common Linking Verbs

am	is	are	was	were	will be
look	feel	taste	smell	seem	appear

Underline the linking verb in each sentence below. Circle each predicate noun or predicate adjective. Write *PN* on the line if the circled word is a predicate noun. Write *PA* if it is a predicate adjective.

Example: I am a swimmer. PN

1. Susan will be a lifeguard someday. ______
2. Lifeguards are brave. ______
3. The ocean breeze smells fresh. ______
4. I am afraid of jellyfish. ______
5. A sea nettle is a jellyfish. ______
6. Ocean water tastes salty. ______
7. That boat is a kayak. ______
8. My grandmother was a diver. ______
9. That stroke seems difficult to me. ______
10. Clayton and Rachel are surfers. ______

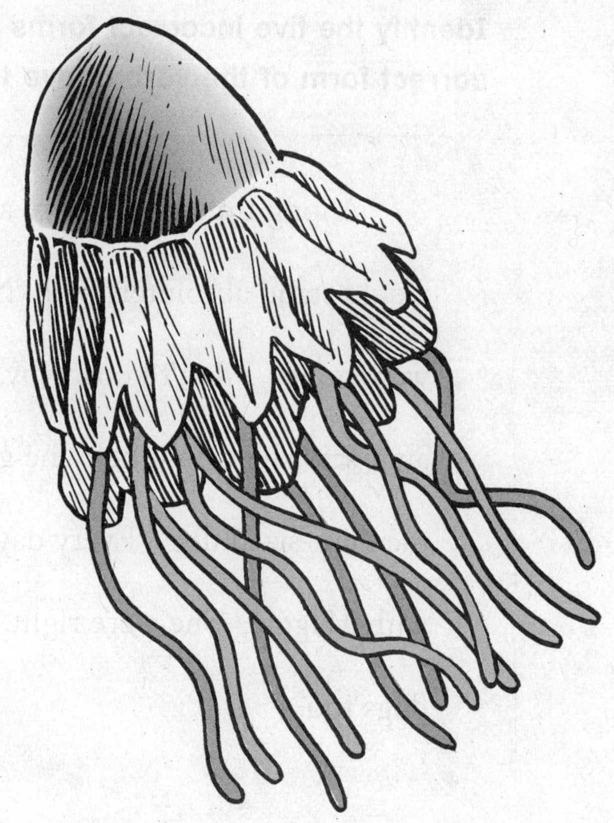

Name ______________________________

Are You Afraid?

Using Forms of the Verb *be* When using *be* as a linking verb, a writer must use the correct form of the verb. Like any other verb, a linking verb must agree with its subject in number.

The Verb *be*

	Present Tense	Past Tense
I	am	was
You	are	were
She/he/it	is	was
We	are	were
You	are	were
They	are	were

Identify the five incorrect forms of the verb *be* in the draft. Write the correct form of the verb above the error.

A long time ago, I were afraid of dogs. Every time I saw a dog I would stand absolutely still. Nobody could make me move until the dog were gone. I don't know why, but dogs was just frightening to me. My aunt said she would help me get to know her dog, Maggie. Maggie are a medium-sized dog. Every day for a month my aunt came to our house with Maggie. She were right. I began to trust Maggie and some other dogs too.

Name ______________________________

Writing a Clarification Composition

Sometimes when you read, you will encounter a quote or statement that expresses a belief but whose meaning is not entirely clear. You can write a **clarification composition** to clarify the statement.

Choose one of the following statements from *The Fear Place* and write it on the clarification map:

- *Anything is possible, but not everything is probable.*
- *So many layers, we never did get to the bottom of it.*
- *Maybe there were places that only fools would tread.*

Then write what you think the statement means, and list reasons, details, and examples from *The Fear Place* that support your opinion.

Statement
Meaning
Reasons, Details, and Examples

Name ______________________________

Combining Sentences with Helping Verbs

Good writers avoid unnecessary repetition in their writing. Sometimes you can improve your writing by combining sentences that repeat the same helping verb into one sentence.

> He **had** reached the ledge. He **had** glanced down at the canyon.
>
> He **had** reached the ledge and glanced down at the canyon.

Revise a postcard that Doug Grillo might have sent. Combine sentences that repeat the same helping verb into a single sentence. Write the revised message on the lines below.

Dear Jim,

We are finishing up our vacation in Colorado. We are coming home next week. I have spotted a snowshoe rabbit. I have studied other wildlife for my merit badge. After a fight, Gordie had hiked up a steep trail. My brother had pitched a tent on a high ridge. I was very scared. I was determined to find my brother. I should have climbed with someone else. I should have turned back before the narrow path curves sharply. Instead, I faced my fear. With the help of Charlie the cougar, I reached my brother safely!

Your friend,

Doug

____

____

____

____

____

____

Mae Jemison, Space Scientist

Key Vocabulary

Name ____________________

Space Is the Place

Write each word from the box on the correct line.

1. spacecraft

____

____

2. people

____

____

3. descriptive words

____

____

4. words about movement

____

____

5. a condition

____

Vocabulary

- artificial
- satellite
- launches *(verb)*
- orbit
- reusable
- mission
- specialist
- space shuttle
- astronaut
- weightlessness

Now choose three words from the box. Use them to write a short paragraph about the launch of a spacecraft.

____

____

____

____

____

____

Name ______________________

Main Idea Chart

Topic: ______________________	
Page 211	On September 12, 1992, Mae Jemison became the first African American woman to fly into space.
Pages 212–213	
Pages 213–214	
Pages 215–216	
Page 217	
Page 218	
Pages 219–221	
Pages 221–222	

Mae Jemison, Space Scientist

Comprehension Check

Name ______________________________

Is It True?

The sentences below tell about Mae Jemison. Write T if the sentence is true, or F if the sentence is false. If a sentence is false, tell why it is false.

1. Mae Jemison developed an interest in science at an early age.

____

____

2. Her parents and teachers all encouraged her to become a scientist.

____

____

3. When she graduated from Stanford University, she applied for admission to the astronaut corps.

____

____

4. Mae never gave up her childhood dream of traveling in space.

____

____

5. At the end of her year of intensive training, Mae Jemison rode a rocket into space.

____

____

6. On September 12, 1992, Mae Jemison became the first African American woman to journey into space.

____

____

Name ______________________________

Exploring the Topic

Read the following passage. Then complete the activity on page 117.

Space Shuttle Science

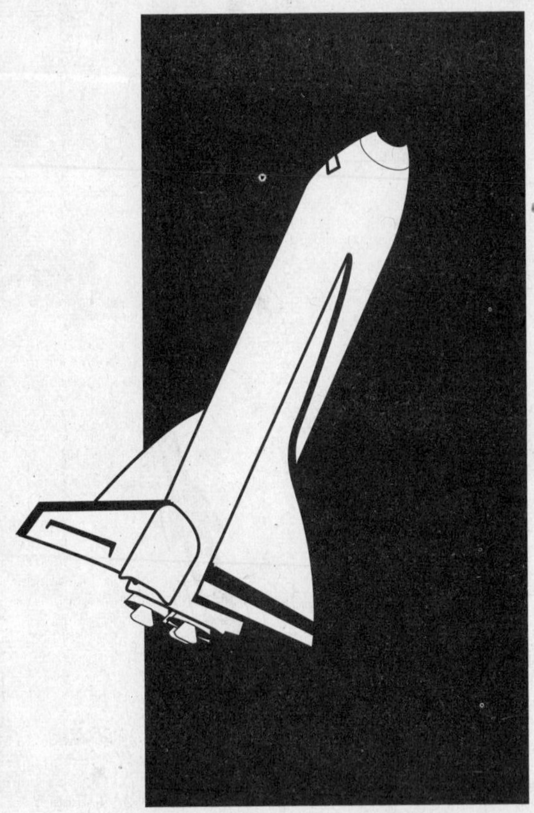

The space shuttle has many important uses. One use is for scientific research. In the weightless environment of space, scientists can carry out experiments they cannot do on Earth.

Inside the shuttle is a complete research laboratory called Spacelab. Spacelab is divided into two parts. One part is inside, where scientists can work. The other is outside and holds telescopes and other instruments that need to be exposed to space.

Most experiments take place in the inner section. Scientists on the space shuttle typically do experiments that make use of microgravity and weightlessness. They make new materials, such as crystals and silicon chips, and they also create medicines. Scientists even use themselves as test subjects, recording how weightlessness affects the human body.

Experiments in the outside section of Spacelab take advantage of being outside Earth's atmosphere. The atmosphere helps prevent radiation from reaching Earth, but it also makes radiation hard to study. Being outside the atmosphere also lets scientists use telescopes to get a clearer "view" of space.

Mae Jemison, Space Scientist

Comprehension Skill Topic and Main Idea

Name ______________________________

Exploring the Topic continued

Complete the chart below by filling in the topic and main ideas of the passage on page 116. Then write two details that support one of the main ideas.

Topic: ______________________________

Main Ideas:	
first paragraph	1. ______________________________
second paragraph	2. ______________________________
third paragraph	3. ______________________________
fourth paragraph	4. ______________________________

Details:

1. ______________________________

2. ______________________________

Mae Jemison, Space Scientist

Structural Analysis Suffixes *-ive* and *-ic*

Name ______________________________

Suffix Shuttle

Choose words from the word boxes to write in the blanks in the paragraph below. Use the clue in parentheses to help you.

-ic
artistic
historic
periodic
realistic

-ive
inventive
massive
positive
supportive

It was a truly (timely) ______________________ event when the shuttle first went up. The scientists who built it had (clever) ______________________ ideas. They were dreamers, but they were (aware of how things are) ______________________ about what was possible. They knew the shuttle's flights would have to be (now and then) ______________________ during the year. But watching the (big) ______________________ rocket rise into the air was breathtaking. Its fiery trail in the sky looked (made with style) ______________________. The entire country was (in favor) ______________________ of their efforts. They were (sure) ______________________ they had a winner!

Name ______________________________

The /ûr/ and /îr/ Sounds

When you hear the /ûr/ sound, think of the patterns *er, ir, ur, ear,* and *or.* When you hear the /îr/ sounds, think of the patterns *eer* and *ear.*

/ûr/ g**er**m, st**ir**, ret**ur**n, **ear**ly, w**or**th

/îr/ st**eer**, sm**ear**

► The /îr/ sound in *pier* differs from the usual spelling patterns. In this word it is spelled *ier.*

Write each Spelling Word under its vowel + *r* sound.

/ûr/ Sound

______________ ______________

______________ ______________

______________ ______________

______________ ______________

______________ ______________

______________ ______________

______________ ______________

____

/îr/ Sound

______________ ______________

______________ ______________

____

Spelling Words

1. smear
2. germ
3. return
4. peer
5. stir
6. squirm
7. nerve
8. early
9. worth
10. pier*
11. thirst
12. burnt
13. rear
14. term
15. steer
16. pearl
17. squirt
18. perch
19. hurl
20. worse

Name ________________________________

Mae Jemison, Space Scientist

Spelling The /ûr/ and /îr/ Sounds

Spelling Spree

Hint and Hunt Write the Spelling Word that answers each question.

1. What does a toy water pistol do?
2. What do you quench with a tall drink?
3. What is one thing you do with a spoon?
4. Where do you go to board a ship?
5. What might a diver find in an oyster?

1. ____________
2. ____________
3. ____________
4. ____________
5. ____________

Spelling Words

1. smear
2. germ
3. return
4. peer
5. stir
6. squirm
7. nerve
8. early
9. worth
10. pier*
11. thirst
12. burnt
13. rear
14. term
15. steer
16. pearl
17. squirt
18. perch
19. hurl
20. worse

Word Maze Begin at the arrow and follow the Word Maze to find ten Spelling Words. Write the words in order below.

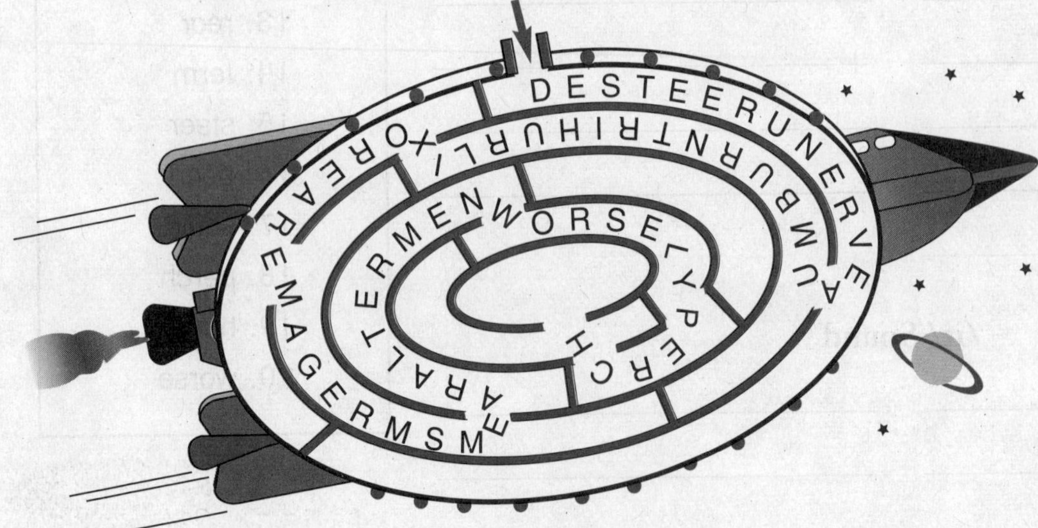

6. ____________
7. ____________
8. ____________
9. ____________
10. ____________
11. ____________
12. ____________
13. ____________
14. ____________
15. ____________

Name ______________________________

Proofreading and Writing

Proofreading Circle the five misspelled Spelling Words in this part of a script for a class skit. Then write each word correctly.

Astronaut: Mission Control, when can we begin our retern to Earth?

Mission Control: Probably erly tomorrow morning. How's it going up there? How much fuel have you burnt?

Astronaut: Not much—we've still got a few days' werth. We're all starting to squerm a bit up here, though. We're ready to go home. Actually, if I per closely through the glass here, I think I can see my house.

Mission Control: That's very funny.

Spelling Words

1. smear
2. germ
3. return
4. peer
5. stir
6. squirm
7. nerve
8. early
9. worth
10. pier*
11. thirst
12. burnt
13. rear
14. term
15. steer
16. pearl
17. squirt
18. perch
19. hurl
20. worse

1. ______________
2. ______________
3. ______________
4. ______________
5. ______________

Write a Newspaper Article You have been asked to write a brief article about Mae Jemison's space shuttle mission for the school newspaper. Did any one of the experiments particularly interest you? Will you include any details about Jemison's personal life?

On a separate piece of paper, write your article about Mae Jemison's mission. Use Spelling Words from the list.

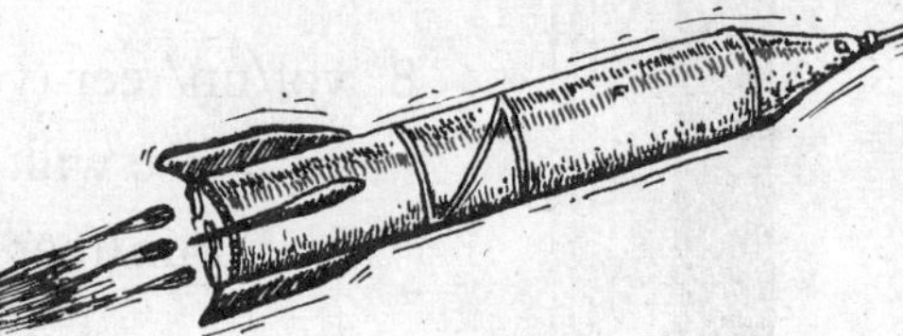

Name ______________________________

Stress on Syllables

Read each dictionary entry. Sound out the entry word three ways, placing stress on a different syllable each time. Circle the choice with the correct stress.

1. ad/ven/ture (ăd vĕn chər) *n.* A bold, dangerous, or risky undertaking.
   AD/ven/ture   ad/VEN/ture   ad/ven/TURE
2. en/gi/neer/ing (ĕn jə nîr ing) *n.* The practical use of scientific knowledge.
   EN/gi/neer/ing   en/GI/neer/ing   en/gi/NEER/ing
3. en/vi/ron/ment (ĕn vī rən mənt) *n.* Surroundings and conditions that affect the growth of living things.
   en/VI/ron/ment   en/vi/RON/ment   en/vi/ron/MENT
4. in/flu/ence (ĭn flo͞o əns) *n.* The power to have an effect without using direct force.
   IN/flu/ence   in/FLU/ence   in/flu/ENCE
5. or/gan/i/za/tion (ôr gən ĭ zā shən) *n.* A group of people united for some purpose or work.
   OR/gan/i/za/tion   or/GAN/i/za/tion   or/gan/i/ZA/tion
6. par/tic/i/pate (pär tĭs ə pāt) *v.* To join with others in doing something; take part.
   par/TIC/i/pate   par/tic/I/pate   par/tic/i/PATE
7. tel/e/vi/sion (tĕl ə vĭ zhən) *n.* The transmission and reception of visual images and sounds as electrical waves through the air or through wires.
   TEL/e/vi/sion   tel/e/VI/sion   tel/e/vi/SION
8. vol/un/teer (vŏl ən tîr) *n.* A person who performs a service of his or her own free will.
   VOL/un/teer   vol/UN/teer   vol/un/TEER

Name ____________________

Mae Jemison, Space Scientist

Grammar Skill Present Tense and Past Tense

Astronauts Travel into Space

Verb Tenses Verbs have forms, or tenses, that tell when the action occurs.

- A **present-tense** verb shows action that happens now, or that happens regularly over time.
- A **past-tense** verb shows that something already occurred.
- To form the **present tense,** add *-s* or *-es* to most verbs if the subject is singular. Do not add *-s* or *-es* if the subject is plural or *I* or *you.*
- To form the **past tense** of most verbs, add *-ed.*

On the line, write the tense of the verb in the first sentence of each pair. Then fill in the blank of the second sentence with the same verb, but change its tense.

Example: Astronauts conducted experiments in space. past
Astronauts conduct experiments in space.

1. My mother studies engineering at the university. ____________
My mother ____________ engineering at the university.
2. You learned about space travel in school. ____________
You ____________ about space travel in school.
3. I worked hard on my science project. ____________
I ____________ hard on my science project.
4. Kate's father designs bridges. ____________
Kate's father ____________ bridges.
5. She followed her dreams. ____________
She ____________ her dreams.

Name ______________________________

Astronauts Will Travel into Space

More about Verbs A **future-tense** verb shows that something is going to happen. Form the **future tense** by using the helping verb *will* or *shall* with the main verb.

Present Tense: I **see** many films about space.

Future Tense: I **will see** many films about space.

Present Tense: He **reads** about Jupiter.

Future Tense: He **shall read** about Jupiter.

Rewrite each sentence. Change each verb from the present or past tense to the future tense.

Example: You go to Cape Canaveral.

You will go to Cape Canaveral.

1. Astronauts fly the space shuttle.

____

2. The space probe landed on Mars.

____

3. You studied physics in college.

____

4. Meteors shoot across the sky.

____

5. We think about the future.

____

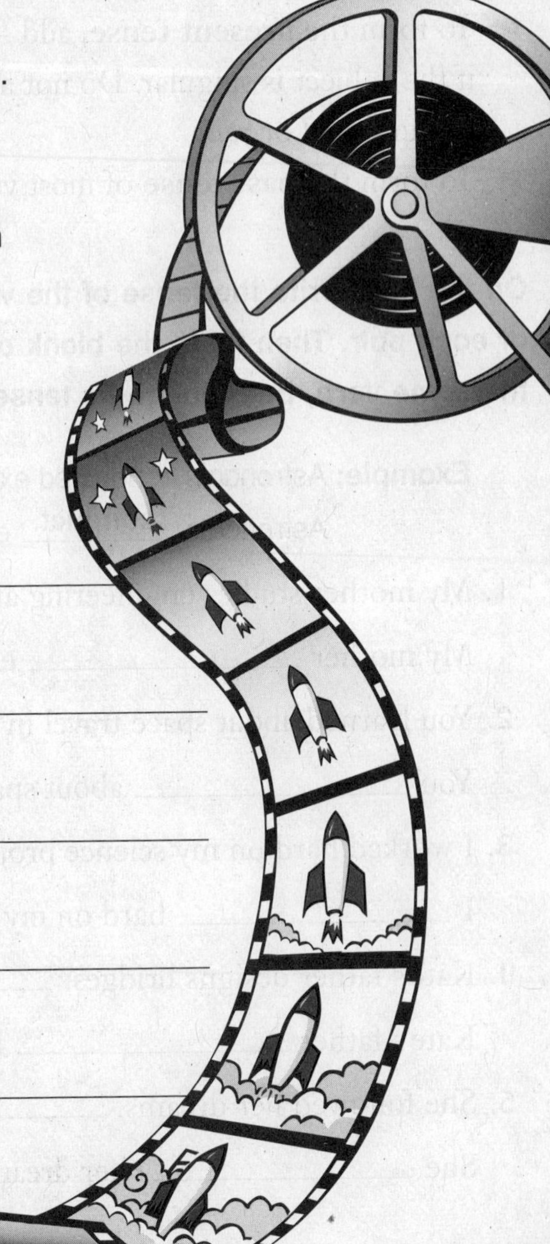

Name ______________________________

I Joined

Using the Right Tense A good writer uses the correct tense to talk about a particular time. Look at the two examples below. The second sentence in each pair makes more sense than the first sentence.

Incorrect: I will clean my room yesterday.
Correct: I cleaned my room yesterday.
Incorrect: Next Thursday Jeremy listens to me on the radio.
Correct: Next Thursday Jeremy will listen to me on the radio.

George has written a paragraph about his dream of joining the Peace Corps, like Mae Jemison and his teacher. Revise the paragraph to correct problems with verb tenses.

will go
Example: Next week, we went to South America.
^

Someday, I joined the Peace Corps. Last month, my teacher Mr. Stinson talks about his experience as a member of the Peace Corps in Ghana. He shows us photographs of the region too. He made many new friends while he was there. In the Peace Corps, my teacher will work to help build a school. Every day now I asked him to tell us more about it.

Name ______________________________

Persuasive Business Letter

Use this idea-support map to plan and organize a letter of recommendation to NASA telling why Mae Jemison would make an excellent astronaut.

Goal:

Reason:

Details:

Reason:

Details:

Reason:

Details:

Mae Jemison, Space Scientist

Writing Skill Improving Your Writing

Name ______________________________

Using the Right Tone

Tone is the attitude that a writer has toward a subject and is conveyed in the choice of words and details. Here are some tips to follow when you write a business letter:

- Use polite language and a formal tone.
- Use correct grammar and complete sentences.
- Avoid the use of slang.
- Do not include personal information.

Fill in the chart with examples of language and details that do *not* strike the proper tone.

144 Primrose Street
Evanston, IL 60201
October 23, 2001

Dr. Mae Jemison
P.O. Box 591455
Houston, TX 77259-1455

Dear Mae,

I am in the fifth grade at Primrose Elementary School. My class will be studying about space and space travel. I got a 91 on my last quiz. We hope you might be able to come talk to our class about your experiences as an astronaut.

It would be the bomb to meet an astronaut in person. My uncle is a pilot. We look forward to hearing from you. Do not give us some lame excuse about why you cannot speak here.

Love,
Karen Aldrin

Slang:
Impolite Language:
Informal Tone:
Personal Information:

Name ______________________________

Filling in the Blank

Use the test-taking strategies and tips you have learned to help you complete these fill-in-the-blank sentences with the correct answer. You may go back to *The Fear Place* if you need to. This practice will help you when you take this kind of test.

Read each item. In the answer row, fill in the circle that best completes each sentence.

1 When Doug climbs higher than nine thousand feet, —

- **A** he will be thirstier.
- **B** it will be harder for him to breathe.
- **C** he will not see any animals.
- **D** it will be easier for him to climb the rocks.

2 Doug predicted that when he reached Gordon's camp, —

- **F** Gordon would be okay.
- **G** Gordon would be gone.
- **H** Gordon's parents would be there.
- **J** Gordon would be in serious trouble.

3 If Doug thought about all the people who had died climbing the mountain, he might —

- **A** slip and fall.
- **B** decide to turn back.
- **C** find the climb more exciting.
- **D** go in the wrong direction.

4 If Doug stopped a while before reaching the Fear Place, he might —

- **F** have more time to conquer his fear.
- **G** see Gordon coming down the mountain.
- **H** find a safer way to climb the cliff.
- **J** be too afraid to continue.

ANSWER ROWS 1 (A) (B) (C) (D) 3 (A) (B) (C) (D)
2 (F) (G) (H) (J) 4 (F) (G) (H) (J)

Name ______________________________

Filling in the Blank continued

5 If Doug fell to the floor of the canyon —

A the cougar would not be able to find him.

B he would be killed.

C his parents would be disappointed.

D he would have to start the climb over.

6 If he hadn't followed the cougar along the ledge, Doug might —

F have gotten lost.

G have found a safer way to go.

H not have made it.

J have gotten chased by the cougar.

7 If Doug tied his shoelace while on the ledge, he might —

A not have the energy to stand up again.

B have lost his balance.

C have caused the ledge to break.

D not have been able to see the cougar.

8 The next time Doug gets to the Fear Place, he will probably —

F not be as frightened.

G have to follow the cougar again.

H be too afraid to make the journey.

J need Gordon to help him make it past this point.

ANSWER ROWS 5 Ⓐ Ⓑ Ⓒ Ⓓ 7 Ⓐ Ⓑ Ⓒ Ⓓ
6 Ⓕ Ⓖ Ⓗ Ⓙ 8 Ⓕ Ⓖ Ⓗ Ⓙ

Name ______________________

Spelling Review

Write Spelling Words from the list on this page to answer the questions.

1–8. Which eight words have the /ou/, /ô/, or /oi/ sounds?

1. ____________ 5. ____________
2. ____________ 6. ____________
3. ____________ 7. ____________
4. ____________ 8. ____________

9–26. Which eighteen words have the /ôr/, /âr/, /är/, /ûr/, or /îr/ sounds?

9. ____________ 18. ____________
10. ____________ 19. ____________
11. ____________ 20. ____________
12. ____________ 21. ____________
13. ____________ 22. ____________
14. ____________ 23. ____________
15. ____________ 24. ____________
16. ____________ 25. ____________
17. ____________ 26. ____________

27–30. Which four compound words have one of these words in them?

end wild test date

27. ____________ 29. ____________
28. ____________ 30. ____________

Spelling Words

1. halt
2. weekend
3. steer
4. gorge
5. first aid
6. smear
7. thousand
8. wildlife
9. hurl
10. brother-in-law
11. perch
12. test tube
13. wheelchair
14. early
15. noisy
16. launch
17. hawk
18. royal
19. worth
20. soar
21. pearl
22. up-to-date
23. tore
24. stir
25. snare
26. flair
27. carve
28. barge
29. coward
30. return

Name ______________________

Spelling Spree

Rhyme Time Write a Spelling Word that rhymes with the underlined word and makes sense in the sentence.

1. Marge, do you see that large ______________?
2. Howard, how did you spell the word ______________?
3. If the plane will ______________, we will roar.
4. Let us forge ahead through the narrow ______________.
5. I wore my new shirt until it ______________.
6. Please ______________ the ball to the girl with the curl.
7. Nate, please rate our new ______________ gate.

The Third Word Write the Spelling Word that belongs in each group.

8. to come back, to revisit, to ______________
9. diamond, ruby, ______________
10. sister-in-law, father-in-law, ______________
11. to balance, to wobble, to ______________
12. ten, hundred, ______________
13. days off, holiday, ______________
14. to start, to begin, to ______________
15. animals, nature, ______________

Spelling Words

1. weekend
2. coward
3. soar
4. up-to-date
5. brother-in-law
6. gorge
7. tore
8. thousand
9. wildlife
10. barge
11. launch
12. return
13. perch
14. pearl
15. hurl

Name ______________________

Proofreading and Writing

Proofreading Circle the six misspelled Spelling Words in this diary entry. Then write each word correctly.

April 18—This weekend I woke up erly to go to the race. At the track, I passed the first ade station and steered my weelchair into place at the starting line. The crowd was noysy. I didn't win, but I felt like a royel princess when I came to a hault at the finish line.

1. ______________ 4. ______________
2. ______________ 5. ______________
3. ______________ 6. ______________

Spelling Words

1. halt
2. noisy
3. early
4. hawk
5. test tube
6. snare
7. wheelchair
8. flair
9. steer
10. carve
11. stir
12. worth
13. smear
14. royal
15. first aid

Revise a Letter Write Spelling Words to complete the letter.

You should have seen me ______________ through the pack during the race! I flew like a ______________. Then I felt like I was caught in a ______________ when I hit some loose gravel. I recovered quickly. Racing is hard, but it is ______________ the effort. I have a real ______________ for it, I think.

School was fun today. For art class, I started to ______________ a horse out of soap. Then in science I had to ______________ a solution and put it in a ______________. Last, we had to ______________ pond water on a slide and look at it under a microscope.

Write an Article On a separate sheet of paper, write a short newspaper article about a race or sport you enjoy. Use the Spelling Review Words.

Name ______________________________

Two Poems

Choose two poems: one that rhymes and follows a pattern, and one that is free verse. On the chart below, compare the two poems by answering the questions.

	Rhyming Poem __________ Title	Free Verse Poem __________ Title
What is the poem about?		
What word or sound patterns are in the poem?		
What word pictures does the poem create?		

Name ______________________________

Poetry Award

You are the poetry editor for a magazine. Choose one poem from *Focus on Poetry* as the Poem of the Year. Tell what makes it a good poem and why people will want to read it.

Poem of the Year

____

I think this poem is the best because

____

____

____

____

____

____

____

____

____

____

____

____

____

____

____

____

Launching the Theme
Selection Connections

Name ______________________________

Voices of the Revolution

After reading each selection, complete the chart below and on the next page to show what you discovered.

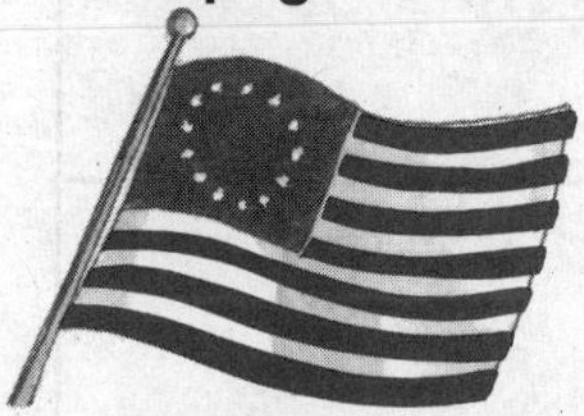

	And Then What Happened, Paul Revere?	Katie's Trunk	James Forten
What kind of writing is this selection an example of?			
Why was this story important to tell?			
What character traits are revealed by the character's actions?			

Name ______________________________

Voices of the Revolution

	And Then What Happened, Paul Revere?	Katie's Trunk	James Forten
What details about colonial life did you learn from the selection?			
What do you think the author's purpose for writing this selection was?			

How did the selections in *Voices of the Revolution* increase your understanding of life in that period?

____

____

____

Name ______________________________

Resisting Oppression

Use the words in the box to complete the paragraphs below.

Vocabulary

- revolution
- express
- cargo
- colonies
- oppose
- liberty
- Patriot
- sentries
- taxes

The residents of America's thirteen ____________________ resented the new ____________________ levied on them by the British government. A group of citizens in the Boston area formed a secret club to ____________________ England's method of governing America. The organization was known as the Sons of Liberty, and every member was a ____________________. The group won a place in history when its members dumped a ____________________ of tea into Boston Harbor to protest the tax on that commodity.

As it became clear that England would never allow the colonists a voice in their own government, Americans began discussing the possibility of ____________________. That kind of talk was dangerous, though, so messages were carried secretly by ____________________ riders from one city to another. The riders had to elude ____________________ or they would be deprived of their ____________________. The communications network they established proved to be very valuable when war finally broke out.

Choose one of the vocabulary words and write a sentence.

____

____

Name ______________________________

Fact or Opinion?

Fill in the chart with facts or opinions from the pages indicated in the first column. Where indicated, explain why the viewpoint is a fact or an opinion.

Page	Statement	Fact or Opinion	Viewpoint Revealed
263	"Of all the busy people in Boston, Paul Revere would turn out to be one of the busiest."	Opinion	This statement shows that the author believes Paul Revere was busy all his life. She seems to be very impressed by him.
264		Opinion	
266		Fact	
269		Fact	
275		Opinion and Fact	

Name ___________________________

When Did It Happen, Paul Revere?

The timeline below lists some important dates in Paul Revere's life. Answer the questions next to each date to help complete the timeline.

1735 What is Boston like when Paul Revere is born?

____

____

____

1756 How does Revere respond when French soldiers and Indians attack the colonies?

____

1773 On the night of December 16, Revere and the other Sons of Liberty are very busy in Boston Harbor. What are they doing?

____

____

1776 On the night of April 18, Revere is sent to Lexington and Concord. What happens on his Big Ride?

____

____

____

1783 By the end of the war, Revere is 48 years old. What does he do?

____

____

1810 What is Boston like now that Revere is 75 years old?

____

____

Name ___________________________

Viewing the Author

Read the passage. Then answer the questions on page 143.

Traitor or Hero?

How should Benedict Arnold be remembered: as a traitor, or as a hero of the American Revolution? I'm not sure this question has a simple answer.

Arnold joined the Patriot militia in 1774. After the Revolutionary War began in 1775, he helped lead the capture of Fort Ticonderoga from the British. Later that year, he led over a thousand soldiers into Canada, was wounded in battle, and earned a promotion for bravery. In October of 1777, he was again seriously wounded as he led his soldiers against the forces of the British general Burgoyne. Arnold's courageous leadership helped the Americans win one of their most important victories in the war.

But in 1780, Arnold worked out a plan with the British to surrender an important American military base in exchange for money. After his plan was discovered, he escaped and joined the British army. Why did he do this? Many historians believe that Arnold felt his country had treated him unfairly. He was disappointed when he was passed over for a promotion. He was also accused of being too easy on Americans who were loyal to the British. This may have angered him.

The British never paid Arnold all the money he asked for. The land they gave him in Canada was not useful to him. When Arnold died in 1801, he had become poor, discouraged, and lonely, for he was a man few people trusted. Arnold was a traitor, it is true. But we should not forget that he performed several heroic acts that helped our nation win its independence.

Name ______________________________

Viewing the Author continued

1. What is the viewpoint of the author of this passage?

____

____

2. Which sentences reveal the author's viewpoint?

____

____

3. What do you think the author's purpose is for writing this passage?

____

____

4. Write a sentence from the passage that shows the author's opinion.

____

5. Write a fact from the passage that helps to support the author's viewpoint.

____

____

6. Write a fact from the passage that might support a different viewpoint about the subject.

____

____

____

____

____

____

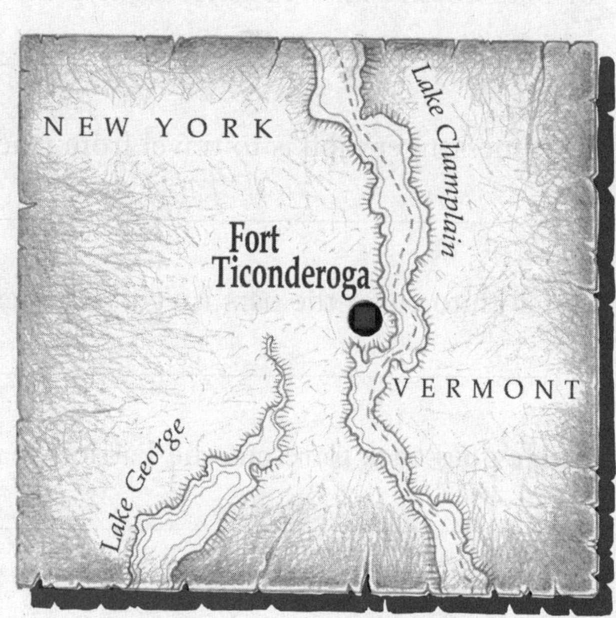

And Then What Happened, Paul Revere?

Structural Analysis
Possessives and Contractions

Name ______________________________

No Apostrophes!

Your school is putting on a play of *And Then What Happened, Paul Revere?* You're sending an e-mail to the script writer, but the apostrophe (') on the computer doesn't work! Change each contraction or possessive to its longer form. Write P for possessive or C for contraction in each box.

1. Paul makes a squirrel's silver collar.

   ______________________________ ☐

2. The writing's sloppy in the letters Paul writes.

   ______________________________ ☐

3. Paul rings the church bells at a moment's notice.

   ______________________________ ☐

4. The English are taxing tea, glass, and printers' inks.

   ______________________________ ☐

5. Paul doesn't miss a chance to help the Sons of Liberty.

   ______________________________ ☐

6. A messenger's job is to travel from place to place on horseback.

   ______________________________ ☐

7. Cloth to cover the oars isn't all Paul leaves behind.

   ______________________________ ☐

8. He goes back to rescue the Patriots' papers.

   ______________________________ ☐

Name ______________________________

And Then What Happened, Paul Revere?

Spelling Final /ər/

Final /ər/

The **schwa sound** is a weak vowel sound that is often found in an unstressed syllable. It is shown as /ə/. When you hear the final /ər/ sound in words of more than one syllable, think of the patterns *er*, *or*, and *ar*.

/ər/ ang**er**, act**or**, pill**ar**

Write each Spelling Word under the pattern that spells its final /ər/ sound.

er	*or*
______	______
______	______
______	______
______	______
______	______
______	______
______	
______	

ar

______

______

______

______

Spelling Words

1. theater
2. actor
3. mirror
4. powder
5. humor
6. anger
7. banner
8. pillar
9. major
10. thunder
11. flavor
12. finger
13. mayor
14. polar
15. clover
16. burglar
17. tractor
18. matter
19. lunar
20. quarter

Name ______________________

Spelling Spree

Find a Rhyme For each sentence write a Spelling Word that rhymes with the underlined word and makes sense.

1. Do me a favor and pick a different _____ of ice cream.
2. I wonder if we'll hear _____ during the rainstorm.
3. The town paved over a field of _____.
4. The butler hung a colorful _____ outside the manor.
5. Put the _____ in the coin sorter.
6. They hope to run the _____ station on solar power.
7. The _____ was a factor in the movie's success.

1. ______________ 5. ______________
2. ______________ 6. ______________
3. ______________ 7. ______________
4. ______________

Spelling Words

1. theater
2. actor
3. mirror
4. powder
5. humor
6. anger
7. banner
8. pillar
9. major
10. thunder
11. flavor
12. finger
13. mayor
14. polar
15. clover
16. burglar
17. tractor
18. matter
19. lunar
20. quarter

Puzzle Play Write the Spelling Word that fits each clue. Then write the circled letters in order below.

8. a farm machine
9. a pointer or a pinky
10. fury
11. a column
12. a thief
13. a surface that reflects
14. place for movies
15. person in charge of a city

Mystery Words: a ___ _____

Name ______________________________

Proofreading and Writing

Proofreading Circle the five misspelled Spelling Words in this notice to British troops. Then write each word correctly.

April 16, 1775

From Boston Headquarters:

We are planning a majer march into the countryside on the evening of the 18th. The current lunor phase will give us a full moon, so there will be plenty of light. If all goes well, we will surprise the rebels and take their supplies of guns and powdur. This mater should be kept secret, of course. Stay calm, and react to any unpleasant situations with humer rather than anger. More details will follow.

1. ______________
2. ______________
3. ______________
4. ______________
5. ______________

Spelling Words

1. theater
2. actor
3. mirror
4. powder
5. humor
6. anger
7. banner
8. pillar
9. major
10. thunder
11. flavor
12. finger
13. mayor
14. polar
15. clover
16. burglar
17. tractor
18. matter
19. lunar
20. quarter

Write Interview Questions If you could interview Paul Revere, what questions would you ask him? Would you like to know more about his work as a silversmith or details of his famous ride?

On a separate piece of paper, write some questions that you would like to ask this famous patriot about his life and the historical events in which he took part. Use Spelling Words from the list.

Name ______________________

Synonym Switch

Find a synonym in the box for each underlined word. Rewrite the sentences using the synonyms.

Vocabulary

arrived
departed
discovered
dragged
earned
hurried
pounded
sneaked
threw
woke

1. In Boston Harbor, ships constantly came and left.

____

____

2. Paul found that money could be made in many ways.

____

____

3. The men hauled the chests to the deck and tossed the tea overboard.

____

____

4. Paul slipped past the sentries and dashed through the snow.

____

____

5. Paul beat on doors in Lexington and aroused the citizens.

____

____

Name ___________________________________

Where's Your House, Paul Revere?

Subject-Verb Agreement A verb must agree in number with its subject. In the present tense, add *-s* or *-es* to the verb if the subject is singular. Do not add *-s* or *-es* if the subject is plural or if the subject is *I* or *you*. If you are using *be* or *have* as helping verbs, use the form that agrees with the subject in number.

Complete each sentence with the present-tense form of the verb in parentheses that agrees with the subject in number.

1. We ______________ visiting Paul Revere's house in Boston. (be)
2. My cousin ______________ the silver teapot on display. (like)
3. I ______________ tankards Paul Revere made. (see)
4. A 900-pound bell ______________ in the courtyard of the Revere house. (stand)
5. The silver cup and tray ______________ brightly. (shine)
6. You ______________ to the Old North Church. (walk)
7. She __________ gazing at the church steeple where the lanterns hung. (be)
8. I ______________ Revere's midnight ride to Lexington. (imagine)
9. Tourists ______________ the Freedom Trail in Boston. (walk)
10. I ______________ learned about American patriots. (have)

Name ______________________________

What Was Your Ride Like, Paul Revere?

Regular and Irregular Verbs To form the past tense of regular verbs, add *-ed* to the verb. Irregular verbs have special forms for the past tense. Do not add *-ed* to irregular verbs.

Tracy and Kim have written an interview to perform in history class. To enjoy the interview, fill in the correct past-tense forms of the verbs in parentheses. You may have to check irregular verbs in your dictionary.

Reporter: We are on the scene with the famous Patriot Paul Revere. Mr. Revere, you have returned from an important mission. What was it like on that ride, sir?

Paul Revere: My midnight ride ____________ (be) exciting. I ____________ (ride) as fast as I ____________ (can)! I don't think I have ever ______________ (ride) so fast before!

Reporter: We have heard that you ______________ (forget) your spurs. Is that true?

Paul Revere: Yes, I ____________ (do), but my faithful dog ________________ (bring) them to me.

Reporter: You also ____________ (row) across the river, right?

Paul Revere: I ____________ (run) as fast as I could, too, and I ______________ (warn) the people about the British.

Reporter: Paul Revere, American Patriot, your country is grateful.

Name ______________________________

What Did You See, Shirley Jensen?

Choosing the Correct Verb Form It is important for a writer to choose the correct form of a verb. For irregular verbs, you may have to check your dictionary.

Shirley keeps a journal on her computer. She recently took a trip to Boston and wants to write an essay about her experience. To get started, she has printed out her journal entries. Proofread the journal entry below and circle the incorrect verb forms. Then write the correct form above the error.

July 15

We arrived at Logan Airport this morning. We taked a subway to Grandma's apartment in Boston. I had took a subway train before in New York City. I wish we haved a subway in Allentown!

Grandma fixes us lunch, but I wasn't hungry because I had ate too many peanuts on the plane. I thinked we might go to the beach in the afternoon, but we goed downtown instead. Grandma shown us the State House with the golden dome. It was beautiful! Then we visit Paul Revere's house. We seen some of the beautiful things he made.

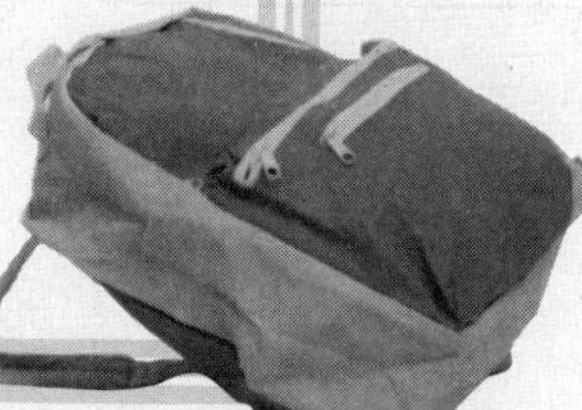

Name ______________________________

Description of a Character

And Then What Happened, Paul Revere? gives many details about Paul Revere, a hero of the American Revolution. These details help you understand what kind of person he was. Using vivid details in your writing can help bring a person to life. A **description of a character** is a written profile that describes how a person looks, acts, thinks, and feels.

Choose a real person from another selection you have read to write about. Use the web to brainstorm details about the character's personality traits, physical appearance, actions, and thoughts.

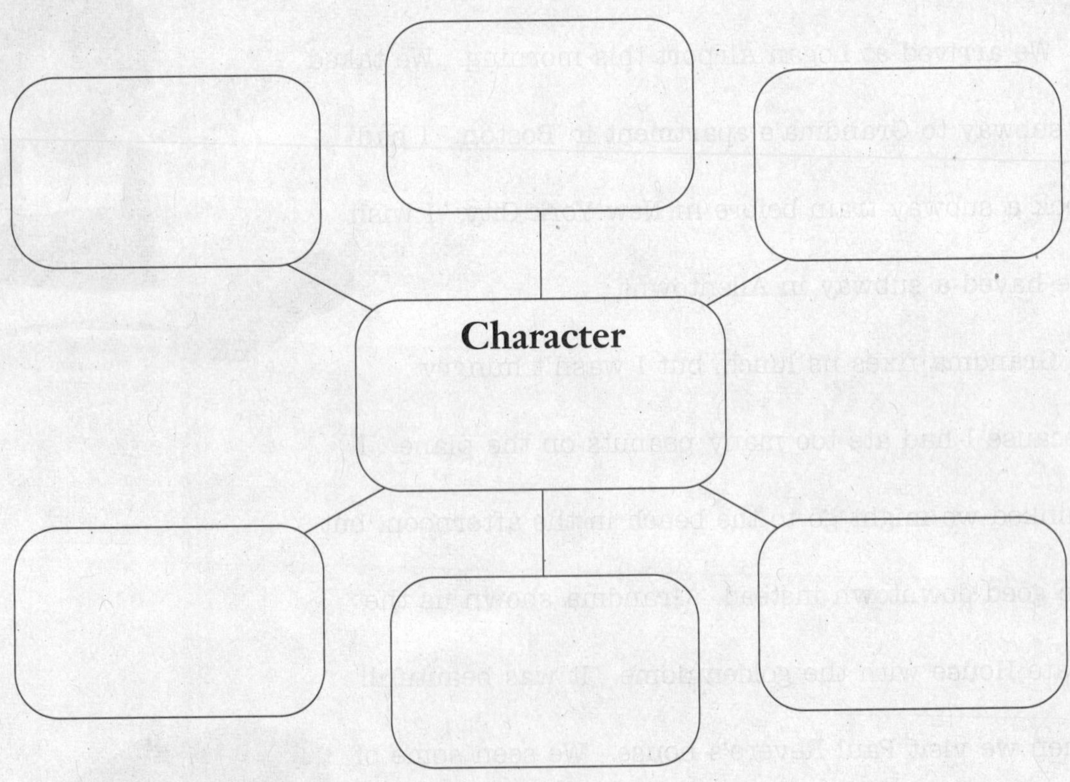

Name ______________________________

Using Exact Nouns and Verbs

Which noun, *lights* or *chandeliers*, is more exact? Which verb, *galloped* or *rode*, is more exact? A good writer avoids using vague nouns and verbs. Exact nouns and verbs like *chandeliers* and *galloped* can make your writing clearer and help readers create a more vivid mental picture of the people, places, and events that you describe.

One fifth-grader drafted these sentences for a description of Paul Revere. Can you help her make her writing clearer and more vivid? Rewrite each sentence on the lines, replacing the underlined vague nouns and verbs with more exact ones from the list below.

More Exact Nouns and Verbs

crafted	careers
hardware store	colonists
opened	warned
tea	silver
pursued	dumped

1. Throughout his life, Paul Revere did many different things.

____

____

2. He made pitchers, candlesticks, and buckles from metal.

____

____

3. With other patriots, he disguised himself as an Indian, boarded a British ship, and put stuff into Boston Harbor.

____

____

4. He became a hero when he told people that British troops were coming.

____

____

Name ______________________________

Revising Your Story

Reread your story. What do you need to make it better? Use this page to help you decide. Put a checkmark in the box for each sentence that describes your story.

Rings the Bell!

- ☐ The setting, characters, and plot are well defined.
- ☐ My story has a distinct beginning, middle, and end.
- ☐ The main character has an interesting conflict to resolve.
- ☐ I use dialogue and exact verbs to make the story's action clear.
- ☐ There are almost no mistakes.

Getting Stronger

- ☐ The setting, characters, and plot could be more clear.
- ☐ My plot isn't always easy to follow.
- ☐ The main character's conflict could be more interesting.
- ☐ I could add more dialogue and exact verbs to make the action clear.
- ☐ There are a few mistakes.

Try Harder

- ☐ The setting and plot are not easy to follow.
- ☐ There is no clear problem.
- ☐ I haven't included details or dialogue.
- ☐ There are a lot of mistakes.

Name ______________________________

Using Exact Verbs

Replace each underlined verb. Circle the letter of the verb that best completes each sentence.

1. Nina <u>rearranged</u> the cards in the deck.
   a. moved b. mixed c. shuffled d. wrinkled
2. "<u>Have</u> one card," she said to Ted. "Then put it back into the deck."
   a. Replace b. Remove c. Repair d. Deliver
3. "Is this your card?" she asked, <u>showing</u> the Queen of Hearts.
   a. flashing b. flushing c. hiding d. presenting
4. Ted <u>moved</u> his head sadly. "No, it's not my card," he said.
   a. rotated b. turned c. stiffened d. shook
5. "Oh goodness," Nina said. "I've <u>done</u> it again."
   a. smiled b. misjudged c. blundered d. coughed
6. Then Nina's hand <u>went</u> behind her ear and pulled out a card.
   a. fell b. darted c. skipped d. grasped
7. "That's my card," Ted <u>said</u>. "The deuce of clubs!"
   a. mentioned b. noted c. exclaimed d. whispered
8. "Thank you very much," Nina said. She bowed to her audience and <u>ran off</u> the stage.
   a. scampered b. slinked c. wriggled d. skipped

Name ______________________________

Spelling Words

Words Often Misspelled Look for familiar spelling patterns to help you remember how to spell the Spelling Words on this page. Think carefully about the parts that you find hard to spell in each word.

Write the missing letters in the Spelling Words below.

1. happ ___ ly
2. min ___ ___ ___
3. b ___ ___ ___ t ___ ful
4. usua ___ ___ y
5. inst ___ ___ d
6. stre ___ ___ ___
7. l ___ ing
8. e ___ ___ ite
9. mil ___ ___ meter
10. d ___ v ___ ___ ___
11. unt ___ ___
12. wri ___ ___ ng
13. tr ___ ___ ___
14. b ___ f ___ ___ ___
15. ___ at ___ ___ day

Study List **On a separate piece of paper, write each Spelling Word. Check your spelling against the words on the list.**

Spelling Words

1. happily
2. minute
3. beautiful
4. usually
5. instead
6. stretch
7. lying
8. excite
9. millimeter
10. divide
11. until
12. writing
13. tried
14. before
15. Saturday

Name ______________________________

Spelling Spree

Phrase Fillers Write the Spelling Word that best completes each phrase.

1. a _____ and true method
2. to yawn and _____
3. wait a _____
4. _____ down for a nap
5. to _____ into two pieces
6. dinner comes _____ dessert
7. _____ a letter

1. ______________
2. ______________
3. ______________
4. ______________
5. ______________
6. ______________
7. ______________

Syllable Scramble Rearrange the syllables to write a Spelling Word. One syllable in each item is extra.

8. til un till
9. ur date day Sat
10. cite ite ex
11. ly u al fer su
12. pi hap an ly
13. in ted stead
14. ti ness ful beau
15. mil time ter li me

8. ______________
9. ______________
10. ______________
11. ______________
12. ______________
13. ______________
14. ______________
15. ______________

Spelling Words

1. happily
2. minute
3. beautiful
4. usually
5. instead
6. stretch
7. lying
8. excite
9. millimeter
10. divide
11. until
12. writing
13. tried
14. before
15. Saturday

Name ______________________________

Proofreading and Writing

Proofreading Circle the five misspelled Spelling Words in this open letter. Then write each word correctly.

Fellow Countrymen:

I am riting these words to urge you all to action. This land cannot spend another minut under the tyrannical rule of the British King! We have tride to plead and reason with him, but he will not listen. Now, insted of talking, we must fight! If we do, it will not be long before we are living hapilly in our own nation. Join the struggle for liberty now!

1. ______________
2. ______________
3. ______________
4. ______________
5. ______________

Spelling Words

1. happily
2. minute
3. beautiful
4. usually
5. instead
6. stretch
7. lying
8. excite
9. millimeter
10. divide
11. until
12. writing
13. tried
14. before
15. Saturday

Slogan Writing Pick three Spelling Words. Then, with each one, write a slogan (such as "Don't Tread on Me" or "Liberty or Death") that could have been used during the Revolutionary War.

Name ______________________________

Some Talk of Revolution

Answer each of the following questions by writing a vocabulary word.

Vocabulary

arming
skittish
just
fierce
skirmish
peered
rebels
kin
drilling

1. Which word means "right" or "fair"?
____
2. Which word names individuals fighting against their government? ______________________
3. Which word means "giving weapons to"?
____
4. Which word means "practicing for battle"?
____
5. Which word is a synonym for *nervous*?
____
6. Which word means "looked"?
____
7. Which word is an antonym for *meek*?
____
8. Which word means "a brief battle"?
____
9. Which word is a synonym for *relatives*?
____

Write a different question using one of the vocabulary words.

____

____

Name ______________________________

Why Did It Happen?

Fill in the columns where indicated with the cause or the effect of the events included in the chart.

Causes	Effects
	The uneasiness and fighting make Katie's family feel skittish, nervous, and worried.
	The family has lost friends and neighbors.
Armed rebels come to Katie's home.	
Katie feels that it is not just for their neighbors to break into their house and ruin their things.	
	Katie hides inside her mother's wedding trunk.
When John Warren searches the trunk and discovers Katie, he calls the rebels away and leaves the lid open so she can breathe.	

Name ______________________________

In the Characters' Words

Read the characters' words in the left column. In the right column, write why each character said what he or she did.

What the Character Said	Why the Character Said It
Mama: "It makes me as skittish as a newborn calf."	
Papa: "Get your mother! Hide in the woods."	
Katie: "It was not right. It was not just. It was not fair."	
The rebels: "This'll be fine pickings!"	
John Warren: "Out! The Tories are coming. Back to the road! Hurry!"	
Katie: "He'd left one seam of goodness there, and we were all tied to it."	

Name ______________________________________

Making Connections

Read the story. Then complete the activity on page 163.

A Dangerous Day

My name is Margaret Tompkins. I work as a nurse in a field hospital here in Virginia. When my brother enlisted as a soldier in the Union army, I, too, wanted to join and help the cause. I decided to become a nurse. I came to this area three months ago when my brother's company was sent here.

For the past few hours, our soldiers have been involved in a fierce battle. After almost ten hours of fighting, they are exhausted and very hungry. Some of the wounded have been brought to the hospital, where the other nurses and I have been treating them. It is hard, heartbreaking work.

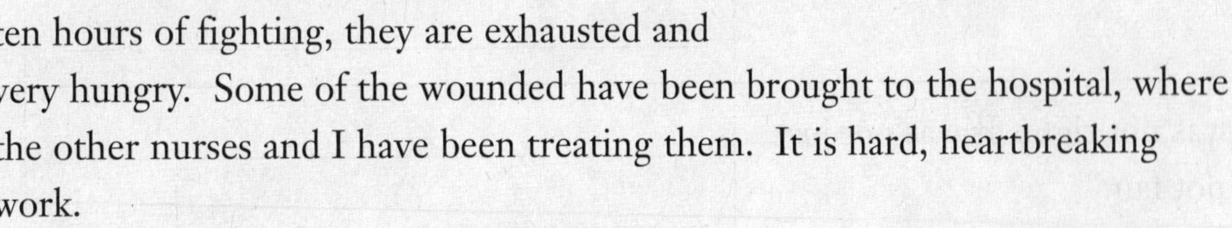

It is now just past three in the afternoon. Over the noise, I suddenly hear my brother's voice calling "Margaret!" I grab a medical bag and run out onto the field. When I reach James, he is sitting next to a cannon, holding his left shoulder.

"What has happened?" I ask him.

"The cannon recoiled and twisted my shoulder out of its socket," he tells me. I tell James I will lead him to the hospital so he can be treated. He shakes his head. "I can't leave here," he says. "Someone has to fire the cannon."

I look around and realize that, for the moment, no one else is nearby. Finally I say, "James, you cannot fire a cannon with a dislocated shoulder. You go. I have watched cannons being fired. I'll take a turn here." He goes.

I feel afraid. But I prepare the cannon. Here is a chance to do more to win the war than just unroll bandages.

Name ______________________________

Making Connections continued

Complete the cause-effect chain to show what caused the events described on page 162, and what happened as a result.

Causes	Effects
Margaret wants to help the Union effort.	______________________
______________________	Margaret travels to Virginia to work in a field hospital and be near him.
______________________	James's shoulder is dislocated.
James refuses to get his shoulder treated because he is the only soldier at the post.	______________________
______________________	Margaret prepares the cannon even though she feels afraid.

Name ______________________________

Signalling Syllables

Rewrite each underlined word, adding slashes between its syllables. Then write a definition of the word.

1. The family usually sat and talked with visitors in the parlor.

   ____

2. Katie's mother is skittish because of the fighting in the area.

   ____

3. Dragonflies would land briefly on the rocks before flying away again.

   ____

4. As she hid in the trunk, Katie heard faraway voices and footsteps.

   ____

5. The incident was just a skirmish, not a major battle.

   ____

6. A large horse went thudding by on the road.

   ____

Name ______________________________

VCCV and VCV Patterns

A **syllable** is a word part with one vowel sound. To spell a two-syllable word, divide the word into syllables. Divide a VCCV word between the consonants. Divide a VCV word before or after the consonant. Look for spelling patterns you have learned, and spell the word by syllables.

VC | CV	VC | CV
ar | rive	**par | lor**
VC | V	V | CV
val | ue	**a | ware**
clos | et	**be | have**

Write each Spelling Word under the heading that tells how it is divided.

Spelling Words

1. equal
2. parlor
3. collect
4. closet
5. perhaps
6. wedding
7. rapid
8. value
9. arrive
10. behave
11. shoulder
12. novel
13. tulip
14. sorrow
15. vanish
16. essay
17. publish
18. aware
19. subject
20. prefer

VC | CV

____
____
____
____
____
____
____
____
____
____

VC | V

____
____
____
____
____

V | CV

____
____
____
____
____

Name ______________________________

Spelling Spree

Syllable Match Match each of the following syllables with one of the numbered syllables to create Spelling Words. Then write the words on the blanks provided.

ar	qual	have	par	a
et	wed	pre	lish	el

1. **nov** ____________
2. **lor** ____________
3. **fer** ____________
4. **clos** ____________
5. **e** ____________
6. **ding** ____________
7. **be** ____________
8. **ware** ____________
9. **rive** ____________
10. **pub** ____________

The Third Word Write the Spelling Word that belongs with each group.

11. sadness, grief, ____________
12. possibly, maybe, ____________
13. worth, price, ____________
14. gather, accumulate, ____________
15. fast, speedy, ____________
16. rose, daffodil, ____________
17. topic, field, ____________
18. paper, report, ____________
19. wrist, elbow, ____________
20. fade, disappear, ____________

Spelling Words

1. equal
2. parlor
3. collect
4. closet
5. perhaps
6. wedding
7. rapid
8. value
9. arrive
10. behave
11. shoulder
12. novel
13. tulip
14. sorrow
15. vanish
16. essay
17. publish
18. aware
19. subject
20. prefer

Katie's Trunk

Spelling VCCV and VCV Patterns

Name ______________________________

Proofreading and Writing

Proofreading Circle the five misspelled Spelling Words in this speech. Then write each word correctly.

Fellow Townspeople!

Recent events have made it clear. The flag of England will soon vannish from our land. We are aware, however, that certain people prefur to remain loyal to King George. This has made some of us angry. Indeed, some people behav as if they don't know their own neighbors. The rappid changes of the past months have stirred up strong feelings, but everyone must remain calm! If you vallue the freedoms of our new land, you will respect your neighbors' homes and property whether or not you share their beliefs.

1. ______________
2. ______________
3. ______________
4. ______________
5. ______________

Spelling Words

1. equal
2. parlor
3. collect
4. closet
5. perhaps
6. wedding
7. rapid
8. value
9. arrive
10. behave
11. shoulder
12. novel
13. tulip
14. sorrow
15. vanish
16. essay
17. publish
18. aware
19. subject
20. prefer

Write a Bulletin-Board Notice You want your classmates to join you in some activity, perhaps organizing a pep rally or raising money for disaster relief or some other worthy cause. How will you get their attention?

On a separate piece of paper, write a notice to tack up on a school bulletin board giving reasons why students should join you in the activity.

Name ______________________________

Turning the Key

Use the spelling table/pronunciation key to figure out how to pronounce the underlined words. Then find a word in the box with the same vowel sound as the underlined word, and write it after the sentence.

Vocabulary

meant
steer
blood
took
town
flour

Sounds	Spellings	Sample Words
/ĕ/	e, ea	shed, breath
/î/	ea, ee, ie, e	dear, deer, pier, mere
/ŭ/	o, u, ou, oo	cut, rough, flood
/o͝o/	u, oo, o	full, book, wolf
/ou/	ou, ow	about, crown

1. Crouched in the underbrush, I felt like an animal in a trap.

____

2. In a fierce whisper, Mama was trying to call me back.

____

3. The men ripped the knocker off the wood.

____

4. The rustle of the clothing in the trunk drowned their words.

____

5. I could hear the drums of the rebels who were marching in town.

____

6. A sudden thread of a song ran through my head.

____

Name ______________________________

Katie's Adventure

Verb Phrases with *have* Many verb phrases begin with a form of *have*, *has*, or *had*. Use *has* with singular subjects. Use *have* with plural subjects or with *I* or *you*. Use *had* with either singular subjects or plural subjects.

Underline the verb phrase in the following sentences.

1. Katie and her family had been friends with their neighbors before the revolution.
2. Political differences now have come between them.
3. It has been difficult for everyone.
4. The rebels have entered the house.
5. Katie has hidden in a trunk.

Fill in the correct form of the verbs in parentheses to complete the following sentences.

6. They have ______________ (break) a precious teapot.
7. It has ______________ (be) a trying time for the family.
8. I have ______________ (enjoy) reading the story about British loyalists.
9. You have ______________ (make) me think.
10. Mr. Roby had ______________ (hope) the class would like the story.

Name ______________________________

Let Us Learn About Lexington

teach, learn; let, leave; sit, set; can, may Some pairs of verbs can be confusing. The meanings of these verbs are related but different. Study the definitions carefully.

teach—to instruct
learn—to be instructed

sit—to rest or stay in one place
set—to put

let—to allow
leave—to go away

can—to have the ability to
may—to have permission

Choose between the two verbs in parentheses to correctly complete each sentence.

1. We will ______________ (teach, learn) about the American Revolution.
2. Ms. Amata will ______________ (teach, learn) us about the Tories.
3. In Lexington, our class ______________ (can, may) see a statue of a Minuteman.
4. You ______________ (can, may) take my picture beside the statue.
5. In Boston, we ______________ (can, may) see the harbor where the rebels dumped the tea.
6. We will ______________ (sit, set) on a bench at the harbor.
7. I'll ______________ (sit, set) my camera on the bench.
8. ______________ (Can, May) I borrow your history book?
9. My teacher ______________ (lets, leaves) me ask many questions.
10. They will ______________ (let, leave) before lunch.

Name ______________________

Uncle Warren's Trunk

Choosing the Correct Verb Michael is writing a letter to his cousin, but he is uncertain about the correct verb to use. Choose the correct verbs from the list to fill in the blanks.

teach
learn
let
leave
sit
set
can
may

Dear Kenya,

I read a story about a girl who had to hide in a trunk. It reminded me of the trunk we saw in Uncle Warren's attic. Do you remember? I talked to Uncle Warren on Sunday, and he said that we ______________ open it next time we visit. I hope we find a Revolutionary War sword inside! If we do, we ______________ try to find out who owned it. We would ______________ a lot about history that way. Uncle Warren doesn't think we will find anything that old, but he said he will ______________ us about the history of our family.

______________ you come next Saturday? If not, will your parents ______________ you come the following Saturday? If you ______________ your house before noon, we ______________ have lunch. I will ______________ on the porch and wait for you. I better ______________ down my pen now and turn out the light.

Your cousin,
Michael

Name ______________________________

Friendly Letter

Katie Gray in *Katie's Trunk* lived in the 1700s during the Revolutionary War. If she wanted to share her experience of hiding in the trunk, Katie could not have called a friend or sent an e-mail message. However, she might have written a friendly letter. A **friendly letter** is a letter that you write to a friend to share news about your life.

Use this page to organize your friendly letter. Follow these steps.

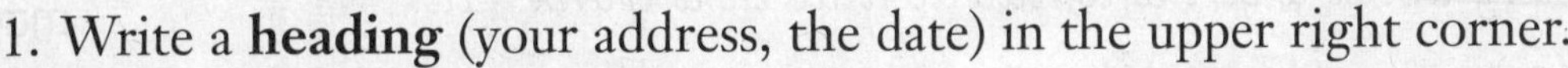

1. Write a **heading** (your address, the date) in the upper right corner.
2. Write a **greeting** (*Dear* and the person's name followed by a comma) at the left margin.
3. Use the chart below to plan the **body** of the letter. Under Events, list the important things that happened. What important details do you recall? List them under Details.

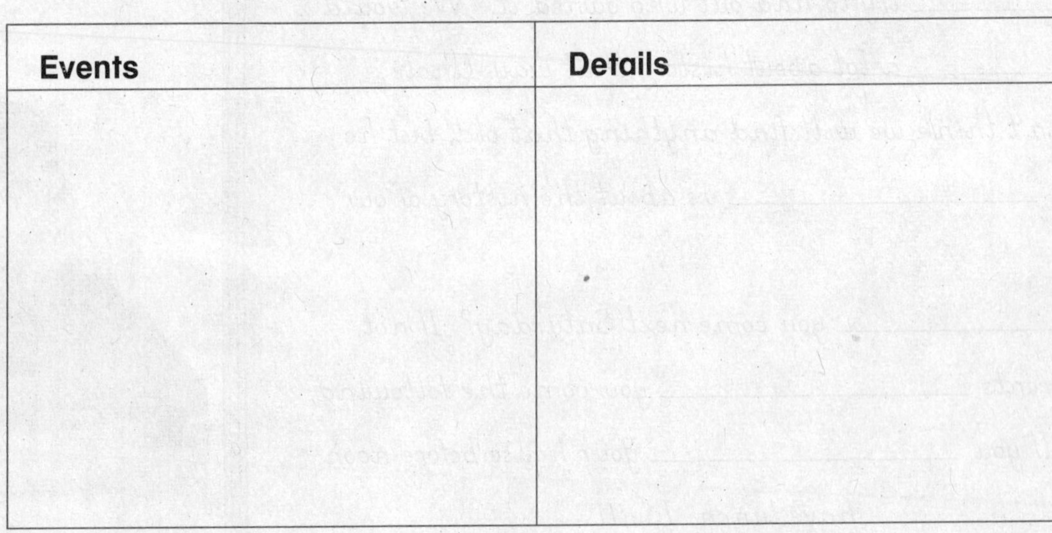

Events	Details

4. Write an informal **closing**, such as *Love* or *Your Friend*, followed by a comma in the lower right corner.
5. Sign your name under the closing.

Name ______________________________

Voice

Every writer has a **voice,** or a unique way of expressing himself or herself. A writer's voice helps reveal what he or she is like as a person. You can sometimes also "hear" a narrator's or a character's voice when you read a work of literature. For example, listen for Mama's voice as you read this sentence from *Katie's Trunk:* "Tea! In the harbor! Wasting God's good food."

You can strengthen your own writing voice when you write by showing more of what you think and feel, and by including expressions you commonly use when speaking, such as *No way!* or *I'm psyched* or *You've got to be kidding.*

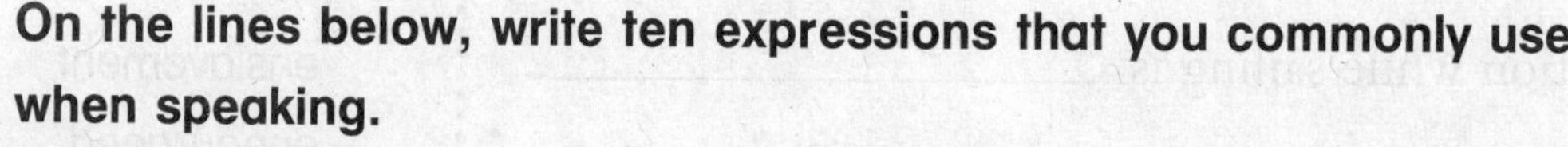

On the lines below, write ten expressions that you commonly use when speaking.

My Common Expressions

______________________ (expression of fear)	______________________ (expression of disgust)
______________________ (expression of surprise)	______________________ (expression of embarrassment)
______________________ (expression of encouragement)	______________________ (expression of affection)
______________________ (expression of confusion)	______________________ (expression of pleasure)
______________________ (expression of doubt)	______________________ (expression of concern)

When you revise your friendly letter, use these expressions to strengthen your writing voice. By adding a few of these expressions, you can make your writing sound more natural — as if you are talking directly to your friend.

Name ______________________________

Drama on the High Seas

Complete each sentence below by writing a vocabulary word from the box.

Vocabulary

captives
dread
abolitionists
influential
privateer
tacking
apprentice
conflict
enslavement
encouraged
assisted

1. Those opposing slavery were called ______________.
2. A group whose views are respected by leaders is considered to be ______________.
3. If you have helped a person, you have ______________ him or her.
4. An argument is one type of ______________.
5. Changing direction while sailing is ______________.
6. If you have told a group that their plan seems solid, you have ______________ them to carry it out.
7. Another word for *prisoners* is ______________.
8. If you feel strong fear, you feel ______________.
9. ______________ is preventing people from living in freedom.
10. A ______________ was a private ship given papers by a government allowing it to attack ships of another country.
11. A person learning a trade is an ______________.

Choose one of the vocabulary words and write a sentence.

____

____

Name ______________________________

James Forten and the Revolutionary War

Complete the chart as you read the selection.

What I Know	What I Want to Know	What I Learned

Name ______________________________

Did It Really Happen?

The sentences below tell about James Forten. Write T if the sentence is true, or F if the sentence is false. If a sentence is false, correct it to make it true.

1. _____ New York, where James Forten was born, was home to many significant abolitionists.

____

____

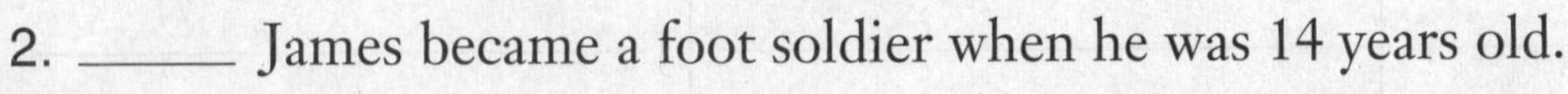

2. _____ James became a foot soldier when he was 14 years old.

____

____

3. _____ On his second voyage, James Forten and the crew of the *Royal Louis* were captured and held captive on board the British prison ship *Jersey*.

____

____

4. _____ James feared he would be killed by the British.

____

____

5. _____ It was probably George Washington's victory over the British that saved Forten.

____

____

6. _____ After the war, James Forten became a wealthy politician and an influential abolitionist.

____

____

Name ______________________________

Step by Step

Read the directions. Then answer the questions on page 178.

"Wild Snake" Marble Game

This marble game provides good marble-shooting practice.

Players: Two or more

Materials: One marble per player; a stick or a piece of chalk

Object: The winner is the last player left in the game.

How to Play:

1. If the game is played on sand, scratch seven circles to form a course. If it is played on cement, draw seven circles with chalk. The course may go in any direction.
2. Make a starting line and place all players' marbles behind it.
3. Taking turns, players try to land their marble in the first circle by flicking it with their thumb or finger.
4. A player who lands a marble in the first circle proceeds to the second one, and so on.
5. A player who gets to the seventh circle must complete the course in reverse.
6. Players who complete the course forward and backward are "wild snakes." This means that they may shoot at the other players' marbles.
7. If a player's marble is hit by the marble of a wild snake, that player is out of the game (even if that player is also a wild snake).
8. If a wild snake's marble lands in a circle while trying to shoot another player's marble, the wild snake is out of the game.

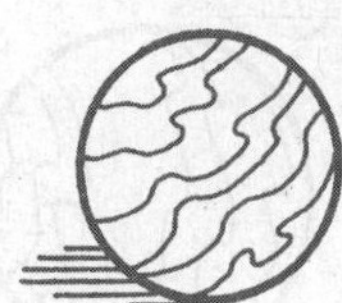

Name ______________________________

Step by Step continued

Answer these questions about the directions on page 177.

1. What do the directions teach readers?

___

___

2. In order to follow these directions, what should you do first?

___

___

3. What does each player need before play can begin?

___

___

4. Why do you need chalk if you are playing the game on cement?

___

___

5. How does a player become a "wild snake"?

___

___

6. What can cause a wild snake to be out of the game?

___

___

7. What would happen if you did step number two before doing step number one?

___

___

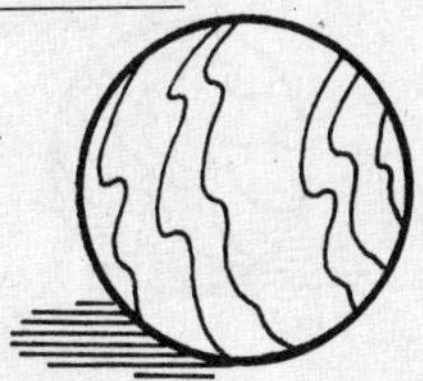

James Forten

Structural Analysis Prefixes *sub-* and *sur-*

Name ______________________________

Prefix Plus

Use the charts to figure out the meaning of each underlined word. Then rewrite the word in the blank space, using the clues. The first one has been done for you.

Prefix	Meaning
sub-	under, below
sur-	over, above

Word Root	Meaning
mit	to cause to go
ject	to throw
vey	to look
merge	to plunge

Base Words
mount (climb)
standard (usual quality)
face (part)
pass

1. The rebels would not submit to unfair British laws.
   The rebels would not go under unfair British laws.
2. The naval officer surveyed the harbor.
   The naval officer ______________ the harbor.
3. A harbor seal submerged near the ship.
   A harbor seal ______________ near the ship.
4. Soon, the seal came to the surface of the ocean.
   Soon, the seal came to the ______________ of the ocean.
5. The prisoners were subjected to punishment.
   The prisoners were ______________ punishment.
6. James thought the tattered sailcloth was substandard.
   James thought the tattered sailcloth was ______________.
7. With his positive attitude, James could surmount any problem.
   James could ______________ any problem.
8. James's sails surpassed any others.
   James's sails ______________ any others.

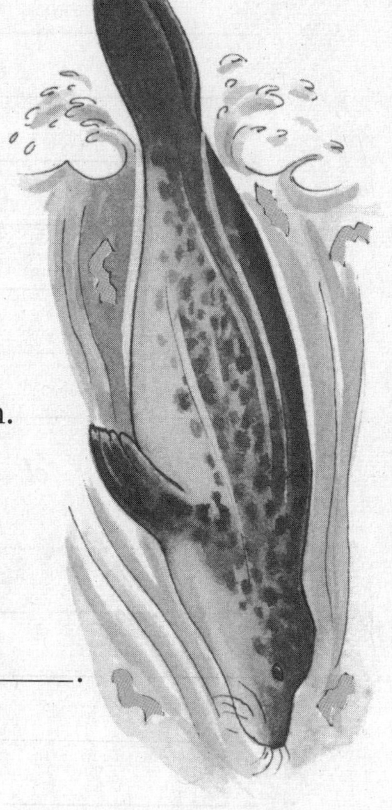

Name ______________________________

Final /l/ or /əl/

The final /l/ or /əl/ sounds are usually spelled with two letters. When you hear these sounds, think of the patterns *le*, *el*, and *al*.

/l/ or /əl/ sparkl**e**, jew**e**l, leg**a**l

► The spellings of *fossil* and *devil* differ from the usual spelling patterns. The /əl/ sounds in these words are spelled *il*.

Write each Spelling Word under its spelling of the final /l/ or /əl/ sound.

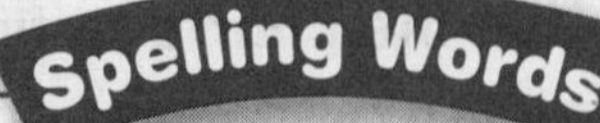

1. jewel
2. sparkle
3. angle
4. shovel
5. single
6. normal
7. angel
8. legal
9. whistle
10. fossil*
11. puzzle
12. bushel
13. mortal
14. gentle
15. level
16. label
17. pedal
18. ankle
19. needle
20. devil*

le

____
____
____
____
____
____
____
____

al

____
____
____
____

Another Spelling

____
____

el

____
____
____
____
____
____

Name ______________________

Spelling Spree

Ending Match For each beginning syllable, choose the correct spelling of the /l/ or /əl/ sound to form a Spelling Word. Then write each word correctly.

1. spar-	-kel	-kle	-kal	1. ______
2. gen-	-tle	-tal	-til	2. ______
3. fos-	-sle	-sal	-sil	3. ______
4. puz-	-zel	-zle	-el	4. ______
5. la-	-bel	-bal	-ble	5. ______
6. whis-	-tel	-tle	-tal	6. ______
7. mor-	-tle	-tel	-tal	7. ______

Crack the Code Some Spelling Words have been written in the following code. Use the code to figure out each word. Then write each word correctly.

CODE:	R	E	N	O	T	V	A	G	B	F	Y	M
LETTER:	A	D	E	G	I	J	K	L	N	P	V	W

8. RBAGN ______
9. GNYNG ______
10. RBONG ______
11. BNNEGN ______
12. RBOGN ______
13. VNMNG ______
14. ENYTG ______
15. FNERG ______

Spelling Words

1. jewel
2. sparkle
3. angle
4. shovel
5. single
6. normal
7. angel
8. legal
9. whistle
10. fossil*
11. puzzle
12. bushel
13. mortal
14. gentle
15. level
16. label
17. pedal
18. ankle
19. needle
20. devil*

Name ______________________________

Proofreading and Writing

Proofreading **Circle the five misspelled Spelling Words in the following Help Wanted advertisement. Then write each word correctly.**

Are you tired of doing dirty work with a shovle? Maybe you're sick of hauling bushal baskets of vegetables to market. We're looking for a hard-working, singel young man or woman to be an apprentice in the sailmaking business. You must be of legil working age, and you should be willing to work with a large needle. **Please apply in person during normel business hours at the office of James Forten, Sailmaker.**

1. ______________________
2. ______________________
3. ______________________
4. ______________________
5. ______________________

Spelling Words

1. jewel
2. sparkle
3. angle
4. shovel
5. single
6. normal
7. angel
8. legal
9. whistle
10. fossil*
11. puzzle
12. bushel
13. mortal
14. gentle
15. level
16. label
17. pedal
18. ankle
19. needle
20. devil*

Write a Character Sketch James Forten had an unusual life. At various times he was a sailor in the Revolutionary War, a sailmaker, a successful businessman, and an abolitionist. Is there anything about his personality that you think would have helped him in the different parts of his life?

On a separate sheet of paper, write a brief character sketch of James Forten. Use Spelling Words from the list.

James Forten

Vocabulary Skill Antonyms

Name ____________________

Journal of Opposites

Read the journal. In each blank, write an antonym of the clue word.

December 31, 1781

This summer I set sail aboard the *Royal Louis*. We were ready to fight the ____________ (powerless) British navy. Soon we were caught up in battle with the ____________ (lightly) armed ship *Active*. I carried gunpowder from ____________ (above) the decks to the guns. In time, the *Active* surrendered by ____________ (raising) its flag. I'll never forget the crowd's excited ____________ (booing) as we took the ship back to Philadelphia. But our next trip out was ____________ (lucky). Our ship surrendered to three British ships, and we crew members were ____________ (set free) as prisoners. At least the boys were ____________ (forbidden) to play marbles. The captain's son joined us, and we became ____________ (enemies). I wonder if this friendship saved me from being ____________ (bought) into slavery.

Name ______________________

What Kind? How Many? Which One?

Adjectives A word that describes a noun or a pronoun is called an **adjective**. It tells what kind or how many. *A*, *an*, and *the* are special adjectives called **articles**. *A* and *an* refer to any item. *The* refers to a particular item. *This*, *that*, *these*, and *those* are **demonstrative adjectives**. They tell which one. *This* and *these* refer to nearby items; *that* and *those* refer to farther away items.

Circle all of the adjectives in the following sentences, including articles and demonstrative adjectives.

1. James sewed straight seams on large, square sails.
2. Those ships needed many sails.
3. Six sailors are pulling on the thick ropes.
4. This huge vessel is impressive.
5. Tired merchants closed the shops.
6. Grateful citizens will raise a cheer for these sailors.
7. An anchor is thrown overboard.
8. A white seagull dives for the slippery fish.
9. That shop sells sails and other equipment for ships.
10. Philadelphia has a proud heritage.

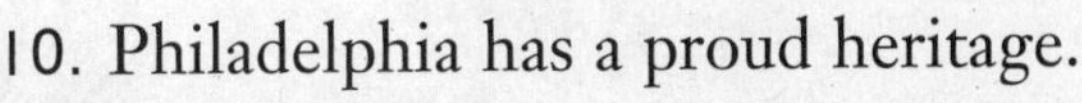

Name ______________________________

Who Settled Where?

Proper Adjectives A **proper adjective** is formed from a proper noun and always begins with a capital letter.

Fill in the blank with the proper adjective formed from the proper noun in parentheses. Check a dictionary if you need to. (Number four is tricky!)

1. The state of Louisiana was once a ______________ colony. (France)
2. The ______________ Revolution was a fight for independence from England. (America)
3. King George III sat on the ______________ throne. (England)
4. There were ______________ settlers in New York. (Holland)
5. ______________ explorers settled parts of Florida. (Spain)
6. Margaret's ______________ ancestors settled in Pennsylvania. (Germany)
7. Many ______________ immigrants came to America in the nineteenth century. (Ireland)
8. James Forten's ancestors were ______________. (Africa)
9. Alaska was once a ______________ territory. (Russia)
10. General Washington fought ______________ soldiers. (Britain)

Name ______________________________

Marvelous Marbles

Expanding Sentences with Adjectives Good writers add interest to their writing by adding adjectives that help readers visualize a scene.

Add adjectives to the following sentences to make them more lively and interesting. Use your imagination!

1. These ______________ children are playing with marbles.
2. That ______________ bag holds ______________ marbles.
3. Alfred sits on the ______________ ground to play.
4. Carla shows Tony a ______________ marble.
5. The players enjoy the ______________ sunshine.
6. Kinley doesn't play marbles, but he collects ______________ cards.
7. That ______________ girl usually wins.
8. The ______________ boy in the ______________ jacket won today!

Name ______________________________

Writing a Biography

In *James Forten*, you read about an African American sailor who served during the Revolutionary War. A **biography** is a written account of important events and significant experiences in a person's life. Before you write a biography of your own, follow these steps:

- ► Choose a real person who lived during the American Revolution.
- ► Research important facts, dates, places, events, and accomplishments in this person's life. Use the Internet, reference books, or history books in your library to gather information.

Record and organize important dates, locations, and events in this person's life on the timeline below.

The Life of ______________________________

DATE	EVENT
________	______________________________
________	______________________________
________	______________________________
________	______________________________
________	______________________________

Name ____________________________

Capitalizing Names of People and Places

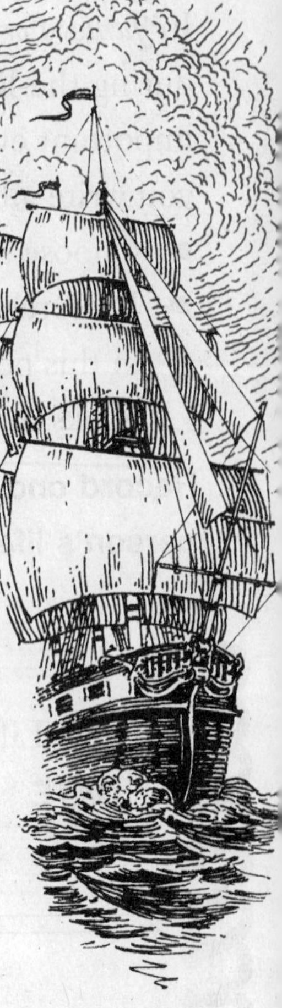

Good biographers proofread their writing to check for correct capitalization of proper names. Imagine you have written a biography of James Forten. The book jacket will include information to interest readers in the book.

Proofread the following book-jacket sentences. Underline the names of people and places that should be capitalized and write them correctly on the lines.

African American sailor james forten was born in philadelphia in 1766.

____

Living on the shores of the atlantic ocean, he dreamed of glory on the high seas.

____

When he was only fourteen years old, he joined the crew of a vessel that was commanded by captain stephen decatur.

____

The *royal louis* was a privateer, or a privately owned ship that the united states used in the war against england.

____

After the British captured his ship in 1781, the teenaged sailor was imprisoned in the filthy hold of a prison ship, the *jersey*, which was anchored off new york.

____

This young patriot feared little — except the bitter chance that he would be sent to the west indies and enslaved.

____

Name ______________________________

Writing a Personal Response

Use the test-taking strategies and tips you have learned to help you answer personal response questions. Take the time you need to decide which topic you will write about and to write an answer. Then read your answer and see how you may make it better. This practice will help you when you take this kind of test.

Write one or two paragraphs about one of the following topics.

a. Many Patriots in the time of the American Revolution took strong actions, such as dumping tea, to protest the taxes imposed by the British. If you had lived in the time of Paul Revere, would you have protested against British laws? If so, what would you have done? If not, why not?

b. Paul Revere interrupted his regular job as a silversmith to do dangerous work as an express rider for the Sons of Liberty. Do you think interrupting your routine to help others is a good definition for heroism? Explain why or why not.

____

____

____

____

____

____

____

____

____

____

____

Name ______________________________

Writing a Personal Response continued

Read your response. Check to be sure that it

- focuses on the topic
- is well organized
- has details that support your response
- includes vivid and exact words
- has few mistakes in capitalization, punctuation, grammar, or spelling

Now pick one way you can improve your response. Make your changes below.

Name ______________________

Spelling Review

Write Spelling Words from the list on this page to answer the questions.

1–12. Which twelve words have the final /ər/ sounds?

1. ________ 7. ________
2. ________ 8. ________
3. ________ 9. ________
4. ________ 10. ________
5. ________ 11. ________
6. ________ 12. ________

13–23. Which eleven words have the final /l/ or /əl/ sounds?

13. ________ 19. ________
14. ________ 20. ________
15. ________ 21. ________
16. ________ 22. ________
17. ________ 23. ________
18. ________

24–30. What syllable is missing from each word? Write each word.

24. sor— ________ 28. —ware ________
25. —have ________ 29. —ue ________
26. wed— ________ 30. pub— ________
27. rap— ________

Spelling Words

1. jewel
2. polar
3. needle
4. humor
5. legal
6. mayor
7. gentle
8. lunar
9. sorrow
10. tractor
11. quarter
12. behave
13. parlor
14. wedding
15. powder
16. actor
17. rapid
18. equal
19. mortal
20. aware
21. matter
22. sparkle
23. shoulder
24. bushel
25. value
26. publish
27. single
28. whistle
29. burglar
30. pedal

Voices of the Revolution: Theme 3 Wrap-Up

Spelling Review

Name ____________________________________

Spelling Spree

Syllable Rhymes Write the Spelling Word that has a first syllable that rhymes with each word below.

1. win ________________
2. car ________________
3. rub ________________
4. push ________________
5. fur ________________
6. den ________________
7. map ________________

Spelling Words

1. humor
2. gentle
3. lunar
4. tractor
5. quarter
6. rapid
7. mortal
8. sparkle
9. bushel
10. publish
11. single
12. burglar
13. pedal
14. jewel
15. mayor

Word Fun Write a Spelling Word to fit each clue.

8. Change the last three letters in *jelly* to make a word meaning "gem." ________________
9. Change the first three letters of *final* to make a word describing what you do to make a bicycle move. ____________
10. Add a consonant to *moral* to make a word meaning "human being." ________________
11. Change the word *quartz* to make it mean "twenty-five cents." ____________
12. Remove two letters from *detractor* to form a word for a farm machine. ________________
13. Replace two consonants in *lunch* to form a word having to do with the moon. ________________
14. Replace two letters in *humid* to make a word that tells what makes people laugh. ________________
15. Change one letter in *major* to make the head of a city. ____________

Name ______________________

Proofreading and Writing

Proofreading **Circle the five misspelled Spelling Words in this report. Then write each word correctly.**

Betsy Ross sat in her parler with a few scraps of cloth, a needel, and some thread. She usually made jackets, weding dresses, and lacy shirts. That day, she made a flag with great valyew for the new nation. It made the colonial army equel to the British.

1. ______________
2. ______________
3. ______________
4. ______________
5. ______________

Title Trouble **Correct the following book titles. Replace each underlined word with a rhyming Spelling Word.**

6. *Soldiers, Keep Your Chowder Close By* ______________
7. *Just Thistle, I'll Come Running!* ______________
8. *The Factor Who Makes History Come Alive* ______________
9. *One Soldier's Borrow; Another's Joy* ______________
10. *Be Compare of Danger Signs* ______________
11. *Manners: How a Soldier Should Shave* ______________
12. *Valley Forge—Cold as Solar Ice* ______________
13. *He Carried His Musket on His Boulder* ______________
14. *The New Flag Really Does Flatter!* ______________
15. *The Regal Papers* ______________

Spelling Words

1. powder
2. polar
3. matter
4. parlor
5. equal
6. aware
7. behave
8. sorrow
9. shoulder
10. value
11. whistle
12. needle
13. legal
14. actor
15. wedding

Write a Diary Entry **On a separate sheet of paper, write a diary entry telling about a colonial American's day. Use the Spelling Review Words.**

Name ___________________________________

Person to Person

The characters in this theme learn about themselves and others. After reading each story, complete the chart below to show what you have learned about the characters.

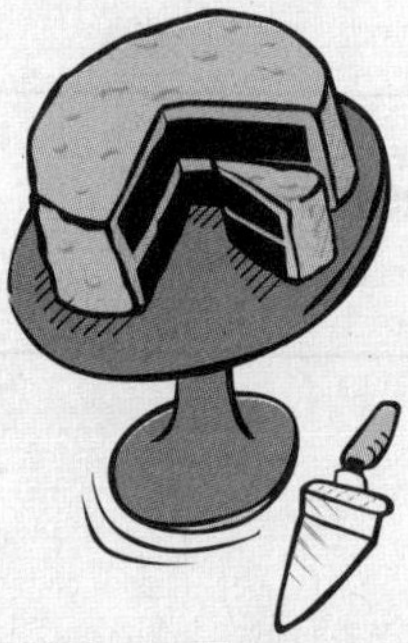

	Mariah Keeps Cool	Mom's Best Friend
Who is the main character or characters?		
How do the story characters try to help each other?		
How do the story characters communicate with each other?		

Name ______________________________

Person to Person continued

	Yang the Second and Her Secret Admirers	Dear Mr. Henshaw
Who is the main character or characters?		
How do the story characters try to help each other?		
How do the story characters communicate with each other?		

What have you learned about working together in this theme?

____

____

____

Name ______________________________

Guests of Honor

Answer each of the following questions by writing a vocabulary word.

Vocabulary

volunteer
amazingly
decorate
celebration
detain
spectators
suspects
festive
reluctant
honor

1. Which word means "make something look nice"? ______________
2. Which word tells what people do when they stop someone and delay him or her for a while? ______________
3. Which word means "people who make up an audience"? ______________
4. Which word means "express a willingness to help"? ______________
5. Which word describes an event with lively music and colorful decorations? ______________
6. Which word is another word for *party*? ______________
7. Which word means "unwilling"? ______________
8. Which word has the same meaning as *astonishingly*? ______________
9. Which word means "believes something is wrong"? ______________
10. Which word means "to show respect for someone publicly"? ______________

Now write the first letter of each of the last five words you wrote above to answer this question.

What noise might tip off a person that he or she is about to be surprised? ______________

Name ______________________________

This Was Their Solution!

Read the problem stated in the left-hand column. Fill in the Solution column with information from the selection.

Problem		Solution
Lynn overhears Mariah say "See you later" to Denise and is curious about why they were going to be together.	→	Mariah tells Lynn that ______
Lynn shows up unexpectedly at Brandon's house while they're making decorations.	→	Mariah, Brandon, and the girls ______
Lynn doesn't want a birthday celebration; she just wants to stay in bed all day.	→	Mariah asks her mother to ______
Mariah forgets to get music for the party.	→	Mariah's father calls Brandon's father because ______
Mariah and the rest of the Friendly Five don't have anyone to dance with.	→	Mariah suggests that they ______

Name ______________________________

Surprise Party Advice

Based on what you've learned from the selection, complete the sentences below giving advice about how to throw a successful surprise party.

- On the party invitations, make sure everyone knows ______________________________
- Speak carefully when you're around the guest of honor, so ______________________________
- If you say something that makes the guest of honor suspicious, be ready to tell a story that ______________________________
- A few days before the party, get others to help you ______________________________
- If the guest of honor unexpectedly appears while party preparations are taking place, figure out ______________________________
- On the day of the party, ask others to help you ______________________________
- If the party is taking place at the guest of honor's house, ask someone to ______________________________
- Be sure to have plenty of ______________ available for your guests.
- If you want to have music at the party, be sure that you have ______________________________
- And remember to ______________ yourself!

Name ______________________________

Think It Through

Read the passage. Then complete the activity on page 201.

Munching on Leaves

Julie's little brother Pablo was obsessed with the movie *Bugs*. This wouldn't have been a problem, except that Aunt Elena bought him the soundtrack, and Pablo listened to it nonstop, especially one song called "The Caterpillar Crawl." The chorus went: "Merrily we crawl along, crawl along, munchin' leaves all day!" It had one of those catchy tunes that sticks in your mind even though it is the last song in the world that you want to sing. Last week Julie's friend Diana had looked at her strangely and asked, "What are you singing? Something about munching *leaves*?" Julie knew she had to do something.

"I can't listen to that CD anymore," she told her father. "Not one more time. If I hear it one more time, I will scream."

Dad sighed. "Yes, I know," he said. "Yesterday at the office I started singing 'Don't Bug Me' during a meeting."

"Can't you tell him not to play it anymore?"

"Well, would it be fair if I told you not to play one of your CDs?"

"It would be if I played one CD over and over and over again."

"What about the time I asked you to stop playing that Screaming Purple Rhinos CD?" Julie could see that her dad had a point.

She went to the library and searched until she found an audiotape of folk songs that she had loved when she was six. She checked it out, brought it home, and started playing it on her own tape player. When Pablo asked what it was, she said, "Never mind," and shut her door.

Soon she heard him tapping. "Can't I listen to that?"

"No, it's mine. Go listen to your *Bugs* CD." She heard him complaining to Dad. Julie came out of her room and said, "Oh, all right. You can listen to it, but you have to give it back right afterwards." Of course, he didn't, which had been her plan all along.

By the time Julie was sick of the folk song tape, it was due back at the library.

Mariah Keeps Cool

Comprehension Skill
Problem Solving

Name ______________________________

Think It Through continued

Answer these questions about the passage on page 200.

1. What problem does Julie have in the story? ______________________________

____

2. What solution does Julie think of first? ______________________________

____

3. After thinking about that solution, what does Julie decide? ______________________________

____

____

4. What solution does she think of next? ______________________________

____

____

5. Do you think her solution is a good one? Why or why not?

____

____

6. Think about the steps to solving a problem. Which steps did Julie follow, and how well did she follow them? ______________________________

____

____

____

Name ______________________________

Divide and Define

Read each sentence. Rewrite the underlined word with a slash (/) to divide the syllables. Then, after it, write a definition or synonym for the word.

1. As you approach the yard, you will smell the hot dogs.

____

2. I'll be ready for the party in an instant.

____

3. Lynn is always hungry when she wakes up in the morning.

____

4. I'll call you when the decorations are complete.

____

5. On his vacation in Maine, Brendan went out on a lobster boat.

____

6. Will you please increase the volume on the CD player?

____

7. Mariah decided to confront Denise about the rumor she had heard.

____

8. The balloons and colored paper make a beautiful display.

____

Name ______________________________

VCCCV Pattern

Two-syllable words with the VCCCV pattern have two consonants that spell one sound, as in *laughter*, or that form a cluster, as in *complain*. Divide a VCCCV word into syllables before or after those consonants. Then look for familiar patterns that you have learned, and spell the word by syllables.

VCC | CV **laugh | ter** VC | CCV **com | plain**

Write each Spelling Word under the heading that shows where it is divided.

VC | CCV

______________ ______________
______________ ______________
______________ ______________
______________ ______________
______________ ______________
______________ ______________
______________ ______________
______________ ______________
____

VCC | CV

______________ ______________
____

Spelling Words

1. district
2. address
3. complain
4. explain
5. improve
6. farther
7. simply
8. hundred
9. although
10. laughter
11. mischief
12. complex
13. partner
14. orphan
15. constant
16. dolphin
17. employ
18. sandwich
19. monster
20. orchard

Name ______________________

Spelling Spree

Syllable Addition Combine the first syllable of the first word with the final syllable of the second word to write a Spelling Word.

1. addition + headdress = _____
2. parting + runner = _____
3. monsoon + youngster = _____
4. farsighted + father = _____
5. command + floodplain = _____
6. concern + instant = _____
7. empire + deploy = _____

1. ______________________ 5. ______________________
2. ______________________ 6. ______________________
3. ______________________ 7. ______________________
4. ______________________

Word Clues Write a Spelling Word to fit each clue.

8. a child whose parents have died
9. two pieces of bread and a slice of cheese
10. an area set aside for a specific purpose
11. where you can find apple trees
12. a reaction to a joke
13. an aquatic mammal
14. a word meaning "even though"

8. ______________________ 12. ______________________
9. ______________________ 13. ______________________
10. ______________________ 14. ______________________
11. ______________________

Spelling Words

1. district
2. address
3. complain
4. explain
5. improve
6. farther
7. simply
8. hundred
9. although
10. laughter
11. mischief
12. complex
13. partner
14. orphan
15. constant
16. dolphin
17. employ
18. sandwich
19. monster
20. orchard

Mariah Keeps Cool

Spelling VCCCV Pattern

Name ______________________________

Proofreading and Writing

Circle the six misspelled Spelling Words in this birthday card that Mariah might have sent. Then write each word correctly.

Dear Lynn,

Let me explane why we threw you a surprise party. It wasn't to create mischeif. Although you said you simplie wanted to stay in bed on your birthday, we had to show how much we care about you. That's why we decided on something more complecks than a simple party. By having the guests bring things for your friends at the shelter, we might be able to improove the lives of the people there. I hope it's the best party you'll ever have, even if you live to be a hunderd!

Your loving sister,

Mariah

1. ____________ 4. ____________

2. ____________ 5. ____________

3. ____________ 6. ____________

Spelling Words

1. district
2. address
3. complain
4. explain
5. improve
6. farther
7. simply
8. hundred
9. although
10. laughter
11. mischief
12. complex
13. partner
14. orphan
15. constant
16. dolphin
17. employ
18. sandwich
19. monster
20. orchard

Write About an Experience Have you ever worked together with your family or friends to surprise someone? What was the surprise? How did you organize it? Were you able to keep it a secret until the end? How did the person being surprised react?

On a separate piece of paper, write a paragraph describing the experience. Use Spelling Words from the list.

Name ______________________________

Inflection Connection

Read each word and its definition. Pay attention to inflected endings such as *-s, -es, -ed, -ing, -er, -est.* Then use inflected forms of each word to complete the sentences below.

dance (dăns) *v.* danced, dancing, dances. To move in time to music.

happy (hăp´ ē) *adj.* happier, happiest. Showing or feeling joy or pleasure.

noisy (noi´ zē) *adj.* noisier, noisiest. Full of or accompanied by noise.

party (pär´ tē) *n.*, pl. parties. A social gathering for pleasure or entertainment.

supply (sə plī´) *v.* supplied, supplying, supplies. To make available for use; provide.

1. Everyone agreed that Rosa's birthday celebration was one of the best ____________ they had been to.
2. Gabe shouted to Danny that he had never been to a ____________ party.
3. Conchita ____________ the music from her large CD collection.
4. Singing and ____________ went on late into the night.
5. Rosa's big smile showed that she was the ____________ person there.

Name ______________________________

Strong, Stronger, Strongest

Comparing with Adjectives Add *-er* to most adjectives to compare two people, places, or things. Use *more* with long adjectives to compare two items. Add *-est* to most adjectives to compare three or more. Use *most* with long adjectives to compare three or more.

1. **Most Adjectives**	Tanya is strong.
Add *-er* or *-est* to the adjective.	Chris is **stronger** than Tanya.
	Pat is the **strongest** of all.
2. **Adjectives with Two or More Syllables**	It is a beautiful view.
	It is a **more beautiful** view from here.
Use *more* or *most*.	It is the **most beautiful** view of all.

Complete each sentence with the correct form of the adjective in parentheses.

1. She is the ______________ person I know. (generous)
2. Denise is a ______________ artist than I am. (skillful)
3. Her mother was the ______________ one there. (calm)
4. It was the ______________ night of the year. (great)
5. I'd like a ______________ slice of cake than that, please. (small)
6. LaToya is the ______________ person I know. (kind)
7. Of all our houses, Marco's house is the ______________ one to the school. (near)
8. Marsha is a ______________ singer than Carlos. (talented)
9. However, Carlos is the ______________ bass player in the school. (gifted)
10. I am a ______________ reader than a writer. (fast)

Name ______________________________

Mariah Keeps Cool

Grammar Skill Comparing with *good* and *bad*

'Tis Better to Give Than to Receive

Comparing with *good* and *bad* The adjectives *good* and *bad* have irregular comparative forms. Use *better* to compare two things, and *best* to compare three or more. Use *worse* to compare two things, and *worst* to compare three or more.

	Good	Bad
Comparing two	This lunch is **better** than yesterday's.	I did **worse** on this test than the last one.
Comparing three or more	It is the **best** lunch I've ever had.	In fact, this is the **worst** I've ever done.

Fill in each blank with the correct form of *good* or *bad*.

1. Donating used clothing is a ______________ act than throwing it away.
2. In fact, it is probably the ______________ thing you can do with old clothing.
3. Icy sidewalks are a ______________ hazard for frail people than for others.
4. Last winter was the ______________ winter on record.
5. Hooray! This month's food drive was a ______________ one than last month's.
6. In fact, it was the ______________ food drive we've ever had.
7. What is the ______________ thing that has ever happened to you?
8. Uncle Sal has a ______________ garden than my mother.
9. In fact, he won an award for the ______________ garden in the neighborhood.
10. She has a ______________ cold than I had.

Mariah Keeps Cool

Grammar Skill Combining Sentences with Adjectives

Name ______________________________

Lighter and Warmer

Combining Sentences with Adjectives To avoid having too many short, comparing sentences, you can combine sentences to make one sentence with two or more comparative adjectives. Here is an example:

Two sentences: This year's swim team is **more enthusiastic** than last year's team. It is a **stronger** team too.

One sentence: This year's swim team is **more enthusiastic and stronger** than last year's team.

Mark wrote a draft of an article for the school paper. Revise the five underlined pairs of sentences by combining them to form sentences with more than one comparative adjective.

I am a member of the swim team. Being on the team has given me a busier life. It has given me a better life too. I get up at 6 A.M. for practice. In the winter, it was darker outside than it had been in the fall. It was colder too. That was hard, but when I got to school I saw my teammates. Pat would tell funny jokes. Dale would tell even funnier jokes. Dale told sillier jokes too.

Now that spring is here, warmer days have arrived. Lighter days have arrived too. It is easy to practice a lot when it is light. We will have a stronger team for our next meet. We will have a faster team too. I love to swim, but the best part of being on the team is working with great friends.

1. ______________________________
2. ______________________________
3. ______________________________
4. ______________________________
5. ______________________________

Name ______________________________

Fictional Narrative

A **fictional narrative** is a story that has characters, settings, and events that are similar to persons, places, and events in real life.

Use this chart to plan your fictional narrative. Follow these steps:

- **Name the characters and describe the setting.**
- **Outline the main events in the story. Be sure to include the conflict that the characters face and how it is resolved at the end.**
- **Make sure you include colorful adjectives that describe your characters, setting, and set the mood of the story.**

Characters	Setting

Plot
Conflict:
Events:
Resolution:

Mariah Keeps Cool

Writing Skill Improving Your Writing

Name ______________________________

Changing Positions Of Adjectives

An **adjective** describes a noun or pronoun. Adjectives may come before or after the nouns or pronouns they describe. Good writers place adjectives in different positions in a sentence to add variety to their writing.

First, underline the adjectives in the following part of a story about Denise and the other party organizers. Then rewrite the body of the story on the lines, changing the positions of some adjectives to add variety. Either place the adjectives before or after the nouns they describe.

They met at Brandon's house on Wednesday. They had decided in advance to make decorations for the party that were pretty but inexpensive. Denise brought scissors and paper to make flowers and banners that were handmade. Mariah wanted to make banners that were long and dramatic, and Brandon had many markers that were colorful. Denise said she often makes decorations that are simple and easy. Denise was excited because she thought the garden would be beautiful and the other party guests would be happy!

____

____

____

____

____

____

Name ______________________________

Revising Your Personal Narrative

Reread your personal narrative. What do you need to do to make it better? Use this page to help you decide. Put a checkmark in the box for each sentence that describes your personal narrative.

Rings the Bell!

- ☐ My story starts with an attention-grabbing beginning.
- ☐ My voice comes through in my telling of the story.
- ☐ I included details that help the reader picture what happened.
- ☐ My use of dialogue makes the story more interesting.
- ☐ I vary the types of sentences in my writing.
- ☐ There are very few mistakes.

Getting Stronger

- ☐ I could have a stronger beginning.
- ☐ Most of it sounds like me, but some of it doesn't.
- ☐ I use details, but I could include more.
- ☐ Maybe I should add more dialogue.
- ☐ I could vary my sentences a bit more.
- ☐ There are quite a few errors that need to be fixed.

Try Harder

- ☐ My beginning needs work.
- ☐ This doesn't sound like the way I would tell a story.
- ☐ I need to add details so it isn't so hard to picture what's happening.
- ☐ I haven't varied the sentence types in my writing.
- ☐ Too many mistakes make the story hard to read.

Name ______________________________

Varying Sentence Types

Read the paragraph. All the sentences are declarative sentences.

Yesterday I had a bad day. I overslept. I didn't have time for breakfast. I missed the bus. I yelled at it to stop. It was too late. No one heard me. I walked all the way to school. I wondered what I had done to deserve this. I was late, and I didn't have a note from my mom. The day went downhill from there.

Now rewrite the paragraph, varying the sentence types. Include at least one question, one exclamation, and one command. You will need to add or delete words to revise the sentences.

____

____

____

____

____

____

____

____

____

____

____

____

____

____

____

Reading-Writing Workshop

Frequently Misspelled Words

Name ______________________________

Spelling Words

Words Often Misspelled Look for familiar spelling patterns to help you remember how to spell the Spelling Words on this page. Think carefully about the parts that you find hard to spell in each word.

Write the missing letters in the Spelling Words below.

1. ____ lot
2. bec ____ ____ se
3. s ____ ____ ool
4. it ____
5. it ____ ____
6. ton ____ ____ ____ t
7. m ____ ____ ____ t
8. r ____ ____ ____ t
9. ____ ____ ite
10. ag ____ ____ n
11. t ____
12. t ____ ____
13. t ____ ____
14. th ____ ____
15. tha ____ ____ ____

Spelling Words

1. a lot
2. because
3. school
4. its
5. it's
6. tonight
7. might
8. right
9. write
10. again
11. to
12. too
13. two
14. they
15. that's

Study List **On a separate piece of paper, write each Spelling Word. Check your spelling against the words on the list.**

Name ______________________

Reading-Writing Workshop

Frequently Misspelled Words

Spelling Spree

Homophone Blanks **The blanks in each of the following sentences can be filled with homophones from the Spelling Word list. Write the words in the correct order.**

1–2. I think _____ too bad that the park lost _____ swimming pool.

3–5. The _____ football players decided that they would try _____ play on the basketball team, _____.

6–7. After she broke her arm, Leslie couldn't _____ with her _____ hand.

1–2. ______________ ______________

3–5. __________ __________ __________

6–7. ______________ ______________

Spelling Words

1. a lot
2. because
3. school
4. its
5. it's
6. tonight
7. might
8. right
9. write
10. again
11. to
12. too
13. two
14. they
15. that's

Crack the Code **Some Spelling Words have been written in the code below. Use the code to figure out each word. Then write the words correctly.**

CODE:	B	P	Y	L	A	T	R	F	D	W	Z	X	V	I	O
LETTER:	a	b	c	e	g	h	i	l	m	n	o	s	t	u	y

8. DRATV — 8. ______________
9. B FZV — 9. ______________
10. XYTZZF — 10. ______________
11. VTBV'X — 11. ______________
12. BABRW — 12. ______________
13. VTLO — 13. ______________
14. PLYBIXL — 14. ______________
15. VZWRATV — 15. ______________

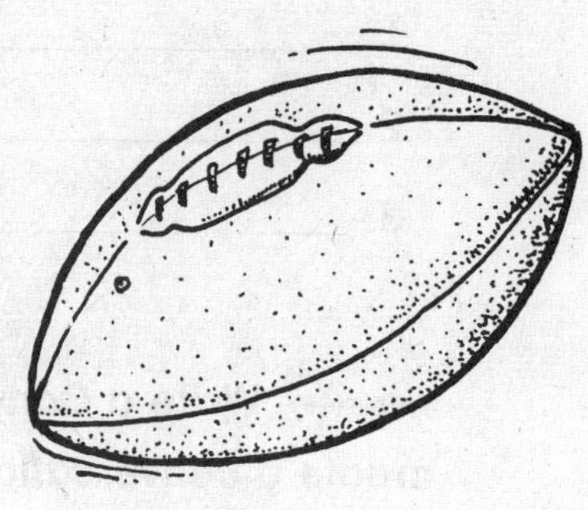

Reading-Writing Workshop

Frequently Misspelled Words

Name ______________________

Proofreading and Writing

Proofreading **Circle the five misspelled Spelling Words in this advertisement. Then write each word correctly.**

Has it been two long since you talked to your best friend? Do you feel like you don't have the time to wright to the people you care about? Then its time to call them, person to person! There's nothing like a conversation to get you back in touch. And it doesn't cost alot, either! Call tonite — you'll be glad you did.

Spelling Words

1. a lot
2. because
3. school
4. its
5. it's
6. tonight
7. might
8. right
9. write
10. again
11. to
12. too
13. two
14. they
15. that's

1. ______________ 4. ______________

2. ______________ 5. ______________

3. ______________

Write a Conversation **Work with one or more classmates to create a conversation. One person writes a sentence, using a Spelling Word, to open the conversation. The next person writes the second sentence, using a Spelling Word. From here, take turns writing sentences, using Spelling Words from the list.**

Name ________________________________

A Friend and a Helper

Use words from the box to complete the paragraphs below.

Vocabulary

attachment
dog guide
mastered
obedience
memorizing
obstacles
instinct
mature
braille
layout

A person who cannot see may use a ______________ as a helper when going from place to place. In order to do this important work, a dog must go through ______________ training. It must learn to ignore its ______________ to chase other dogs. It must also learn to help its master avoid ______________ and cross streets safely. Only a ______________ dog can be trained effectively. Once a dog has ______________ the basic skills, it can go to live with its master and begin developing an ______________ to that person.

Dogs are helpful in a number of ways, but people who cannot see still must spend time ______________ the ______________ of a building in which they will be spending time. They also must depend on their listening skills and their ability to read ______________ in order to acquire new knowledge and be more independent.

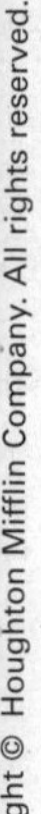

Name ______________________________

Tell Me All the Details!

Look for details in the selection, and fill in each Details column. Read the prompts in the far left-hand column to determine if the details belong *before, while,* or *after* Mom went to The Seeing Eye.

	Details about Mom	Details about Narrator	Details about Ursula
Before Mom returns to The Seeing Eye			
While Mom is at The Seeing Eye			
After Mom returns from The Seeing Eye			

Write one sentence with details about The Seeing Eye.

____

____

Name ______________________________

Trace the "Route" of the Selection

Complete the sentences in the boxes below to show the steps in Ursula's training process.

1. Mom returns to ______________________
____
____
where she gets her new guide dog, Ursula.

2. After making mistakes in her early lessons, Ursula ______________________
____

3. In addition to training with Ursula, Mom spends her time at The Seeing Eye ______________________
____

4. When Mom brings Ursula home, she continues ______________________
____
____

5. When Ursula finally feels comfortable in her new home, Mom starts ______________________
____

6. Ursula soon becomes ______________________
____

Name ______________________________

Reading Carefully

Read the passage. Then complete the activity on page 221.

Louis Braille

Louis Braille was born in France in 1809. At the age of three, he had an accident in his father's workshop and became blind. His father wanted young Louis to become educated and successful, so he enrolled Louis in the Royal Institute for Blind Youth in Paris when Louis was ten years old. The Institute was a school that specialized in teaching blind students.

Louis proved himself to be an outstanding student. He learned to read, though books for people who were blind were rare and hard to use at that time. The Institute had only three books in its library. Each book was divided into twenty parts, and each part weighed more than twenty pounds. A person read the text by touching the huge raised letters on each page.

Shortly after Louis came to the Institute, a military officer named Charles Barbier brought his own system of writing to the attention of the school. He had invented a system he called "night writing." It consisted of raised dots and dashes on thin cardboard and was used by night watchmen to send and receive messages. Louis was fascinated with the system, and he decided to try to improve it.

Louis worked day and night. He used only the dots and found that a "cell" made up of up to six dots could be changed to form sixty-three different patterns. Using his six-dot cell, Louis made a separate pattern for each letter of the alphabet, for numbers, punctuation marks, and even musical notes. This system, which became known as *braille*, is used in countries throughout the world.

Name ______________________________

Mom's Best Friend

Comprehension Skill Noting Details

Reading Carefully continued

Read each statement below. Write a detail from the passage on page 220 to support the statement.

Conclusions	Supporting Details
1. Louis was intelligent and hard-working.	1. ____________
2. Louis had sensitive fingers and could learn new things.	2. ____________
3. Before the invention of braille, books for people who were blind were hard to read.	3. ____________
4. Louis was creative and liked to try new things.	4. ____________
5. Louis was patient and determined.	5. ____________
6. The invention of braille affects the lives of many people.	6. ____________

Mom's Best Friend

Structural Analysis
Syllabication VV Pattern

Name ________________________________

Viva Vowels!

Read the letter. Notice that each underlined word has two vowels with the VV pattern. If the vowels should be kept together in a syllable, circle the vowels. If the vowels should be divided between syllables, draw a line between the vowels. Two examples have been done for you.

actual
believer
pause
create
complains
librarian
laziest

Dear kids,

Today could not have been much crazier! I spent so much time with Prince, my dog guide, that both of us were exhausted. And Prince still had to see the veterinarian.

I can't wait for you to meet Prince. He is a golden retriever. I wish I could explain to him what our routine at home will usually involve. I do not think he realizes that he is soon going to end his training.

Love, Mom

Now use the VV words in the word box to complete these sentences.

1. After a short ____________ for a sip of water, the speaker continued.
2. The ____________ told me that the latest *Billy Burton* mystery just came in!
3. "You are the ____________ animal I've ever known," I said to my sleeping cat.
4. I didn't think you could win the race, but you've made me a ____________.
5. Our neighbor ____________ that the garbage collector comes too early in the morning.
6. This is not a copy of the Gilroy diamond; it is the ____________ jewel!
7. I asked the puppeteer how she was able to ____________ such lifelike puppets.

Name ______________________________

VV Pattern

When the two vowels in a VV pattern spell two vowel sounds, divide the word into syllables between the vowels. Look for familiar patterns that you have learned, and spell the word by syllables.

V | V — po | em

V | V — cre | ate

► The word *quiet* has three vowels that appear together. In this word, the *u* goes with *q* to make the consonant sound /kw/.

Write each Spelling Word. Draw a line between the two vowels in each VV syllable pattern.

V | V

______________	______________
______________	______________
______________	______________
______________	______________
______________	______________
______________	______________
______________	______________
______________	______________
______________	______________
______________	______________

Spelling Words

1. poem
2. idea
3. create
4. diary
5. area
6. giant
7. usual
8. radio
9. cruel
10. quiet*
11. diet
12. liar
13. fuel
14. riot
15. actual
16. lion
17. ruin
18. trial
19. rodeo
20. science

Name ______________________________

Spelling Spree

Phrase Fillers Write the Spelling Word that best completes each phrase.

1. a nutritious, low-fat ______
2. to call an untruthful person a ______
3. a ______ by jury
4. the ______ of biology
5. a ______ with four verses
6. an ancient, crumbling ______
7. a fairy tale with a towering ______
8. the mane of a ______
9. an ______ for a new product

1. ______________ 6. ______________
2. ______________ 7. ______________
3. ______________ 8. ______________
4. ______________ 9. ______________
5. ______________

1. poem
2. idea
3. create
4. diary
5. area
6. giant
7. usual
8. radio
9. cruel
10. quiet*
11. diet
12. liar
13. fuel
14. riot
15. actual
16. lion
17. ruin
18. trial
19. rodeo
20. science

Syllable Scramble Rearrange the syllables to write a Spelling Word. One syllable in each item is extra.

Example: ish ble fin *finish*

10. ra dis o di ______________
11. al u ent su ______________
12. ru ot ri ______________
13. a di sci ry ______________
14. tu re ac al ______________
15. de o ro ant ______________

Name ____________________

Proofreading and Writing

Proofreading Circle the five misspelled Spelling Words in this set of guidelines. Then write each word correctly.

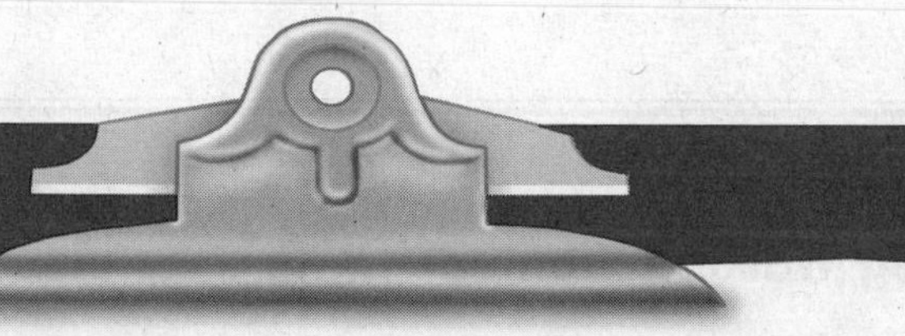

Tips on Caring for Your New Dog Guide

1. Be sure to creat a comfortable home environment for your dog. A calm and quiete atmosphere is best.
2. Feed your dog a healthy diet. Just as food gives you energy, a dog's food is its fule too.
3. Discipline your dog firmly but kindly.
4. Never be crual to your dog—or to any animal!
5. Focus on walks in the areea around your neighborhood until your dog becomes familiar with the territory. Then try some longer trips.

1. ____________ 4. ____________
2. ____________ 5. ____________
3. ____________

Spelling Words

1. poem
2. idea
3. create
4. diary
5. area
6. giant
7. usual
8. radio
9. cruel
10. quiet*
11. diet
12. liar
13. fuel
14. riot
15. actual
16. lion
17. ruin
18. trial
19. rodeo
20. science

Write a Want Ad What qualities make a good dog guide? What natural instincts does a dog guide have to learn to overcome?

On a separate sheet of paper, write a want ad for *Working Dog Weekly* describing the job of dog guide. Use Spelling Words from the list.

Name ______________________

The Meaningful Word

Read the advertisement. Then use each underlined word to complete the numbered sentences. Be careful! The underlined words have more than one meaning.

Dog Walkers Wanted

Helping Hound, the biggest guide dog school in the state, is looking for young people like you. We need your help to train our future guide dogs. You can take a dog on a trip to the park or around the block. You can play with your dog, teach it not to bark at other dogs, and help break it of other bad habits. You'll be training your dog to suit a new owner. You'll have fun as you help your helping hound pass its final exams! Apply today.

1. I covered my ears to ______________ out the sound of the jackhammer.
2. Be careful not to ______________ on that curb.
3. If you ______________ your teacher for less homework, you might get more instead!
4. My father bought us tickets for a ______________ ride this weekend.
5. If you get tired, take a ______________ before you go back to work.
6. Could you please ______________ me the potatoes?
7. Every day, my mother wears a ______________ to work.
8. We drove around looking for a place to ______________ the car.
9. Speak into the microphone and ______________ your name clearly.
10. The thin white ______________ of the birch tree feels soft, like tissue paper.

Name ______________________________

Commas, Commas, and More Commas!

Commas in a Series A **series** is a list of three or more items. Use commas to separate the items in a series. Put a comma after each item in a series except the last one. Use *and* or *or* before the last item in a series.

I like cats, dogs, rabbits, **and** all kinds of animals.

Add commas to the sentences below that have items in a series. If the sentence does not contain a series, write *none* after the sentence.

1. German shepherds golden retrievers and other breeds can be trained as dog guides.
2. Dogs and monkeys are trained to help people with disabilities.
3. Our dogs are named Riley Maggie and Midnight.
4. My cousin takes her dog to visit nursing homes retirement centers and hospitals.
5. Parakeets parrots cockatoos and mynah birds can learn to talk.
6. In our classroom are fish turtles and a snake.
7. Other classrooms have guinea pigs hamsters and gerbils.
8. Our calico cat is black brown white and orange.
9. Marla's cat is orange and white.
10. Tim's cat is black gray and white.

Name ______________________________

Yes, I Can

More Uses for Commas Use commas to set off the words *yes*, *no*, and *well* when they appear as introductory words at the beginning of a sentence. Also use a comma or commas to set off the names of people who are addressed directly.

Introductory word:	**Yes,** Mr. Baxter's dog is devoted to him.
Direct address:	**Kristin,** please help Mr. Baxter with the door.
	Would you walk the dog, **Jamie**?
Introductory word and direct address:	**Well, Kristin,** that is a good idea.

Add commas where needed in the sentences below.

1. I'm afraid I'm not feeling well today Jamie.
2. Well Mr. Baxter I'll walk Buster for you.
3. Thank you Jamie.
4. Why isn't Mr. Baxter walking Buster Kristin?
5. Well I guess Jamie wants to help him.
6. It's nice of you Jamie to help Mr. Baxter.
7. Well Kristin Mr. Baxter is a helpful neighbor.
8. Yes he is Jamie.
9. Kristin have you ever walked Buster?
10. No Myron I haven't.

Name ______________________________

I Feed, Groom, and Pet My Cat

Combining Sentences by Creating a Series A good writer puts items in a series in one sentence, instead of mentioning them in separate sentences.

Awkward: Dogs make good pets. Cats make good pets. Birds do too.

Revised: Dogs, cats, and birds make good pets.

Sophie is drafting an essay. Revise the essay by putting items into a series where needed. Write your revision below.

My cat, Buzz, greets me at the door when I come home from school. He greets me when I come home from a friend's house. He greets me when I come home from an appointment. Buzz meows. He purrs. He rubs against my legs. Then I pick him up. Buzz purrs while I tell him about the spelling test. He purrs while I tell him about my friend's cat or events of the day.

I like to take care of Buzz. I feed him. I groom him. I play with him. He can make me feel calm. He can make me feel loved. He can make me feel special. Buzz is like a patient person with fur. He is like a person with long whiskers. He is like a person with a tail.

____

____

____

____

____

____

____

____

Name ___________________________

Summary

If you were asked to summarize the second part of *Mom's Best Friend*, you would probably tell what happened when Mom brought Ursula home and how the family grew to love her. A summary is a brief account of a story or selection. Writing a summary is a good way to share what a selection is about and to recall main events, ideas, and characters.

Think about the most important events or ideas in the second half of *Mom's Best Friend*. Then add them to the graphic organizer below.

Idea/Event	Idea/Event	Idea/Event

Name ______________________________

Combining Sentences by Using Introductory Phrases and Clauses

Good writers avoid using a string of short, choppy sentences to express their ideas. One way to streamline your writing is to combine two choppy sentences into one sentence with an introductory phrase or clause.

Mom will walk solo with Ursula.
She will do this after ten practice runs with Pete.
After ten practice runs with Pete, Mom will walk solo with Ursula.

Read the instructions for being a sighted guide. Rewrite them on the lines below, combining two short sentences into a single sentence.

Techniques for Being a Sighted Guide

Let the person grasp your arm just above the elbow. Do this at the start. Walk where the person wants to go. Use a comfortable pace. Stay slightly ahead. Guide with your words and body movement. The person needs to know what is ahead, such as stairs or a curb. Tell them when you are approaching an obstacle. The person needs to know when to turn right or left. Do this just before turning. You will reach your destination. The person will release his or her grasp.

Techniques for Being a Sighted Guide

____

____

____

____

____

____

____

Name ______________________________

It's a Secret

Write each word from the box in the correct category.

Vocabulary

- heritage
- impressed
- traditions
- opera
- accompaniment
- demonstration
- noble
- rhythmic

things done in front of an audience

____

____

parts of a culture

____

____

describing words

____

____

action word

____

word for musical support

____

Choose two words from the box and write a sentence using both words.

____

____

Name ______________________________

Different and Alike

Fill in the diagram to compare and contrast Second Sister and Yingtao.

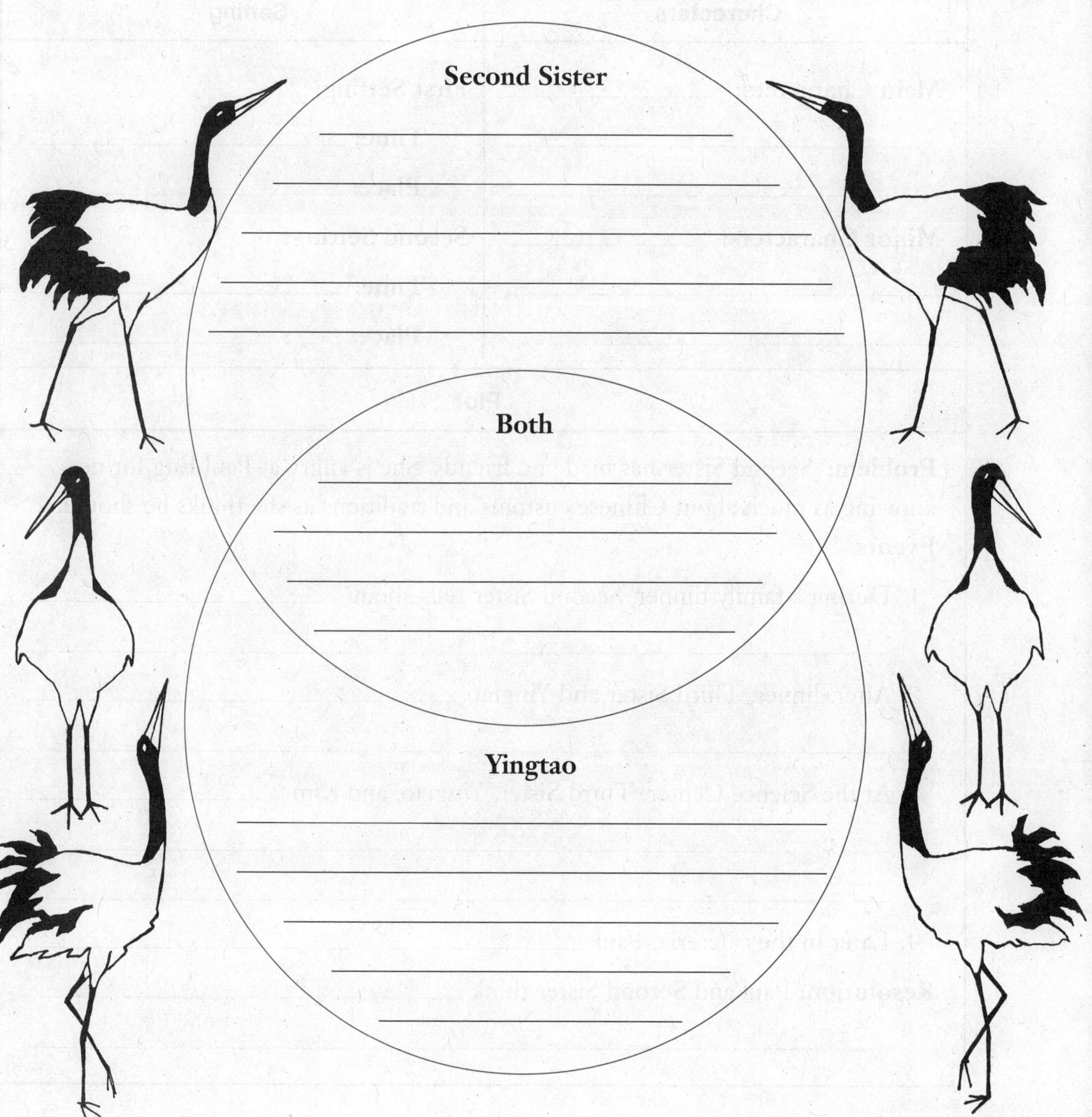

Name ______________________________

Plot the Trick

Complete the story map below to show the main elements of the story.

Characters	Setting
Main Characters: ____________ ____________ ____________	**First Setting:** **Time:** ____________ **Place:** ____________
Minor Characters: ____________ ____________ ____________	**Second Setting:** **Time:** ____________ **Place:** ____________

Plot

Problem: Second Sister has made no friends. She is angry at Paul Eng for not knowing as much about Chinese customs and traditions as she thinks he should.

Events:

1. During a family dinner, Second Sister tells about ____________
____

2. After dinner, Third Sister and Yingtao ____________
____

3. At the Science Center, Third Sister, Yingtao, and Kim ____________
____
____

4. Later in the cafeteria, Paul ____________

Resolution: Paul and Second Sister think ____________
____

Name ____

Similarity Search

Read the passage. Then complete the activity on page 236.

Trevisa's Favorite Teachers

Trevisa had two favorite teachers: Mr. Yetto, her third-grade teacher, and the fifth-grade teacher, Mrs. McIlvaine, who was Trevisa's teacher now.

Mr. Yetto was young and athletic. He had played football in college and still liked sports, just like Trevisa. He was kind and often called on Trevisa to answer questions during class discussions to help her get over her shyness. But Mr. Yetto could also be strict, and he did not accept excuses. If a student didn't turn in his or her homework on time, he marked that student's grade down. On Fridays Mr. Yetto did yo-yo tricks for the class after lunch. He saved new tricks to show them for the weeks when they had worked especially hard.

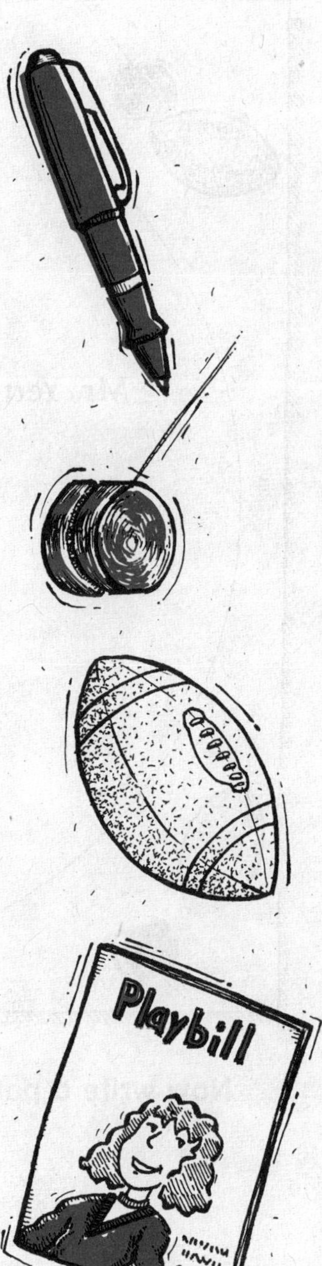

Unlike Mr. Yetto, Mrs. McIlvaine was older. She did not like sports, but she loved stories and plays. On Fridays she allowed her students to perform skits during class. Once Danny Pine and David Ginsburg performed a skit in which Danny wore a white wig and played the role of Mrs. McIlvaine herself. He imitated her voice and even remembered certain phrases she used. Mrs. McIlvaine laughed and laughed. But like Mr. Yetto, Mrs. McIlvaine could also be strict. Once, when Trevisa tried writing a book report in very tiny handwriting, just to see if she could do it, Mrs. McIlvaine made her rewrite it. "I can't even read this!" she wrote across the page in red ink. But after Trevisa rewrote her report and turned it in again, Mrs. McIlvaine wrote, "I'm glad I can read this now, because it is just marvelous!"

Name ___________________________

Similarity Search continued

Fill in the Venn diagram below to show some ways Mr. Yetto and Mrs. McIlvaine are alike and different.

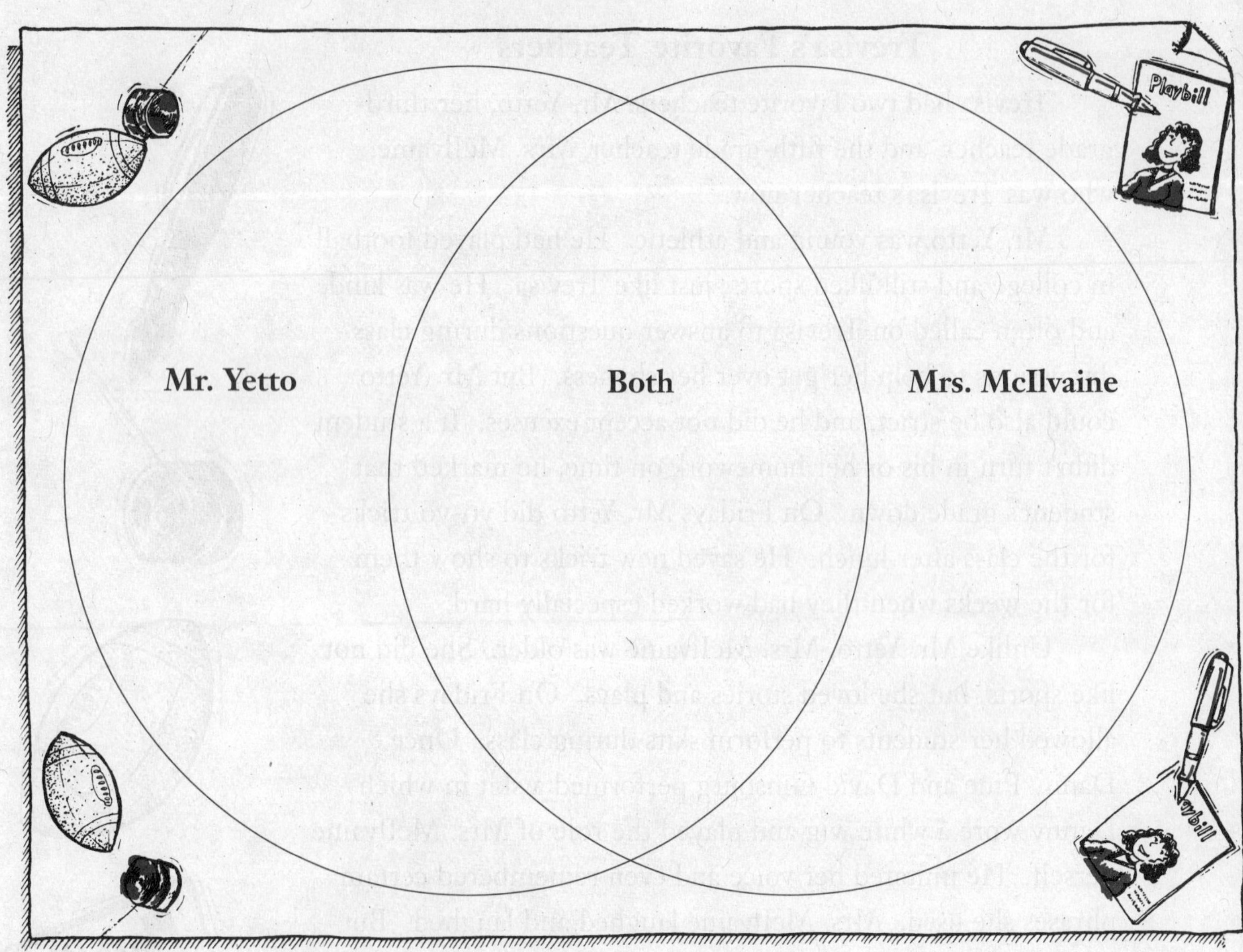

Now write a paragraph in which you describe how the two teachers are alike.

____

____

____

Name ______________________________

Tricky Endings

Read the speech below. Circle the *-ed* and *-ing* endings of the underlined words. Then write those words on the lines with each *-ing* ending changed to an *-ed*, and each *-ed* to an *-ing*. Use the new words to complete the sentences at the bottom of the page.

It's too bad that Tanya keeps ignoring Raul! He was admiring how hard she studied for the math test. He's always dropping by to say, "Do you think she noticed me at the wrestling match?"

____

____

____

____

____

____

Tanya ______________ by my locker today. She didn't know that Raul ______________ on the school team. I told her not to feel bad if he ______________ her in class. He's too busy ______________ to be ______________ anyone! She said she really ______________ his hard work.

Yang the Second and Her Secret Admirers

Spelling Words with *-ed* or *-ing*

Name ____________________

Words with *-ed* or *-ing*

A **base word** is a word to which endings can be added. When a base word ends with *e*, you usually drop the *e* when *-ed* or *-ing* is added. If a base word does not end with *e*, you usually add the ending *-ed* or *-ing* without a spelling change.

amuse + ing = amus**ing**　　direct + ing = direct**ing**

When a one-syllable word ends with a vowel and a consonant, you usually double the consonant when adding *-ed* or *-ing*. When a two-syllable word ends with a vowel and a consonant, you often do not double the consonant when adding *-ed* or *-ing*.

plan + ed = plan**ned**　　cover + ed = cover**ed**

► The spelling of *mixed* differs from the usual spelling pattern. Although *mix* is a one-syllable word, the final consonant is not doubled when *-ed* is added.

Write each Spelling Word under the heading that shows what happens to the base word when *-ed* or *-ing* is added.

Final *e* Dropped	No Spelling Change
________	________
________	________
________	________
________	________
________	________
Final Consonant Doubled	________
________	________
________	________
________	________
________	________
________	

Spelling Words

1. covered
2. directing
3. bragging
4. amusing
5. offered
6. planned
7. rising
8. deserved
9. visiting
10. mixed*
11. swimming
12. sheltered
13. resulting
14. spotted
15. suffering
16. arrested
17. squeezing
18. ordered
19. decided
20. hitting

Name ______________________________

Spelling Spree

Ending Clues Write the Spelling Word that fits each clue.

1. What *-ing* word is causing others to smile?
2. What *-ed* word was arranged ahead of time?
3. What *-ing* word is moving through water?
4. What *-ed* word was all stirred up?
5. What *-ing* word is pressing hard on something?
6. What *-ing* word is coming about as a consequence?
7. What *-ed* word was commanded?
8. What *-ing* word is striking?

1. ______________ 5. ______________
2. ______________ 6. ______________
3. ______________ 7. ______________
4. ______________ 8. ______________

Spelling Words

1. covered
2. directing
3. bragging
4. amusing
5. offered
6. planned
7. rising
8. deserved
9. visiting
10. mixed*
11. swimming
12. sheltered
13. resulting
14. spotted
15. suffering
16. arrested
17. squeezing
18. ordered
19. decided
20. hitting

Finding Words Each word below is hidden in a Spelling Word. Write the Spelling Word.

9. serve ______________
10. rest ______________
11. over ______________
12. off ______________
13. pot ______________
14. rag ______________
15. she ______________

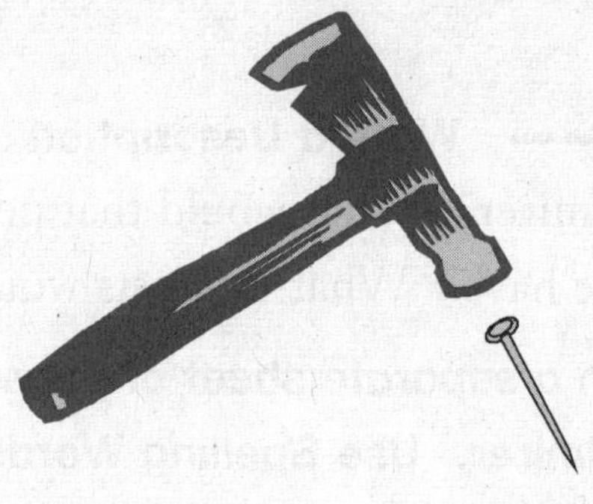

Yang the Second and Her Secret Admirers

Spelling Words with *-ed* or *-ing*

Name ______________________

Proofreading and Writing

Circle the five misspelled Spelling Words in this diary entry that Yinglan might have written. Then write each word correctly.

Dear Diary,

Well, I'm still suffring from shyness around Paul Eng. Today I spotted him in the hall, visitting with some other students. Although nervous, I desided to go say hello. I was only a few steps away when Paul saw me. Suddenly, I felt all my blood riseing to my face. I ended up direckting my eyes straight at the floor and walking right past Paul. Why on earth am I so afraid of him?

1. ______________ 4. ______________
2. ______________ 5. ______________
3. ______________

Spelling Words

1. covered
2. directing
3. bragging
4. amusing
5. offered
6. planned
7. rising
8. deserved
9. visiting
10. mixed*
11. swimming
12. sheltered
13. resulting
14. spotted
15. suffering
16. arrested
17. squeezing
18. ordered
19. decided
20. hitting

Write a Description Have you ever wanted to have a secret admirer? What would that person look like? What qualities would he or she have? What interests would you have in common?

On a separate sheet of paper, write a description of your ideal secret admirer. Use Spelling Words from the list.

Name ______________________________

Pinpointing Prefixes

Read the dictionary entries. Then in the sentences below, underline the word with a prefix. Write the definition of the word after the sentence.

in- or *im-* A prefix that means "not."

re- A prefix that means "again" or "back."

un- A prefix that means "not."

1. After waiting so long, the people were impatient for the play to begin.
   ____
2. My uncle likes to refresh himself with a nap before going out to dinner. ______________________________
3. Nina thought it was unfair to have a science test the morning after the school concert. ____________________
4. I wrote down the incorrect directions and got lost.
   ____
5. The mayor used words we didn't understand, so we asked her to rephrase what she said. ____________________
6. When she feels unhappy, Brenda cheers herself up by playing soccer with her friends. ____________________
7. Jesse's visits to the doctor are infrequent, because he rarely gets sick. ____________________
8. When I'm in the city, I like to revisit my old neighborhood. ____________________

Name ______________________________

Hey! Let's Play!

Interjections An *interjection* is a word or words that express strong feeling. An interjection usually appears at the beginning of a sentence. It can be followed by either a comma or an exclamation point, depending on how strong a feeling is expressed.

Common Interjections						
Well	Wow	Hey	Ouch	Whew	Oh, no	Oh

Write an interjection and appropriate punctuation on each blank line below.

1. ________________ Where is the music for our rehearsal?
2. ________________ here it is.
3. ________________ let's start with the piece by Brubeck.
4. ________________ I have a long trumpet solo!
5. ________________ I made it all the way through without any big errors.
6. ________________ that was beautiful.
7. ________________ I stubbed my toe on this chair.
8. ________________ we're going to practice the hardest part.
9. ________________ let's get started.
10. ________________ We're good!

Name ______________________________

"What Kind of Music Do You Like?" I Asked

Quotations A *direct quotation* gives a speaker's exact words. Set off exact words with quotation marks. Begin each quotation with a capital letter. Place end punctuation inside quotation marks. Use commas to separate most quotations from the rest of the sentence. If a quotation is two sentences, use a period after the speaker's name.

Clara said, "I like to listen to all kinds of music."

"Yesterday," she said, "I heard a recording of Chinese opera."

"I liked it," said Clara. "Where can I see a performance?"

Rewrite each quotation below, adding needed punctuation marks and capital letters.

1. Sara asked what did the music of ancient Greece sound like

____

____

2. nobody really knows said Ms. Walter.

____

3. Lacey said I like the new music from African musicians.

____

____

4. Lacey, Ms. Walter asked, where can I hear new music from Africa?

____

____

5. you can hear it on the radio said Lacey it's on a program called World Music Today

____

____

Name ______________________________

Yang the Second and Her Secret Admirers

Grammar Skill Punctuating Quotations

Grandma said, "Yes."

Punctuating Quotations A good writer is careful to punctuate sentences correctly. An incorrectly punctuated sentence is easily misunderstood.

Incorrect: Mrs. Voss said Ana please help me.

Corrected: "Mrs. Voss," said Ana. "Please help me."

Corrected: Mrs. Voss said, "Ana, please help me."

Megan is writing about a visit with her grandmother. She has included exactly what she said and exactly what her grandmother said. Proofread Megan's dialogue, correcting any mistakes in punctuating quotations.

"Your great-grandfather was born in Ireland, Nana said.

I said Wow, I never knew that!"

His parents Nana said owned a small store where all the family worked.

"Didn't my great-grandfather want to work in the store" I asked.

There were, Nana explained already two older sisters working in the store, and there would not be enough work for him.

I asked "What did he do?

He had read so much about America that he decided he wanted to see it for himself," Nana said The next time you visit, I'll tell you about his first job in New York City."

Name ______________________________

Writing a How-To Paragraph

When you want to tell readers how to do something, write instructions.

Use this page to plan and organize a set of instructions. First, choose a topic like how to wash dishes, how to make a pizza, or how to tie a certain knot. Next, list the materials that are needed. Then outline each step, giving details that readers need to know to do each one. Doing the activity yourself will help you outline each step.

Instructions for: ______________________________

Materials: ______________________________

Step 1

↓

Step 2

↓

Step 3

↓

Step 4

↓

Step 5

Name ______________________________

Using Order Words

A careful writer uses **order words** such as *first*, *next*, and *finally* in a set of instructions. Order words help readers understand a process and keep track of the sequence of steps.

Read the following instructions. Then rewrite the instructions on the lines, adding order words and phrases from the list to make the sequence of steps clearer and to help readers follow the process. Be sure to use correct capitalization and punctuation when you add order words and phrases or combine two sentences.

To clean chopsticks, you will need a big pan, hot water, and dishwashing liquid. Fill the pan with hot water. Add about a teaspoon of dishwashing liquid. Drop the dirty chopsticks in the hot, soapy water. Grab a handful of chopsticks and roll them together like a stack of pencils between your two hands. You hear a burrrr sound. This means the chopsticks are getting really clean! Rinse the chopsticks with clean water.

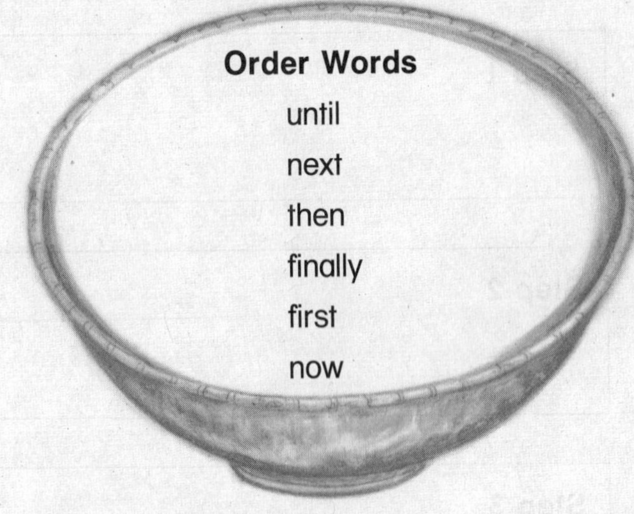

____

____

____

____

____

____

____

Name ___________________________

A Writer's Words

Write each word from the box beside the phrase that describes it.

Vocabulary

diary
experience
understanding
prose
snoop
disappointed
submitted
splendid
rejected

1. very wonderful ________________
2. writing that is not poetry ________________
3. a person who invades the privacy of others ________________
4. a book not to be read by others without permission ________________
5. how you feel when you're not able to do something you've been wanting to do ________________
6. a thing that happens to you ________________
7. what you have done when you have given an article to a newspaper for publication ________________
8. the opposite of *accepted* ________________
9. knowing why things are the way they are ________________

Now write three sentences about being a writer. Use at least one vocabulary word in each sentence.

____

____

____

____

____

____

Dear Mr. Henshaw

Graphic Organizer
Inferences Chart

Name ______________________________

Reading Between the Lines

Read the prompt in the first column. Use evidence from the story and your own experiences to make inferences about Leigh.

	Evidence from the Story	Own Experiences	Inferences
• **What kind of person is Leigh?**			
• **How does Leigh feel about his house?**			

Name ______________________________

The "Write" Connection

What relationship did each person have with Leigh in *Dear Mr. Henshaw*? Answer in complete sentences.

Miss Neely ______________________________

____

____

Leigh's dad ______________________________

____

____

Barry ______________________________

____

Leigh's mom ______________________________

____

____

____

Angela Badger ______________________________

____

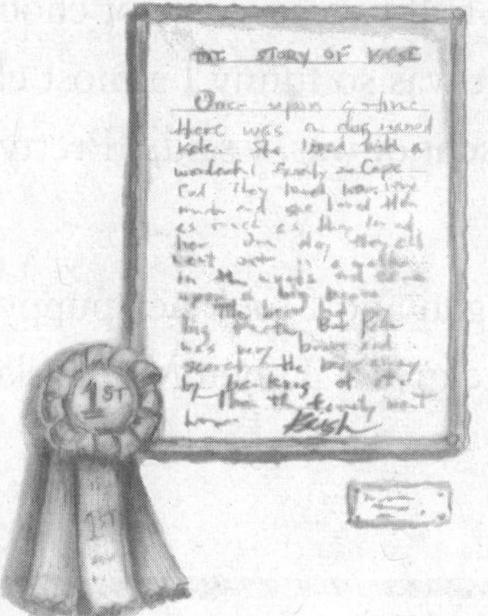
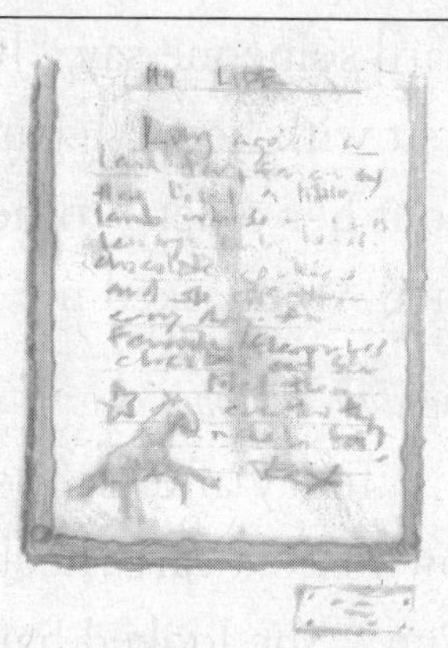
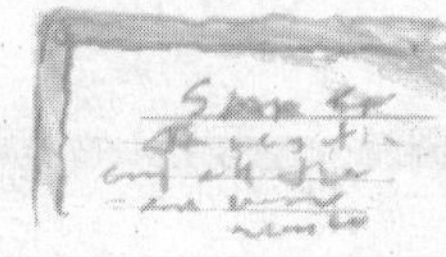

Name ______________________________

Connecting Clues

Read the diary entries that might have been written by Julia. Then complete the activity on page 251.

Monday, October 1

Today was my first day at George Washington Elementary School. My old school's name was better: Woodside. I miss the stretch of woods nearby where my best friend Laura and I would go to skip stones in the creek and look for frogs. The area around this school is made out of concrete, even the playground. I sat by myself at lunch.

Tuesday, October 2

Today my teacher, Mrs. Langley, asked me to stand up in front of the class and tell one exciting fact about where I moved from. My face felt like it was on fire. I said I was from Illinois and on the license plate it says "Land of Lincoln." I thought I saw Mrs. Langley hide a laugh behind her sleeve, but I can't be sure. After that, I was glad I have a desk in the back of the room. When I got home, Mom asked me how school was. I gave her the same answer I'd given the day before, "Okay."

Thursday, October 4

Today at lunch they had chocolate pudding. I took two because chocolate pudding is my favorite. I was sitting alone (again) reading a book (again) when I heard someone say, "Julia?" It was Megan, the girl with the loud laugh, asking me to sit with her. Megan also had two servings of chocolate pudding. She told a story about her older brother that was so funny I almost choked on my broccoli. Today when Mom asked me how school was, I said, "Pretty good."

Tuesday, October 9

Today after school Megan and I took her puppy to the park. She showed me how to do a cartwheel in the grass. When Mom asked me how my day was, I said, "Fun." She looked happy.

Name ____________________

Connecting Clues continued

Answer each question about the passage on page 250. Below your answer, write the clues and what you know from your own experience that helped make the inference.

1. How does Julia feel after the first day at her new school?

____

Story Clues	+	My Own Experience

2. How does Julia feel about talking in front of the class?

____

Story Clues	+	My Own Experience

3. How do Julia's feelings change after the first week of school?

____

Story Clues	+	My Own Experience

Name ______________________________

Thanks with Suffixes

Read this letter that Leigh might have written. In the underlined words, circle the suffixes *-ly, -ness, -ment, -ful,* and *-less*.

April 3

Dear Mrs. Badger,

I couldn't believe it when I heard the announcement that I could go to the writers' lunch today. It was wonderful to meet you. Before today, I felt hopeless about my fitness to be a writer. I was doubtful what I should write. My ideas mostly went nowhere. But you gave me encouragement. Now I feel fearless when I write. I think I'll be in the writing business for a long time.

Sincerely yours,
Leigh Botts

Now, write each word with a suffix beside its correct definition.

1. ______________________: for the most part
2. ______________________: without hope
3. ______________________: profession
4. ______________________: truly; honestly
5. ______________________: message
6. ______________________: great
7. ______________________: a lift in confidence
8. ______________________: without fear
9. ______________________: suitability
10. ______________________: full of doubts

Name ______________________________

Words with Suffixes (*-ly, -ness, -ment, -ful, -less*)

A **suffix** is a word part added to the end of a base word. A suffix adds meaning to the word. The word parts *-ly*, *-ness*, *-ment*, *-ful* and *-less* are suffixes. The spelling of the base word is usually not changed when the suffix begins with a consonant.

safe + ly = safe**ly**
pale + ness = pale**ness**
enjoy + ment = enjoy**ment**
cheer + ful = cheer**ful**
speech + less = speech**less**

Spelling Words

1. dreadful
2. enjoyment
3. safely
4. watchful
5. speechless
6. paleness
7. breathless
8. government
9. cheerful
10. actively
11. closeness
12. lately
13. goodness
14. retirement
15. forgetful
16. basement
17. softness
18. delightful
19. settlement
20. countless

Write each Spelling Word under its suffix.

-ness or *-ment*	*-ful* or *-less*
______	______
______	______
______	______
______	______
______	______
______	______
______	______
______	______
______	______

-ly		
______	______	______

Name ______________________________

Spelling Spree

Adding Suffixes **Write the Spelling Word that contains each base word below.**

1. soft ____________
2. retire ____________
3. good ____________
4. forget ____________
5. govern ____________
6. breath ____________
7. settle ____________

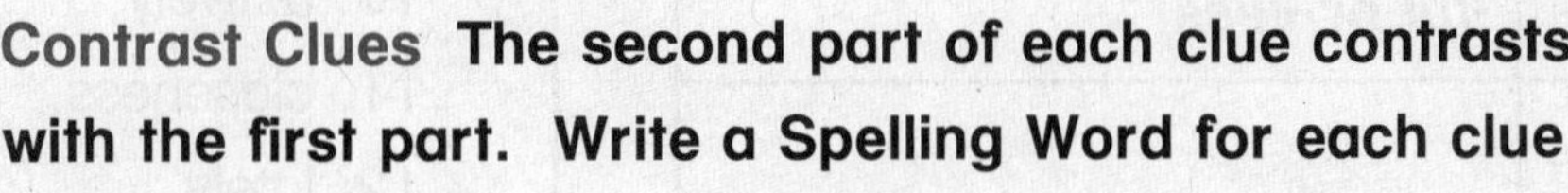

Contrast Clues **The second part of each clue contrasts with the first part. Write a Spelling Word for each clue.**

Example: not weak, but *powerful*

8. not long ago, but ____________
9. not talkative, but ____________
10. not careless, but ____________
11. not distance, but ____________
12. not grouchy, but ____________
13. not wonderful, but ____________
14. not darkness, but ____________
15. not few, but ____________

Spelling Words

1. dreadful
2. enjoyment
3. safely
4. watchful
5. speechless
6. paleness
7. breathless
8. government
9. cheerful
10. actively
11. closeness
12. lately
13. goodness
14. retirement
15. forgetful
16. basement
17. softness
18. delightful
19. settlement
20. countless

Dear Mr. Henshaw

Spelling Words with Suffixes *-ly, -ness, -ment, -ful, -less*

Name ____________________

Proofreading and Writing

Proofreading Circle the five misspelled Spelling Words in the following newspaper article. Then write each word correctly.

Young Writers Meet Famous Author

The winners of the Young Writers' Yearbook contest had a delightfull lunch with Mrs. Angela Badger last week. Some students were speechless upon meeting the popular author, but others acttively sought her attention and talked easily with her. Mrs. Badger was impressed by the number of our students who read and write for their own injoyment. Everyone had a wonderful time, and our young writers returned safly to the school. If any students have not yet read the winning stories, copies of the yearbook are available in the supply room in the school basment.

1. ____________
2. ____________
3. ____________
4. ____________
5. ____________

Spelling Words

1. dreadful
2. enjoyment
3. safely
4. watchful
5. speechless
6. paleness
7. breathless
8. government
9. cheerful
10. actively
11. closeness
12. lately
13. goodness
14. retirement
15. forgetful
16. basement
17. softness
18. delightful
19. settlement
20. countless

Write an Opinion Leigh was disappointed because his story received an honorable mention instead of a prize. In the end, though, it was his story that Mrs. Badger remembered. If you were in Leigh's position, would you rather have won the contest or received Mrs. Badger's praise?

On a separate piece of paper, write a paragraph describing how you would have felt if you were in Leigh's place and why. Use Spelling Words from the list.

Name ______________________________

That's Good or Bad?

A script for *Dear Mr. Henshaw* might contain a scene in which Leigh tells his mother about meeting Angela Badger. Rewrite each sentence by first replacing the underlined word with a positive connotation. Then, write the sentence again replacing the word with a negative connotation. Choose your words from the list below.

odd	aroma	chatted	notorious
famous	inventive	stink	jabbered

1. "Mom, Mrs. Badger called my story original!"

____

____

2. "She liked what I wrote about the smell of grapes in the sun."

____

____

3. "We asked her what it felt like to be a well-known author."

____

____

4. "The other kids talked with Mrs. Badger more than I did."

____

____

Name ______________________________

Make It Shorter!

Abbreviations An **abbreviation** is a shortened form of a word. Most abbreviations begin with a capital letter and end with a period. Most abbreviations should only be used in special kinds of writing, such as in addresses and lists.

Common Abbreviations					
Mr.	Mister	St.	Street	Co.	Company
Mrs.	married woman	Ave.	Avenue	Inc.	Incorporated
Ms.	any woman	Apt.	apartment	WV	West Virginia
Dr.	Doctor	P. O.	Post Office	TX	Texas
Jr.	Junior	Dec.	December	CA	California
Sr.	Senior	Mon.	Monday	ME	Maine

Rewrite each group of words using abbreviations where possible.

1. Morgan Glass, Incorporated ______________________________
2. Mister David Kowalsky, Junior ______________________________
3. Wednesday, February 28, 2004 ______________________________
4. 2557 Hastings Avenue, Apartment 4 ______________________________
5. Bangor, Maine ______________________________
6. Post Office Box 1287 ______________________________
7. Star, West Virginia ______________________________
8. 25 Westgate Road, Apartment 6

____

Name ______________________

Titles, "Titles," and *More Titles*

Titles Capitalize the first, the last, and each important word in the titles of books, movies, or newspapers. Capitalize forms of the word *be*, including *is*, *are*, and *am*. Capitalize words like *and*, *in*, *of*, *to*, *a*, and *the* only when they are the first or last word in a title. Put titles in italic type or underline them. Titles of short works, such as short stories, poems, articles, songs, and chapters of books are enclosed in quotation marks.

Newspaper: My mother reads The Wall Street Journal every day.
Book: I read Make Way for Ducklings to my younger brother.
Chapter: The first chapter of this book is called "On the Beach."

Each of the sentences below contains a title. Rewrite each title correctly.

1. The book The cat in the hat was a childhood favorite of mine.

____

2. Lester read a book called the second floor mystery.

____

3. The disappearance of the ladder is the name of the first chapter.

____

4. Chris saw the old movie My friend flicka.

____

5. Have you seen the review in The gladeview gazette, our school paper?

____

6. Do you know the words to the song America?

____

7. Deer at dusk is one of my favorite poems

____

Name ______________________________

Using Abbreviations

A good writer uses abbreviations only in special kinds of writing, such as lists and addresses. Marcus used abbreviations where he should have written out the entire word, and wrote out words that should be abbreviated.

Rewrite and correct the address. Then proofread the body of the letter. Correct each error above the line.

Marcus Chester, Junior ______________________

218 Mulberry Street ______________________

Bowen, California ______________________

Dear MisterVasquez:

I am a big fan of your work. Last Sat. I read your latest mystery. It was exciting. When Randolph and Kildare chased Brad and Chris down the rd., I read as fast as I could to find out what would happen next.

Have you ever thought of setting a story in NC? If you came here to do research, I could help you. My family lives in an apt. in Charlotte, and we would be happy to have you stay with us. Our st. has a big, dark old house you would like. My friends and I saw something mysterious there last Aug.

Thanks for writing such great books.

Your fan,

Marcus

Marcus Chester

Name ______________________________

Writing a Journal Entry

Use this flow chart to organize your journal entry. First, choose a topic. Next, write the main events in time order, one in each box. Finally, write details about each event. Include personal thoughts, feelings, reactions, questions, and ideas.

Topic: ______________________

Event:

Details:

↓

Event:

Details:

↓

Event:

Details:

Name ______________________________

Expanding Sentences with Adjectives

An **adjective** like *plump* or *icy* describes a noun or pronoun. Good writers use adjectives to create a clear, vivid picture of what they are describing or narrating.

Read this journal entry that Leigh Botts might have written after a day of hiking. Then rewrite it on the lines, adding adjectives from the list to bring Leigh's description to life. Use as many adjectives as you can, joining related adjectives with *and* or a comma if appropriate.

Saturday, March 10

Today I took a hike through the woods. A cloud of monarch butterflies fluttered through the air. As I leaned quietly against the bark of a tree trunk, they landed in the leaves above. Soon the afternoon sun appeared like a coin against the hills. I knew it was time to go home for supper, but the gas station is so noisy compared with the silence of the forest.

Adjectives

dark	lonely
distant	orange
huge	green
delicate	short
scratchy	busy
golden	cool
crowded	small
shiny	

____

____

____

____

____

____

____

____

Name ______________________________

Vocabulary Items

Use the test-taking strategies and tips you have learned to help you answer vocabulary items. This practice will help you when you take this kind of test.

Read each pair of sentences below. Then choose the word that correctly completes both sentences. Fill in the circle for your answer at the bottom of the page.

1 The _______ led the class on a tour through the museum.
The instructor will _______ us in doing the project.

A teacher **C** lead
B guide **D** instructor

2 Lee made her sandwich on the kitchen _______.
Kevin put the last math _______ in his notebook.

F chair **H** table
G block **J** book

3 Our best runner was struck out at first _______.
The _______ of the statue was cracked and uneven.

A floor **C** base
B arm **D** basket

4 The dogs played and _______ in the park.
Which candidate _______ the best race?

F sat **H** won
G limped **J** ran

ANSWER ROWS	1 Ⓐ Ⓑ Ⓒ Ⓓ	3 Ⓐ Ⓑ Ⓒ Ⓓ
	2 Ⓕ Ⓖ Ⓗ Ⓙ	4 Ⓕ Ⓖ Ⓗ Ⓙ

Name ______________________

Vocabulary Items continued

5 Rita thought the math test was a ______.
The boy tightened the ______ so the saddle would not fall off the horse.

A rope **C** girth
B cinch **D** nightmare

6 The girl wanted to find a pet that would ______ her.
Dad wore his blue ______ to the meeting.

F suit **H** like
G uniform **J** comfort

7 Grandpa taught me how to ______ my own problems.
Don't touch the ______ on the hot frying pan.

A lid **C** handle
B solve **D** understand

8 Every person has to learn how to make ______ decisions.
The meat was too ______ to chew.

F tender **H** stringy
G wise **J** tough

ANSWER ROWS 5 (A) (B) (C) (D) 7 (A) (B) (C) (D)
6 (F) (G) (H) (J) 8 (F) (G) (H) (J)

Person to Person: Theme 4 Wrap-Up

Spelling Review

Name ______________________

Spelling Review

Write Spelling Words from the list on this page to answer the questions.

1–9. Which nine words have the VCCCV pattern?

1. ______ 6. ______
2. ______ 7. ______
3. ______ 8. ______
4. ______ 9. ______
5. ______

10–17. Which eight words have a VV pattern that makes two vowel sounds?

10. ______ 14. ______
11. ______ 15. ______
12. ______ 16. ______
13. ______ 17. ______

18–32. Which fifteen words have suffixes or end in *-ed* or *-ing*? Underline two words that also have the VCCCV pattern.

18. ______ 26. ______
19. ______ 27. ______
20. ______ 28. ______
21. ______ 29. ______
22. ______ 30. ______
23. ______ 31. ______
24. ______ 32. ______
25. ______

Spelling Words

1. complain
2. planned
3. mischief
4. countless
5. laughter
6. rodeo
7. decided
8. offered
9. delightful
10. farther
11. sandwich
12. actively
13. riot
14. amusing
15. radio
16. lately
17. government
18. actual
19. improve
20. goodness
21. hitting
22. diary
23. fuel
24. address
25. visiting
26. cruel
27. covered
28. watchful
29. usual
30. ordered

Name ______________________

Spelling Spree

Phrase Fillers Write the Spelling Word that best completes each phrase.

1. loud ______________ after a joke
2. working to ______________ my grades
3. music on the ______________
4. a ______________ number of stars
5. running out of ______________
6. a cowboy starring in the ______________
7. a ham and cheese ______________

Word Detective Use the following clues to figure out each Spelling Word. Write the word on the line.

8. Not kind, but ______________
9. Not out of the ordinary ______________
10. Tells where you live ______________
11. A disturbance of the peace ______________
12. A daily written record ______________
13. Funny ______________
14. The way a nation is ruled ______________
15. Real, true, and factual ______________

Spelling Words

1. sandwich
2. cruel
3. address
4. actual
5. countless
6. government
7. laughter
8. amusing
9. fuel
10. usual
11. riot
12. diary
13. improve
14. rodeo
15. radio

Name ______________________

Proofreading and Writing

Proofreading **Circle the six misspelled Spelling Words in this e-mail message. Then write each word correctly.**

Dear Aunt Leslie and Uncle Alex,

My goodnes! I am excited about visiding you. Dad orderd me a new suitcase, so it has been hard laitly to wait until it is time to pack. I have been preparing activly for this vacation. I want to practice my pitching under Uncle Alex's wachful eye.

See you soon, Roy

1. ____________ 4. ____________

2. ____________ 5. ____________

3. ____________ 6. ____________

Spelling Words

1. ordered
2. complain
3. goodness
4. farther
5. visiting
6. offered
7. lately
8. decided
9. covered
10. delightful
11. hitting
12. planned
13. watchful
14. mischief
15. actively

Finish the Entry **Complete the list by writing Spelling Words that make sense on the lines.**

7. Uncle Alex ____________ to help me with baseball.
8. We will practice ____________ baseballs.
9. Bring a gift for the party they have ____________.
10. I will be ____________ from home than I've ever been.
11. Do not get into ____________.
12. Bring my camera. Their beautiful garden will be ____________ with flowers.
13. I have ____________ to try fishing this year.
14. My aunt and uncle are ____________ people.
15. Don't ____________ about anything.

Write a Letter **On a separate sheet of paper, write a letter to someone you would like to visit. Use the Spelling Review Words.**

Name ______________________________

Setting Up a Scene

Think about a sequel for *The Case of the Runaway Appetite* in which Joe Giles visits Princess Veronica in her own country. What would be the new setting for the opening scene? Which new characters would you introduce? What new problem could the characters face? Fill in a description of the setting, the characters, and the problem in the chart below. Be as precise as you can.

Opening Scene	Description
Setting **Time:** **Place:**	
Characters:	
Problem:	

Name ______________________________

Comparing Productions

Think of a movie, play, or television show you have enjoyed. Compare it to *The Case of the Runaway Appetite.* Make sure to think about the characters, the setting, the plot, and other details. Write about each production in the Venn diagram below. Remember to use the intersecting part of the circles for the things that both productions have in common.

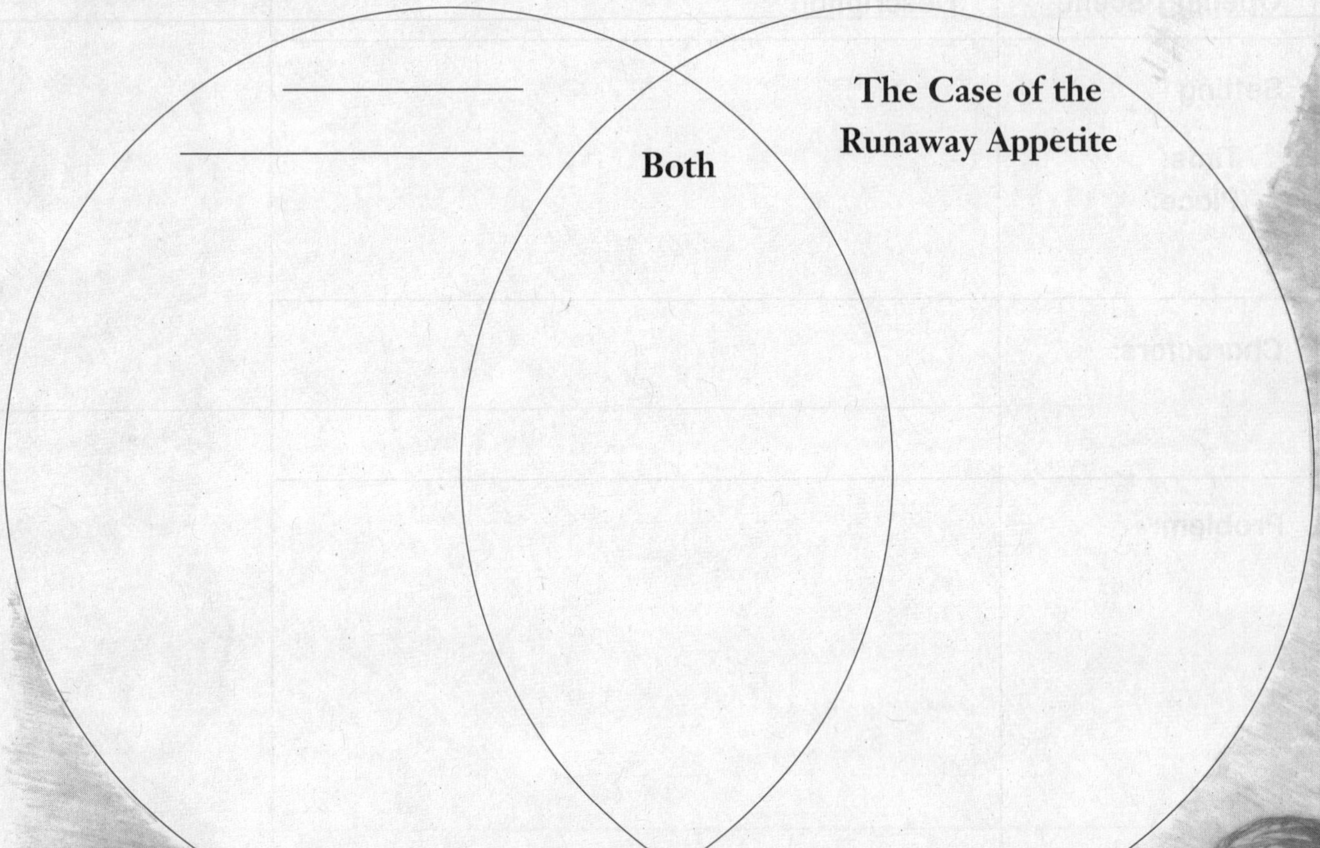

____

____

Both

The Case of the Runaway Appetite

Name ______________________________

One Land, Many Trails

After reading each selection, complete the chart to show what you learned about the people who lived on the American frontier long ago.

	Pioneer Girl	A Boy Called Slow
Tell who the main character in this selection is, and give one important fact about that person.		
What special challenges did this person face in the selection?		
What traits helped this person successfully overcome the challenges?		
How did this person's efforts contribute to America's past?		

Name ______________________________

One Land, Many Trails

	Black Cowboy Wild Horses	Elena
Tell who the main character in this selection is, and give one important fact about that person.		
What special challenges did this person face in the selection?		
What traits helped this person successfully overcome the challenges?		
How did this person's efforts contribute to America's past?		

What have you learned about the contributions different people have made to America's culture and heritage?

____

____

____

Name ______________________________

Path of the Warrior

Read the paragraph below. Use the words in the box to fill in the blanks.

Vocabulary

- customs
- reputation
- inherited
- raid
- extended
- vision
- determination
- respect

Physical abilities are mostly ______________ from parents and grandparents, but character is developed through life experiences. How could a young brave earn a ______________ as a courageous warrior? One way was to lead a ______________ against an enemy camp. Another was to engage a rival group in battle and touch their leader with a coup stick. Still another was to show ______________ in completing a difficult mission. Earning the ______________ of both the ______________ family and the tribal elders was very important to young braves. This could only be done by faithfully observing the traditions and ______________ of the people. One important tradition was going alone on a wilderness journey to seek a ______________. Sometimes this would provide the brave with a new name, one that carried strength and power.

Name ______________________________

Conclusions Chart

Story Clues			=	Conclusions
page 471	+		=	
pages 472–475	+		=	Slow probably has the makings of a good leader.
pages 476–479 Slow wrestles and practices hunting. He becomes strong. He kills a buffalo at age ten.	+	Slow is careful and deliberate. People stop teasing him. He decides to join a battle against the Crow.	=	
pages 480–483 Slow announces that he will join the raid. Instead of waiting, he races ahead toward the Crow.	+	Slow touches a Crow warrior with his coup stick and knocks an arrow out of his hand. The Crow warriors flee.	=	

What predictions can you make about the kind of person Slow will grow up to be?

____

____

Name ______________________________

Slow's Early Life in a Line

The timeline below shows some important events in Sitting Bull's early life. Answer each question to tell about each event.

1. **1831:** Who has a son?

1. ______________________________

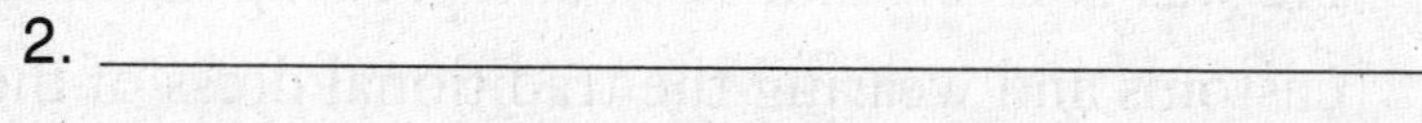

2. **First Months of Life:** What name do Returns Again and his wife give their son? Why?

2. ______________________________

3. **Age Seven:** How does Slow feel about his name? What does he dream of?

3. ______________________________

4. **The Hunting Trip:** What happens when Returns Again goes hunting?

4. ______________________________

5. **Age Ten:** What big thing does Slow do? What else does he do to prepare himself for adulthood?

5. ______________________________

6. **Age Fourteen:** What does Slow decide to do? What happens as a result?

6. ______________________________

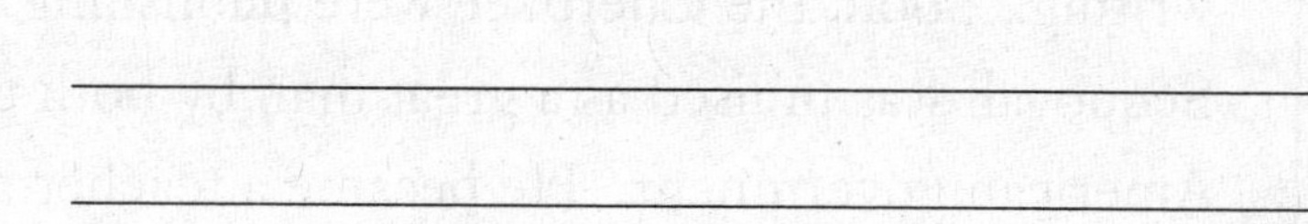

Name ______________________________

Why Do You Think . . . ?

Read the following passage. Then complete the activity on page 277.

Sequoyah

When he was a child, few people would have guessed that Sequoyah would one day be hailed as a genius and a savior of the Cherokee nation. He was born around 1760 and grew up in Tennessee, following Cherokee customs and wearing the traditional dress of the Cherokee people. A childhood illness left him partially disabled, but he managed to acquire the skills of a silversmith and blacksmith.

Sequoyah never learned to speak, read, or write in English. However, he became fascinated with English writing. In fact, he believed that the secret of the white settlers' success was their written language.

Sequoyah figured out that each letter in the English alphabet represented a sound. In 1809 he set out to create a similar alphabet for the Cherokee language. On scraps of tree bark, he scratched symbols to stand for the sounds of Cherokee. His wife did not approve.

"Why are you wasting your time?" she complained. "You should be working, not drawing pictures!"

Sequoyah ignored her. He knew that his work could be important for the Cherokee people. Finally, after many years, he had created a set of eighty-five characters to represent all the sounds of the Cherokee language. When he showed the members of his tribe, however, they laughed at him.

"What do we need an alphabet for?" they said.

Sequoyah didn't lose faith, though. He traveled to Georgia to show his work to the top Cherokee chiefs. They were impressed. The alphabet was easy to learn, and it allowed people to communicate in writing. Soon, the Cherokee were publishing their own newspaper. Sequoyah was praised as a great man by both the Cherokee and the American government. He became a teacher and a highly respected leader of the Cherokee people.

Name ______________________________

Why Do You Think . . .? continued

Answer these questions about the passage on page 276.

1. Why do you think Sequoyah was considered a genius?

____

____

2. In what ways might the Cherokee alphabet have helped to preserve Cherokee customs and ways of life?

____

____

3. Why do you think Sequoyah continued working on the alphabet despite the fact that other members of his tribe did not approve?

____

____

4. Why do you think the Cherokee people changed their minds about the alphabet?

____

____

5. What character traits did Sequoyah possess? Use details from the passage to help you answer.

____

____

____

____

Name ______________________________

Word Parts Match

Read each sentence. Match a prefix or suffix from the box on the left with a base word from the box on the right to form a word that completes the sentence. Write the word in the blank. (The prefixes and suffix may be used more than once.)

dis-	in-	-ion
re-	un-	

accurate	agreed	aware	cooperate
direct	like	possess	turned

1. As they grew older, many of the boys began to ______________ their childhood names and wish for new ones.
2. Returns Again earned his name when he ______________ to protect his people from an enemy raid.
3. The low rumbling noise came from the ______________ of the trail.
4. Returns Again ______________ with the others, who wanted to take out their weapons.
5. Unlike Returns Again, the other men were ______________ of what the big bull buffalo's sounds meant.
6. Slow struck the Crow warrior's arm with his coup stick to make his aim ______________.
7. After their victory, the Lakota Sioux warriors took ______________ of the enemy's horses and weapons.
8. Their spirit of ______________ helped the Lakota Sioux people provide for and protect each other.

Name ______________________

A Boy Called Slow

Spelling Words with a Prefix or a Suffix *(un-, dis-, in-, re-; -ion)*

Words with a Prefix or a Suffix *(un-, dis-, in-, re-; -ion)*

A **prefix** is a word part added to the beginning of a base word or a word root. It adds meaning to a word. Some of the Spelling Words contain the prefixes *un-*, *dis-*, *in-*, or *re-*. To spell these words, find the prefix and the base word or the word root.

Prefix + Base Word: **un**able **dis**cover

Prefix + Word Root: **re**port **in**spect

A **suffix** is a word part added to the end of a base word. The suffix *-ion* can change verbs into nouns. When a verb ends with *e*, drop the *e* and add *-ion*. If a verb does not end with *e*, just add *-ion*.

VERB: promote react NOUN: promot**ion** react**ion**

Write the Spelling Words. Underline the prefixes *un-*, *dis-*, *in-*, and *re-*. Circle the suffix *-ion*.

______________________ ______________________

______________________ ______________________

______________________ ______________________

______________________ ______________________

______________________ ______________________

______________________ ______________________

______________________ ______________________

______________________ ______________________

______________________ ______________________

______________________ ______________________

Spelling Words

1. unable
2. discover
3. report
4. disaster
5. unaware
6. remind
7. televise
8. television
9. inspect
10. inspection
11. react
12. reaction
13. tense
14. tension
15. correct
16. correction
17. promote
18. promotion
19. express
20. expression

Name ______________________________

A Boy Called Slow

Spelling Words with a Prefix or a Suffix *(un-, dis-, in-, re-; -ion)*

Spelling Spree

Meaning Match Write the Spelling Word that has each meaning and word part below.

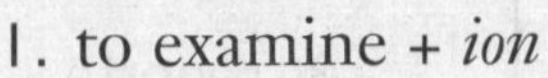
1. to examine + *ion*

2. *dis* + a container lid
3. to broadcast + *ion*
4. *re* + to do something
5. to make right + *ion*
6. *un* + capable of doing something
7. nervous + *ion*
8. to move to a higher position + *ion*

1. ______________ 5. ______________

2. ______________ 6. ______________

3. ______________ 7. ______________

4. ______________ 8. ______________

Hidden Words Write the Spelling Word that is hidden in each row of letters. Don't let the other words fool you!

9. c o r e a c t i o n c e
10. g l e e x p r e s s u r e
11. c h a i n s p e c t r i p
12. a r c o r r e c t a n g l e
13. h o t e l e v i s e n s e
14. d a m p r o m o t e a m
15. h a r d i s a s t e r n

9. ______________ 13. ______________

10. ______________ 14. ______________

11. ______________ 15. ______________

12. ______________

Spelling Words

1. unable
2. discover
3. report
4. disaster
5. unaware
6. remind
7. televise
8. television
9. inspect
10. inspection
11. react
12. reaction
13. tense
14. tension
15. correct
16. correction
17. promote
18. promotion
19. express
20. expression

A Boy Called Slow

Spelling Words with a Prefix or a Suffix *(un-, dis-, in-, re-; -ion)*

Name ______________________________

Proofreading and Writing

Circle the five misspelled Spelling Words in this part of a script for a class play. Then write each word correctly.

Slow: How much longer will we have to be called by these names? Every time I hear mine, all it does is remined me that the elders think of me as just a child. These days, whenever anyone calls my name, I get very tens.

Hungry Mouth: I know what you mean. I have the same reaction. I'd like a name that's an expresion of something more than the fact that I have a big appetite. But what can we do? It's not like the elders are unawear of our feelings.

Slow: That's true, but they're still waiting for us to do something worthy of a new name. The next time they form a war party we should repport for duty.

1. ______________
2. ______________
3. ______________
4. ______________
5. ______________

Spelling Words

1. unable
2. discover
3. report
4. disaster
5. unaware
6. remind
7. televise
8. television
9. inspect
10. inspection
11. react
12. reaction
13. tense
14. tension
15. correct
16. correction
17. promote
18. promotion
19. express
20. expression

Write a Summary If a friend were to ask you what *A Boy Called Slow* is about, what would you say? What happens in the story? Who are the main characters? What details are most important in understanding the events of the story?

On a separate piece of paper, write a brief summary of the story. Use Spelling Words from the list.

Name ______________________

Slow Is to Boy as . . .

Read each analogy. Write the word that best completes each analogy.

1. *Share* is to *hoard* as *gain* is to ______________.
   collect lose heavy surrender
2. *Inherited* is to *received* as *yelled* is to ______________.
   hushed anger argued shouted
3. *Son* is to *relative* as *pony* is to ______________.
   mane saddle animal stirrups
4. *Courage* is to *warriors* as *wisdom* is to ______________.
   elders infants smart college
5. *Retreat* is to *advance* as *speak* is to ______________.
   chatter listen silent command
6. *Slow* is to *name* as *winter* is to ______________.
   summer frozen snow season
7. *Follow* is to *trail* as *protect* is to ______________.
   guard warn attack watch

Use any three of the words in the box to write an incomplete analogy on a separate piece of paper. Challenge a partner to complete it with one of the remaining words. Sample answer shown.

climb	deep	flat	mountains
oceans	peaked	plains	swim

8. *Plains* is to *flat* as *mountains* is to *peaked*.

Name ____________________

We Object to It

Subject and Object Pronouns A pronoun is a word that replaces a noun. *I, you, he, she, it, we,* and *they* are subject pronouns. *Me, you, him, her, it, us,* and *them* are object pronouns. Use a subject pronoun as the subject of a sentence or after forms of *be*. Use an object pronoun as the object of an action verb or after words like *to, for,* or *with.*

Underline the pronoun in parentheses that correctly completes each sentence.

1. (I/me) have a nickname.
2. My family gave (I/me) the nickname Skeeter.
3. My brother Michael is called Apple because (he/him) has red cheeks.
4. People give apples to (he/him) all the time.
5. (They/Them) think Michael always wants an apple.
6. My sister Cheryl is called Cookie by (we/us).
7. Everyone gives cookies to (she/her).
8. If anyone likes cookies, it is (she/her).
9. Cheryl thanks (they/them).
10. Michael and Cheryl share apples and cookies with (we/us).

Name ______________________________

Should It Be *I* or *Me*?

Using *I* and *Me* Use *I* as the subject of a sentence and after forms of *be*. Use *me* after action verbs and after words like *to, in, for,* and *with*. When using the pronouns *I* and *me* with nouns or other pronouns, name yourself last.

Incorrect: **Jack and me** went to the movies.
Incorrect: **I and Jack** went to the movies.
Correct: **Jack and I** went to the movies.

Incorrect: That was a treat for **Jack and I**.
Incorrect: That was a treat for **me and Jack**.
Correct: That was a treat for **Jack and me**.

Underline the words in parentheses that correctly complete each sentence.

1. (Latisha and I/Latisha and me) found shiny, black arrowheads near the creek.
2. (She and I/Her and me) went to the library to learn about arrowheads.

3. The librarian told (Latisha and I/Latisha and me) that our arrowheads were made of obsidian, a kind of volcanic glass.
4. (You and I/You and me) should meet Latisha at the creek tomorrow.

5. Another discovery would be fun for (Latisha and I/Latisha and me).
6. If Latisha finds one, she will give it to (you and me/you and I).
7. (Her and I/She and I) have found broken arrowheads before.
8. But yesterday (I and she/she and I) found two perfect specimens!
9. The arrowhead collection gathered by (her and me/she and I) is growing.
10. Soon (she and I/her and me) will have the largest collection around.

Name ______________________________

We're Pronoun Pros

Good writers are careful to use a subject pronoun as the subject of a sentence or after a form of *be*. They use an object pronoun after an action verb and after a word like *to*, *for*, *with*, or *in*.

Gloria is writing for the school newspaper. Proofread her draft. Cross out each incorrect pronoun or pronoun phrase and write the correct pronoun or phrase above it.

Last Saturday, George, Nan, Kathy, and me followed a trail in the woods on Prospect Hill. Kathy and me asked George and Nan to lead us. The hiking club gave he and she trailblazing badges. I and Kathy knew they would keep us on the path. George knew a special place at the end of the trail. It was him who suggested the hike.

The trail was thick with brambles, but George and Nan kept us on the right path. After half an hour of walking, him and her called out to Kathy and I. The sun shone brightly on wildflowers and bushes full of fat, juicy blackberries. George picked four berries and washed they with water. Nan held out her hand and George gave one berry to she and one to each of us. Nothing has ever tasted so good. Us will go back soon!

Name ______________________________

Writing a Persuasive Speech

In *A Boy Called Slow*, a fourteen-year-old Lakota boy courageously protects his people from a Crow war party and earns himself a new name. His father, Returns Again, gives a very brief speech about Slow's bravery. Now you will write a persuasive speech in which Returns Again describes his son's courage in the battle against the Crow and persuades the listeners that Slow deserves a new name.

Use the chart below to help you get started. First, identify the goal of the speech and the audience to whom you will deliver it. Then list two or more specific reasons why Slow deserves a new name. Include evidence to support your reasons.

Goal	Audience	Reasons

Name ______________________________

Using Quotations

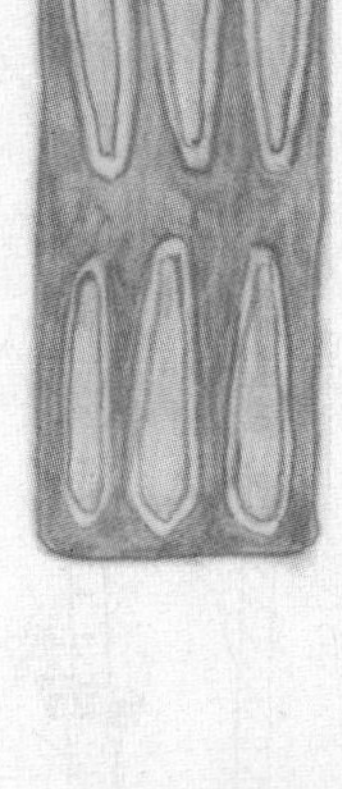

Good speechwriters make their speeches more lively and powerful by including **direct quotations** made by people who have something important to say about the topic. When you use a direct quotation in your own writing, make sure to do the following:

- Write the exact words the person said.
- Use quotation marks to separate the direct quotation from the rest of the sentence.
- Give the name of the person who is responsible for the quotation.
- Check that the spelling of the quoted person's name is correct.

Carefully read these quotations by well-known Native Americans.

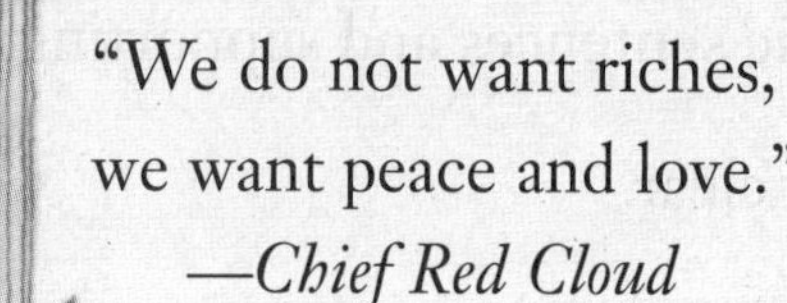

"We do not want riches, we want peace and love."
—*Chief Red Cloud*

"The earth and myself are of one mind."
—*Chief Joseph*

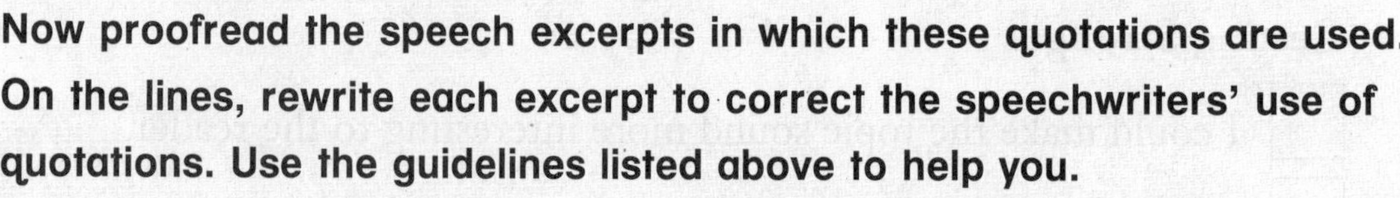

Now proofread the speech excerpts in which these quotations are used. On the lines, rewrite each excerpt to correct the speechwriters' use of quotations. Use the guidelines listed above to help you.

1. Scott Franklin will now share remarkable slides of his round-the-world camping trip. Mr. Franklin's experiment in living echoes Cheif Josef's belief that The earth and myself are of one mind.

____

____

____

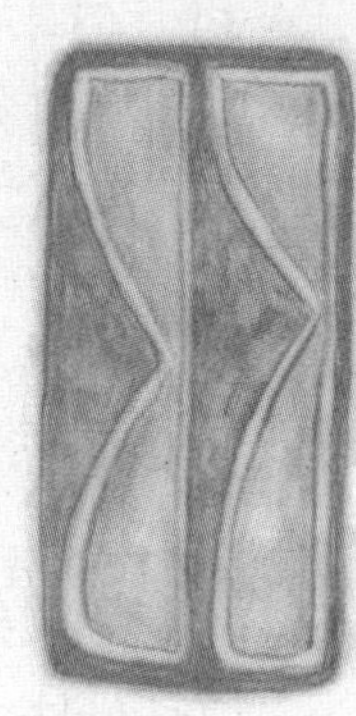

2. Our neighborhood group opposes the proposed development because, as someone said, We do not want riches, we want peace and love.

____

____

____

Name ______________________________

Revising Your Research Report

Reread your research report. What do you need to do to make it better? Use this page to help you decide. Put a checkmark in the box for each sentence that describes your research report.

Rings the Bell!

- ☐ I chose an interesting topic to research.
- ☐ I used different, reliable sources to find information on the topic.
- ☐ I took careful notes and used them to write my report.
- ☐ My paragraphs contain topic sentences and supporting facts.
- ☐ My pronoun references are clear.
- ☐ There are very few mistakes.

Getting Stronger

- ☐ I could make the topic sound more interesting to the reader.
- ☐ More sources might help me make sure I have the facts right.
- ☐ I need to follow my notes more closely.
- ☐ Some of my pronoun references are unclear.
- ☐ There are quite a few errors that need to be fixed.

Try Harder

- ☐ My topic isn't very interesting.
- ☐ I didn't use enough sources to find my facts.
- ☐ I didn't take careful notes on what I found out.
- ☐ Too many mistakes make the report hard to read.

Reading-Writing Workshop

Improving Your Writing

Name ______________________________

Pronoun Reference

Pronouns are words that replace nouns or other words. Write the word or words that the underlined pronoun refers to in each exercise.

1. Gems are hard to find. They are usually embedded in ordinary-looking rocks.
2. Without impurities, gems would be colorless crystals. The color of a gem depends on the type of impurities it contains.
3. The metal chromium gives a green color to one kind of crystal, turning it into an emerald.
4. Gems can be harder than the rock that surrounds them.
5. Rock hunters often find gems in riverbeds. They look for places where the surrounding rock has been eroded away.
6. Sapphires are a fiery blue. They get their color from a mixture of titanium and iron.
7. Rubies have chromium as an impurity. It gives them a deep red color.
8. Once a gem is found, it must be cut by gem-cutters.

1. ______________________ 5. ______________________

2. ______________________ 6. ______________________

3. ______________________ 7. ______________________

4. ______________________ 8. ______________________

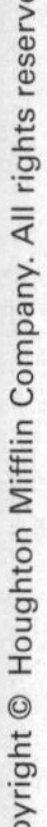

Reading-Writing Workshop

Frequently Misspelled Words

Name ______________________________

Spelling Words

Words Often Misspelled Look for familiar spelling patterns to help you remember how to spell the Spelling Words on this page. Think carefully about the parts that you find hard to spell in each word.

Write the missing letters in the Spelling Words below.

1. ___ ___ ile
2. ___ ___ ole
3. ___ ___ ___ way
4. ___ n ___ one
5. ___ n ___ thing
6. favor ___ ___ ___
7. on ___ ___
8. su ___ ___ ose
9. ev ___ ___ ___ body
10. ev ___ ___ ___ one
11. r ___ ___ ___ ___ y
12. m ___ ___ ning
13. ___ ___ so
14. ___ ___ ways
15. f ___ rst

Spelling Words

1. while
2. whole
3. anyway
4. anyone
5. anything
6. favorite
7. once
8. suppose
9. everybody
10. everyone
11. really
12. morning
13. also
14. always
15. first

Study List On a separate piece of paper, write each Spelling Word. Check your spelling against the words on the list.

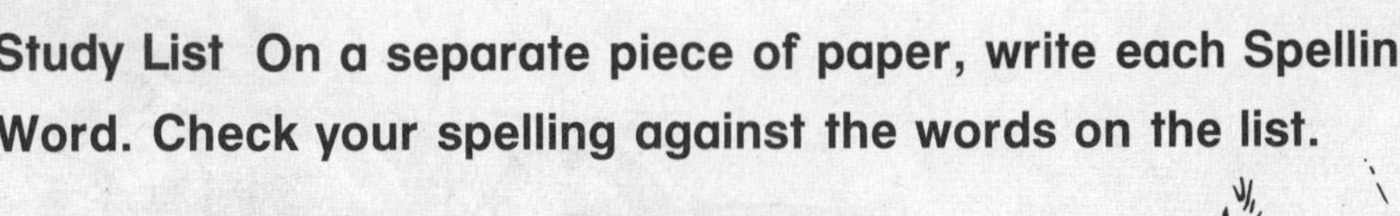

Name ______________________________

Spelling Spree

Contrast Clues **The second part of each clue contrasts with the first part. Write a Spelling Word for each clue.**

1. not evening, but _____
2. not lots of times, but _____
3. not never, but _____
4. not a fraction, but a _____
5. not a specific thing, but _____
6. not last, but _____

1. ______________ 4. ______________

2. ______________ 5. ______________

3. ______________ 6. ______________

Spelling Words

1. while
2. whole
3. anyway
4. anyone
5. anything
6. favorite
7. once
8. suppose
9. everybody
10. everyone
11. really
12. morning
13. also
14. always
15. first

Hidden Words **Write the Spelling Word that is hidden in each row of letters. Don't let the other words fool you!**

7. neverybodyes
8. catsupposeat
9. storeallying
10. towhilearn
11. sieveryonear
12. manywayak
13. mealsound
14. alfalfavoritent
15. canyoneed

humorningoat

7. ______________ 12. ______________

8. ______________ 13. ______________

9. ______________ 14. ______________

10. ______________ 15. ______________

11. ______________

Name ___________________________

Proofreading and Writing

Proofreading **Circle the four misspelled Spelling Words in this song. Then write each word correctly.**

The sun was burning bright this mornning
while I was working my field alone
I didn't have anyon to help me
My favorit dog had gone
I realy wish I had the money
to buy my ticket home.

Spelling Words

1. while
2. whole
3. anyway
4. anyone
5. anything
6. favorite
7. once
8. suppose
9. everybody
10. everyone
11. really
12. morning
13. also
14. always
15. first

1. ____________________ 3. ____________________

2. ____________________ 4. ____________________

Write Tag-Team Poetry **Pair up with a classmate. Then create a poem about the West by taking turns writing lines. Use Spelling Words from the list.**

Name ________________________________

Starting Anew

Read the paragraph below. Fill in each blank with a word from the box. You will use one word twice.

Vocabulary

- homestead
- claims
- immigrants
- sod
- discouraged
- convinced
- heifer
- fertile
- prairie

During the second half of the nineteenth century many ________________ from Europe traveled west across America to begin new lives. Families filed ________________ on pieces of land. There they could establish a ________________ and raise crops and livestock. Advertisements paid for by the railroads said that the flat, treeless ________________ had ________________ soil for growing crops. These ads ________________ many families that they would have success farming in the region. Some did succeed, but others became ________________ and returned to the East. Many who stayed built homes from squares of prairie ________________. With a home built, crops growing, and a healthy ________________ grazing in a ________________ field nearby, a family was off to a good start.

Name ______________________________

Pioneer Life

What I Know	What I Want to Know	What I Learned

Name ______________________________

Pioneer Girl

Comprehension Check

Across-the-Prairie Crossword

Use these clues to complete the crossword puzzle about *Pioneer Girl*.

Across

3. Most homesteaders near the McCances were _____.
5. material for making dresses
8. prairie in the wetter eastern part of the Midwest
11. A common job for children was _____ cows.
12. prairie in the dry western part of the Midwest
14. Much of the Great Plains is bare and _____.
15. The McCances' Christmas "tree" was decorated with _____ chains.

Down

1. grassy land
2. When a prairie fire approached, farmers set _____.
4. The McCances used this to decorate their Christmas "tree."
6. The hungry children had to wait for _____ table on holidays.
7. Grace made a mad _____ to escape from the heifer.
9. the real first name of "Pete"
10. Wild geese stole precious _____.
13. The cows made a cave in this.

Name ______________________________

Join Up!

Read the following fliers, which are modeled on handbills from the 1870s. Use them to answer the questions on page 297.

1

Join the Grange Now!
All Your Neighbors Are!

As a member, you benefit from cooperative prices on farm products and tools. Plus, you can take part in Grange social and educational events.

2

Act Now!
Fight the Big City Bosses!

The railroad bosses say they barely make a profit, but don't you believe it! While we struggle to make ends meet, they are all living lives of luxury in the big cities.

3

Farmers Unite!
It Will Make Your Work Easier!

The Grange is the farmer's friend. It is the one organization created by farmers to improve farmers' lives.

4

Ulysses S. Grant Says,
"Join the Grange!"

Do you listen to your President? You should! President Grant approves of the Grange.

5

Fight the Railroads!
Jefferson and Jackson Would Have!

Rise up, fellow farmers! Join the movement that feeds the great nation of Presidents Thomas Jefferson and Andrew Jackson.

Name ______________________________

Join Up! continued

Answer each question about the fliers on page 296. Then fill in the blanks with the propaganda technique that each flier uses.

Propaganda Techniques

Overgeneralization: making general statements with no basis in fact
Testimonial: using the words of a famous person to support a cause
Bandwagon: persuading people to act because everyone else is
Transfer: associating a famous person with a product or cause
Faulty cause and effect: suggesting that this will make life better

1. How does the first flier persuade farmers to join the Grange?

   ____

   Propaganda Technique: ______________________________

2. What does the second flier say about all railroad bosses?

   ____

   Propaganda Technique: ______________________________

3. What does the third flier promise?

   ____

   ____

   Propaganda Technique: ______________________________

4. Why does the fourth flier quote President Grant?

   ____

   Propaganda Technique: ______________________________

5. What association does the fifth flier make?

   ____

   ____

   Propaganda Technique: ______________________________

Pioneer Girl

Structural Analysis Stressed and Unstressed Syllables

Name ______________________________

Stress That Syllable!

Read each sentence. Say the underlined word several times, placing stress on a different syllable each time. Circle the choice that shows the correct stress for the underlined word. (The stressed syllable is shown in capital letters.)

1. Grace and Florrie wore dresses made of calico.

   CAL i co   cal I co   cal i CO

2. They sweetened their cereal with molasses.

   MO las ses   mo LAS ses   mo las SES

3. The family's Christmas tree was decorated with paper chains.

   DEC o rat ed   dec O rat ed   dec o RAT ed   dec o rat ED

4. Spring was their favorite time of year.

   FA vor ite   fa VOR ite   fa vor ITE

5. Nebraska's population grew rapidly.

   POP u la tion   pop U la tion   pop u LA tion   pop u la TION

6. Poppie was determined to make a success of the farm.

   DE ter mined   de TER mined   de ter MINED

7. The homesteaders began making preparations for the long winter.

   PREP a ra tions   prep A ra tions   prep a RA tions   prep a ra TIONS

8. The harsh weather did not discourage them.

   DIS cour age   dis COUR age   dis cour AGE

Name ______________________

Unstressed Syllables

To spell a two-syllable or three-syllable word, divide the word into syllables. Spell the word by syllables, noting carefully the spelling of the unstressed syllable or syllables.

doz | en /dŭz′ ən/ **dis | tance** /dĭs′ təns/

de | stroy /dĭ **stroi**′/

When you hear the final /ĭj/, /ĭv/, or /ĭs/ sounds, think of these patterns:

/ĭj/ *age* (voy**age**) /ĭv/ *ive* (nat**ive**) /ĭs/ *ice* (not**ice**)

► The /ĭj/ sound in *knowledge* is spelled *-edge*, and differs from the usual spelling pattern.

Write each Spelling Word under the heading that shows which syllable is stressed. Underline the unstressed syllable or syllables.

Spelling Words

1. dozen
2. voyage
3. forbid
4. native
5. language
6. destroy
7. notice
8. distance
9. carrot
10. knowledge*
11. captive
12. spinach
13. solid
14. justice
15. ashamed
16. program
17. message
18. respond
19. service
20. relative

First Syllable Stressed

______	______
______	______
______	______
______	______
______	______
______	______
______	______
______	______

Last Syllable Stressed

______	______
______	______

Name ______________________________

Pioneer Girl

Spelling Unstressed Syllables (including Final /ĭj/, /ĭv/, and /ĭs/)

Spelling Spree

Write a Spelling Word by combining the beginning of the first word with the ending of the second word.

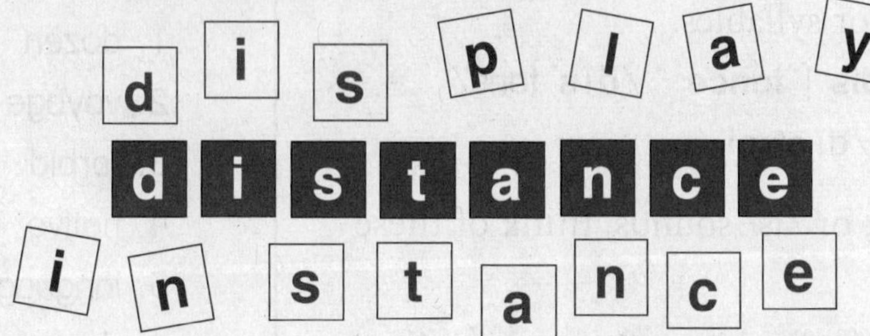

1. capture + olive
2. ashen + framed
3. knowing + pledge
4. nation + forgive
5. languish + passage
6. respect + fond
7. justify + practice
8. serving + office
9. spine + reach
10. progress + madam

1. ______________
2. ______________
3. ______________
4. ______________
5. ______________
6. ______________
7. ______________
8. ______________
9. ______________
10. ______________

Spelling Words

1. dozen
2. voyage
3. forbid
4. native
5. language
6. destroy
7. notice
8. distance
9. carrot
10. knowledge*
11. captive
12. spinach
13. solid
14. justice
15. ashamed
16. program
17. message
18. respond
19. service
20. relative

Word Magic Write a Spelling Word to fit each clue.

11. Add two letters to *relate* to write a word for a family member.
12. Replace two letters in *formed* to write a word meaning "to refuse to allow."
13. Insert one consonant into *doze* to write a word meaning "a set of twelve."
14. Replace one letter in *carry* with two to write a word for a root vegetable.
15. Change the ending of *voice* to write a synonym for *journey*.

11. ______________
12. ______________
13. ______________
14. ______________
15. ______________

Name ______________________________

Pioneer Girl

Spelling Unstressed Syllables (including Final /ĭj/, /ĭv/, and /ĭs/)

Proofreading and Writing

Proofreading Circle the five misspelled Spelling Words in this journal entry. Then write each word correctly.

October 11, 1891

Every day I notise something new and different about this strange land, but I still do not know if I will like it here. There is certainly something beautiful about the way the earth and sky stretch into the distence as far as the eye can see. At the same time, you live with the knowledge that the land can distroy you at any moment. It makes you wish for something more sollid than a sod house to call home. The loneliness is hard too. It takes all day just to send a mesage to the next farm. I should not complain, though. Our lives are good, and I believe that they will only get better.

1. ______________
2. ______________
3. ______________
4. ______________
5. ______________

Spelling Words

1. dozen
2. voyage
3. forbid
4. native
5. language
6. destroy
7. notice
8. distance
9. carrot
10. knowledge*
11. captive
12. spinach
13. solid
14. justice
15. ashamed
16. program
17. message
18. respond
19. service
20. relative

Write About a Photograph The photographs used to illustrate the selection show scenes from life on the Great Plains in the 1800s. Choose one that you find interesting. Who are the people in the photograph? What do they seem to be doing? Based on what you read in the selection, what do you think their lives were like?

On a separate piece of paper, write a brief paragraph describing the photograph. Use Spelling Words from the list.

Pioneer Girl

Vocabulary Skill Dictionary: Suffixes

Name ______________________________

Sentences Using Suffixes

Read the dictionary definition for each suffix. Combine each base word in the box with one of the suffixes and write a sentence using the new word. Use each suffix at least once.

Vocabulary

constant
encourage
happy
hard
short
usual

-er **suff.** To a greater degree; more so: *neater; slower.*
-est **suff.** To the most extreme degree; the most: *greatest; earliest.*
-ly **suff.** In a specified manner: *gradually.*
-ment **suff.** 1. Act, action, or process. 2. State of being acted upon.
-ness **suff.** State, condition, or quality.

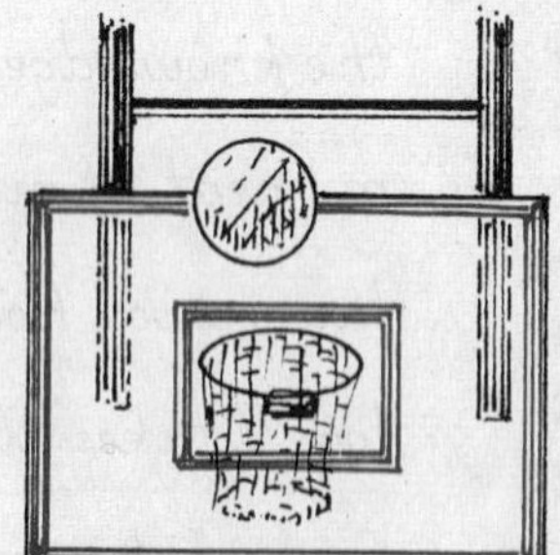

1. ______________________________

2. ______________________________

3. ______________________________

4. ______________________________

5. ______________________________

6. ______________________________

Name ______________________________

Possessive Messages

Possessive Pronouns A **possessive pronoun** shows ownership. *My*, *your*, *his*, *her*, *its*, *our*, and *their* appear before nouns that are subjects. *Mine*, *yours*, *his*, *hers*, *its*, *ours*, and *theirs* stand alone and replace nouns in sentences.

Possessives Used with Nouns		Possessives That Stand Alone	
my	This is **my** cup.	**mine**	This cup is **mine.**
your	**Your** cup is blue.	**yours**	**Yours** is blue.
his	**His** jacket is torn.	**his**	The torn jacket is **his.**
her	**Her** dress is new.	**hers**	**Hers** is the new dress.
its	**Its** food is in the trough.	**its**	The food in the trough is **its.**
our	Please visit **our** farm.	**ours**	The farm is **ours.**
their	We walk by **their** fields.	**theirs**	Those fields are **theirs.**

Underline the pronoun in parentheses that correctly completes each sentence.

1. (Their/Theirs) favorite place is the meadow.
2. (My/Mine) is the apple orchard.
3. (Our/Ours) is the orchard on Harrow Road.
4. What is (your/yours) favorite place?
5. Molly's favorite place is (her/hers) room.
6. The books are (theirs/their).
7. The yellow one is (my/mine).
8. (Our/Ours) favorite place is nearby.
9. (Her/Hers) is nearby too.
10. Where is (your/yours)?

Name ______________________________

Contraction Reactions

Contractions with Pronouns A **contraction** is a shortened form of two words. You can combine pronouns with the verbs *am*, *is*, *are*, *will*, *would*, *have*, *has*, and *had* to form **contractions**. Use an apostrophe in place of the dropped letter or letters.

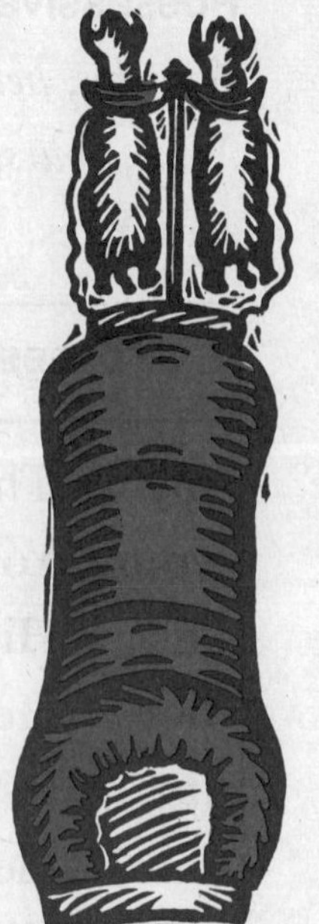

Contractions with Pronouns			
I am	I'm	I have	I've
he is	he's	he has	he's
it is	it's	it has	it's
you are	you're	you have	you've
they are	they're	they have	they've
I will	I'll	I had	I'd
you will	you'll	you had	you'd
we would	we'd	we had	we'd

Rewrite each sentence below, replacing the pronoun and verb with a contraction.

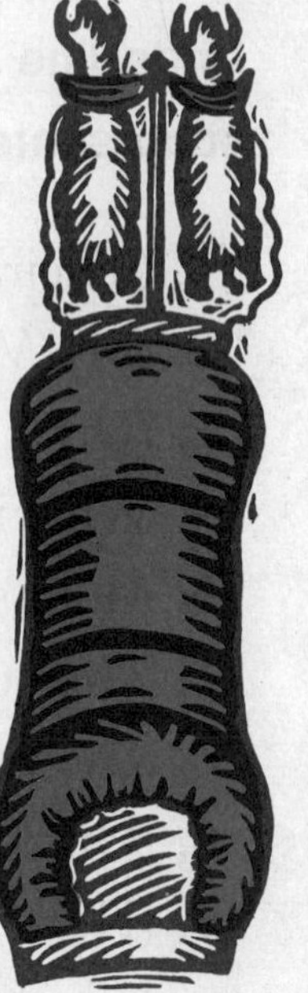

1. It is fun to read about early settlers.
____
2. I have read two books about pioneer life.
____
3. You would like this story about settlers in Oklahoma.
____
4. We will visit my grandfather in Oklahoma next summer.
____
5. He has lived there all his life.
____

Pioneer Girl

Grammar Skill Using *Its* and *It's*

Name ______________________________

It's a Great Invention!

Using *Its* and *It's* A good writer is careful not to confuse the possessive pronoun *its* with the contraction *it's*.

The cat licked **its** paws. **possessive**

It's time for the cat's dinner. **contraction**

Jon wrote this page in his journal. Proofread the copy below and correct the places he has confused the possessive pronoun *its* with the contraction *it's*. Write the correction above each error.

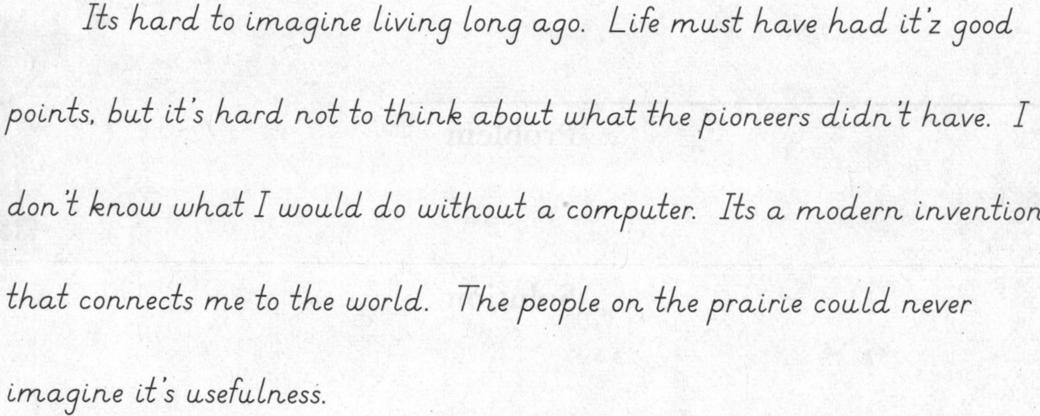

Its hard to imagine living long ago. Life must have had it'z good points, but it's hard not to think about what the pioneers didn't have. I don't know what I would do without a computer. Its a modern invention that connects me to the world. The people on the prairie could never imagine it's usefulness.

Its great for doing research. All I have to do is make sure its plugged in and turn on it's monitor. Then I can find out what pioneer life was like. Its not quite the same as living back then, but its the best I can do. Its a resource pioneers didn't have. In fact, it's a resource even my parents didn't have.

Name ______________________________

Writing a Problem-Solution Essay

A **problem-solution essay** outlines a problem and then gives details about the steps leading to its solution.

Prepare to write a problem-solution essay. First, choose a topic. Then fill in the chart, identifying the problem, the solution, details about the steps that led to the solution, and the outcome.

Choose one of these topics or another one you have discussed: how prairie settlers got water, how they got supplies, and how they made a holiday festive when goods were scarce.

Problem
Solution
Steps toward the solution
Outcome

Name ______________________________

Combining Sentences

Good writers streamline their writing by combining short, choppy sentences that have repeated pronouns or nouns into one sentence.

The prairie **fire** raged all night long. **It** scorched the shortgrass. **It** burned down barns and homes. **It** injured some horses.

Raging all night long, the prairie fire scorched the shortgrass, burned down barns and homes, and injured some horses.

Read this letter that Grace McCance might have written. Then revise the body of the letter by combining short, choppy sentences that have repeated pronouns or nouns into one sentence. Write the revised letter on the lines.

Dear Dora,

How are you? I am still getting used to prairie life. We live in a one-room house made of "Nebraska marble." Poppie made the house himself. He cut blocks of tough prairie earth. He stacked the blocks to construct the walls. He also used a layer of sod for the roof. Our soddy is dark. It is warm in the winter. It is cool in the summer. It is definitely not waterproof, however! Yesterday in a rainstorm, rain leaked right through the roof. Sometimes I really miss Missouri. Write soon!

Your friend,

Grace

____

____

____

____

____

____

Name ______________________________

Tracking Wild Horses

Read the labels below. Write each word from the box under the label that fits it.

Vocabulary

mares	milled	herd
skittered	mustang	remorse
stallion	bluff	ravine

Kinds of Horses

______________ ______________ ______________

Landforms

______________ ______________ ______________

Actions of Horses

______________ ______________ ______________

Feelings

______________ ______________ ______________

Groups of Animals

______________ ______________ ______________

Use at least three words from the box to write directions for rounding up wild horses.

____

____

____

Black Cowboy Wild Horses

Graphic Organizer Judgments Chart

Name ___________________________

Judgments Chart

	Facts from the Selection	Own Values and Experience	Judgment
What kind of person is Bob Lemmons?			
What are some of his character traits?			
What are some more of his character traits?			
What are some of Bob's values?			
What kind of person is Bob Lemmons?			

Name ______________________

What's So Important About . . . ?

Tell why each item listed was important in the story of how Bob Lemmons brought in the herd of wild mustangs.

1. tracks in the dirt ______________________

2. the lightning ______________________

3. the rainstorm ______________________

4. the river ______________________

5. the rattlesnake ______________________

6. the battle of the stallions ______________________

7. the corral ______________________

Name ______________________________

You Be the Judge

Read the following passage. Then answer the questions on page 312.

Bill Pickett: Master Cowboy

One of the greatest cowboys who ever lived was an African American man named Bill Pickett. He was born in 1870 in west Texas, where he learned to rope and ride early in life. As a young man he worked as a ranch hand and then became a trick rider and rodeo star. He later joined Zack Miller's 101 Ranch Wild West Show—a touring cowboy act—and became the star performer. Miller called him "the greatest sweat and dirt cowhand that ever lived, bar none."

Pickett is credited with inventing the rodeo sport known as bulldogging, also known as steer wrestling. Legend has it that Pickett was herding cattle in 1903, when an ornery steer started tearing around the pasture, scattering the other cattle. Losing his patience, Pickett raced after the steer on his horse, leaped onto its back, and wrestled it to the ground. He later perfected this technique and made bulldogging a regular part of his rodeo act.

One of the most famous incidents involving Pickett occurred in New York's Madison Square Garden. There, Pickett was bulldogging with a young assistant, Will Rogers, who later became a show business star himself. Suddenly, a steer bolted out of the ring and charged into the grandstand. The terrified spectators panicked, but Pickett and Rogers stayed calm. They jumped into the stands and wrestled the giant steer back down to the ring. They not only saved lives that day but also put on a great show!

Name ______________________________

Black Cowboy Wild Horses

Comprehension Skill
Making Judgments

You Be the Judge continued

Answer these questions about the passage on page 311.

1. What judgment about Bill Pickett does the author make in the first paragraph?

2. Do you agree with this judgment? Why or why not?

3. In the rodeo bull wrestling is done purely for sport. Do you think this is right? Give reasons for your judgment.

4. Circle each trait below that you think Bill Pickett possessed. Next to each trait you circle, tell why that trait applies to him.

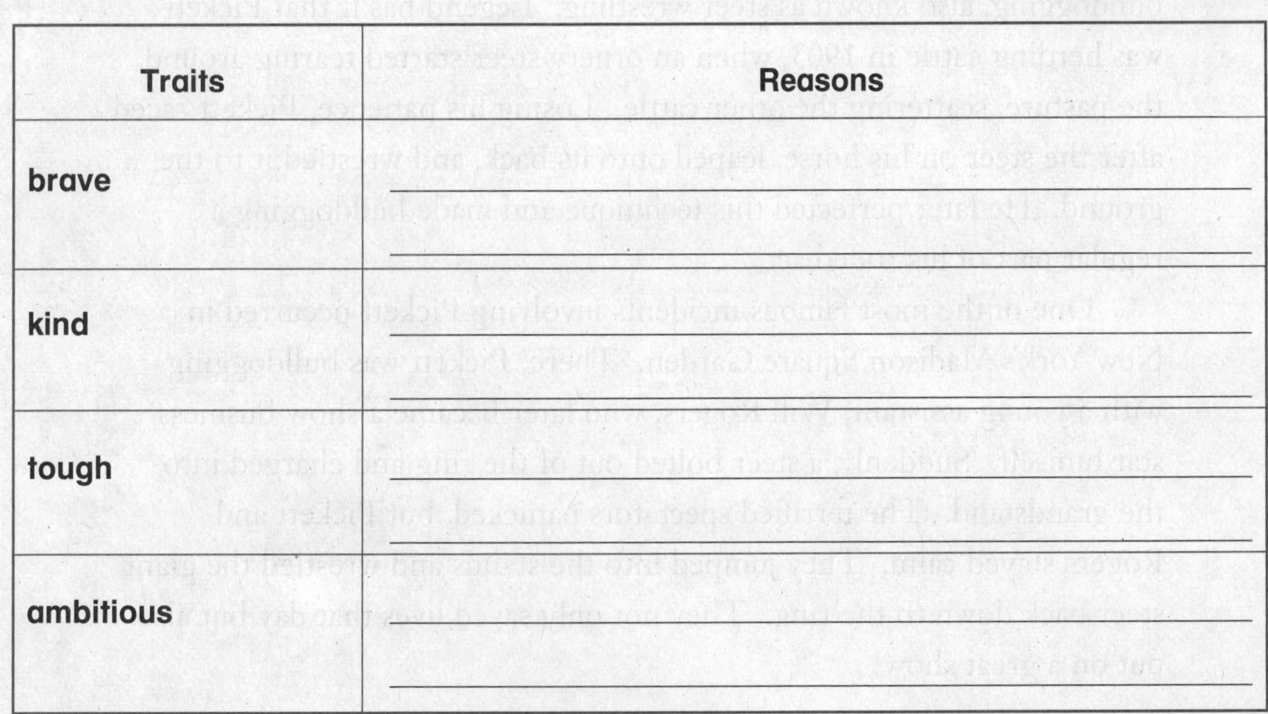

Traits	Reasons
brave	
kind	
tough	
ambitious	

Black Cowboy Wild Horses

Structural Analysis Review of Syllabication

Name ______________________________

Saddle Up Those Syllables!

Read each sentence. On the line below the sentence, divide the underlined word into syllables, using slashes between the syllables. Then write another sentence using the word. The first one is done for you.

Example: Bob awoke as soon as the sun came over the horizon.

ho/ri/zon On the ocean, nothing blocks a view of the horizon.

1. At daybreak, Bob was immediately awake and ready to ride.

____

____

2. Bob Lemmons held his shoulders high as he rode Warrior.

____

____

3. A rattlesnake doesn't always give a warning before it strikes.

____

____

4. Warrior neighed triumphantly after challenging the stallion.

____

____

Name ______________________________

Final /n/ or /ən/, /chər/, /zhər/

Each of these words has the final /n/, /ən/, /chər/, or /zhər/ sounds. When you hear these final sounds, think of these patterns:

/n/ or /ən/ *ain* (capt**ain**) /chər/ *ture* (cul**ture**)

/zhər/ *sure* (trea**sure**)

► The /ən/ sound in the starred words *surgeon* and *luncheon* is spelled *eon* and does not follow the usual spelling pattern.

Write each Spelling Word under its final sound.

Final /n/ or /ən/ Sound

______________________ ______________________

______________________ ______________________

______________________ ______________________

Final /chər/ Sound

______________________ ______________________

______________________ ______________________

______________________ ______________________

______________________ ______________________

______________________ ______________________

____

Final /zhər/ Sound

______________________ ______________________

____

Spelling Words

1. mountain
2. treasure
3. culture
4. fountain
5. creature
6. captain
7. future
8. adventure
9. moisture
10. surgeon*
11. lecture
12. curtain
13. pasture
14. measure
15. vulture
16. feature
17. furniture
18. pleasure
19. mixture
20. luncheon*

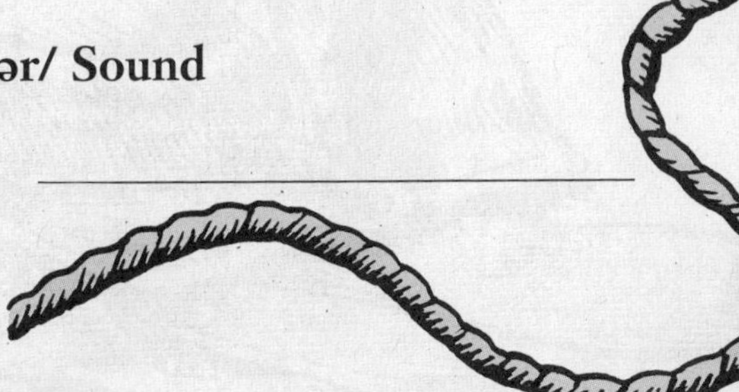

Name ______________________

Black Cowboy Wild Horses

Spelling Final /n/ or /ən/, /chər/, /zhər/

Spelling Spree

Word Root Hunt Write the Spelling Word that has the same root as each word below.

1. pleasing 1. ______
2. collect 2. ______
3. furnish 3. ______
4. capital 4. ______
5. cultivate 5. ______
6. surgery 6. ______
7. pastoral 7. ______

Ending Match Write Spelling Words by matching word parts and endings. Be sure to write each ending correctly.

<a> /n/ *or* /ən/ <b> /chər/ <c> /zhər/

8. vul<b> 8. ______
9. fu<b> 9. ______
10. trea<c> 10. ______
11. curt<a> 11. ______
12. mix<b> 12. ______
13. mea<c> 13. ______
14. lunch<a> 14. ______
15. fount<a> 15. ______

Spelling Words

1. mountain
2. treasure
3. culture
4. fountain
5. creature
6. captain
7. future
8. adventure
9. moisture
10. surgeon*
11. lecture
12. curtain
13. pasture
14. measure
15. vulture
16. feature
17. furniture
18. pleasure
19. mixture
20. luncheon*

Black Cowboy Wild Horses

Spelling Final /n/ or /ən/, /chər/, /zhər/

Name ____________________

Proofreading and Writing

Proofreading Circle the five misspelled Spelling Words in this travelogue. Then write each word correctly.

The corral sits at the foot of a rise—more than a hill, but not quite a mountin. The land doesn't get much moisure, and every living creacher is always on the lookout for its survival. It is here that Bob Lemmons lives and works. I had the pleasure of meeting Mr. Lemmons shortly after he had captured a herd of mustangs. He has a special way of getting his work done. The most remarkable featur of his method is that he gets the horses to accept him as one of them, rather than as a human being. It seemed like quite an adveture to me, but to Mr. Lemmons it was all in a day's work.

1. ____________________
2. ____________________
3. ____________________
4. ____________________
5. ____________________

Spelling Words

1. mountain
2. treasure
3. culture
4. fountain
5. creature
6. captain
7. future
8. adventure
9. moisture
10. surgeon*
11. lecture
12. curtain
13. pasture
14. measure
15. vulture
16. feature
17. furniture
18. pleasure
19. mixture
20. luncheon*

Write a Character Sketch Bob Lemmons was an unusual person who had a very special way of capturing wild mustangs. How would you describe his work? What was his relationship with Warrior like? What were his most outstanding qualities?

On a separate piece of paper, write a character sketch about Bob Lemmons. Use Spelling Words from the list.

Black Cowboy Wild Horses

Vocabulary Skill Dictionary: Parts of Speech

Name ______________________________

Using Parts of Speech

Read the dictionary entries. For each entry word, write two sentences, using the word as a different part of speech in each sentence.

clear (klîr) *adj.* Free from clouds, mist, or haze. *v.* To make free of objects or obstructions.

close (klōs) *adj.* Near in space or time. *v.* (klōz) To move so that an opening or a passage is blocked; shut.

faint (fānt) *adj.* Lacking brightness or clarity; dim; indistinct. *v.* To lose consciousness for a short time.

print (prĭnt) *n.* A mark or an impression made in or on a surface by pressure. *v.* To write in block letters.

1. ______________________________

____

____

2. ______________________________

____

____

3. ______________________________

____

____

4. ______________________________

____

____

Black Cowboy Wild Horses

Grammar Skill Double Subjects

Name ______________________________

Double Trouble

Double Subjects Do not use a double subject (a noun and a pronoun) to name the same person, place, or thing. Use either the noun or the pronoun as the subject, but not both.

Incorrect: Lenny he is my brother.
Correct: Lenny is my brother.
Correct: He is my brother.

Each sentence below has a double subject. Cross out one unneeded subject, and write your new sentence on the line.

1. My aunt and uncle they have a cattle ranch.
____
2. My aunt she runs the business end of things.
____
3. The ranch it is big.
____
4. The animals they are taken care of by my uncle.
____
5. Kurt he is my cousin.
____
6. The horse she trusts Kurt.
____
7. Uncle Henry he trains horses.
____
8. The stable it is home to six horses.
____

Name ___________________________________

We or Us?

Using *We* and *Us* with Nouns Sometimes a writer may need to use a pronoun before a noun to make clear who is being talked about. Use *we* with a noun subject or after a linking verb. Use *us* with a noun object (a noun that follows an action verb) or after words like *to, for, with, at,* or *in*.

subject: We boys are going to pitch hay.

object: The cows will be herded by **us girls.**

Write either *we* or *us* in each blank to correctly complete each sentence.

1. The ranch hands showed ________ kids how to rope a calf.
2. The best riders were ________ girls.
3. ________ cooks made big meals for the ranch hands.
4. It's a great outdoor life for ________ cowboys.
5. ________ boys went to the rodeo on Friday.
6. The owners held a square dance for ________ visitors.
7. ________ fiddlers need to tune up.
8. The caller shook hands with ________ greenhorns.
9. ________ dancers whirled and twirled.
10. Saying good-night was hard for ________ guests.

Name ______________________

Who Is He?

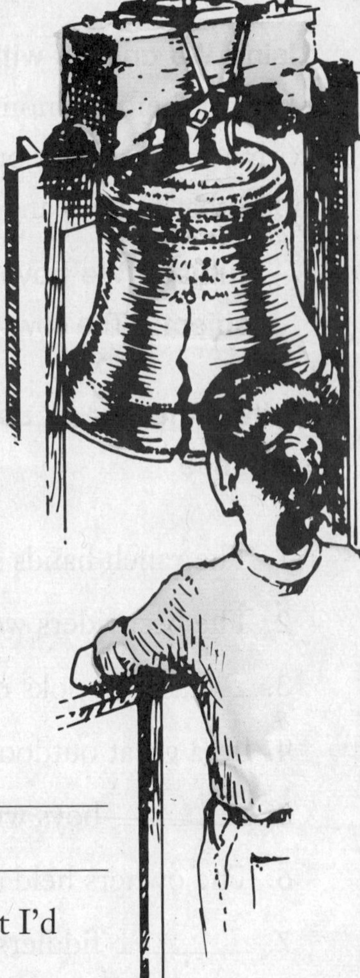

Writing Clearly with Pronouns A good writer makes clear to whom each pronoun refers.

Unclear: After Mel turned hard on the key in the lock, it broke.

What broke—the key or the lock?

Clear: After Mel turned hard on the key in the lock, the lock broke.

Clear: After Mel turned hard on the key in the lock, the key broke.

Shirley wrote the following messages to her friends. Rewrite each sentence with unclear pronoun references to make the references clear.

1. Phil and Bill visited Philadelphia and Pittsburgh. He thinks it has an interesting history.

____

____

2. Julie and Karen joined us in Mississippi. She is my cousin, but I'd never met her before.

____

____

3. This morning, I fixed breakfast. Then I saw a skunk! The skunk turned around, and I was able to eat it.

____

____

Name ______________________________

Writing an Explanation

Black Cowboy Wild Horses explains who Bob Lemmons was and how he tracked animals. The purpose of an explanation is to explain one of the following:

- who or what something is
- what is or was important about something or someone
- how something works or worked
- the steps of a process
- why something happens or happened

Prepare to write several paragraphs explaining how Bob Lemmons was able to capture an entire herd of wild horses by himself. To plan and organize your explanation, use the graphic organizer below. First, write the topic at the top. Then list the steps Lemmons took and details about the process he used. If necessary, look back at the selection to recall how one step led to another.

Topic or Title: ______________________________

Step/Details

↓

Step/Details

↓

Step/Details

↓

Step/Details

Black Cowboy Wild Horses

Writing Skill Improving Your Writing

Name ______________________

Organizing Information

A good writer organizes ideas in a logical way so that readers understand his or her writing. You can organize ideas in your own writing by sequence of events, by causes and effects, or by main ideas and details.

This explanation by an animal tracker like Bob Lemmons has been scrambled. Put the sentences in an order that makes sense. Then rewrite the explanation on the lines.

How to "Read" Animal Tracks

One way to locate an animal is by finding and studying its tracks. Once you identify what animal left a particular track, you can determine how long ago it passed by. To find tracks, try starting near water. A fresh, soft, sharply outlined track means an animal was recently in the area, but a hard, dry, less clearly defined track indicates that time has passed since the animal was there. After you've discovered a set of tracks, you can study their shape and size to figure out what kind of animal made them. Animals often leave tracks on the muddy banks of streams and ponds where they come to drink or hunt food.

____

____

____

____

____

____

____

____

Name ______________________________

Ride Those Riddles

Write a word from the box to answer each riddle.

Vocabulary

- rugged
- wounds
- sombrero
- urgently
- notorious
- condolences
- dictator
- transformed

1. Which word names a type of hat?

   ____

2. Which word names injuries?

   ____

3. Which word means "completely changed"?

   ____

4. Which word describes someone who is well known for something bad? ______________________________

5. Which word describes something rough, difficult, or uneven? ______________________________

6. Which word means "expressions of sympathy"?

   ____

7. Which word means "without delay"?

   ____

8. Which word names a kind of ruler?

   ____

Name ______________________

Story Map

<table>
<tr><th colspan="2">Characters</th></tr>
<tr><td>The family: Elena, Pablo, and their children: Rosa, the narrator, ______</td><td>Other Characters: the villagers, ______</td></tr>
<tr><th colspan="2">Setting</th></tr>
<tr><td>Where the story takes place: rural Mexico; ______</td><td>When the story takes place: ______</td></tr>
<tr><th colspan="2">Plot</th></tr>
<tr><td colspan="2">Problem: ______

Events:
1. ______
2. ______
3. ______
4. ______
5. ______
6. ______

Resolution: ______</td></tr>
</table>

Name ______________________________

A Portrait of Elena

Complete the sentences below to show how Elena's feelings and character traits are revealed through her actions. The first sentence has been completed for you.

In Mexico, in the family's home village	On the way to the United States	In California
Example: Elena shows her **deep love for her husband** when she strokes his hand and speaks gently to him while he is dying.	In the plaza, just before leaving the village, Elena shows **generosity** when she ______	Elena shows she is **hard-working** when she ______
Elena shows **her grief** when she ______	In Ciudad Juárez, Elena shows **love for her son** Esteban when she ______	Elena shows that she **values education** when she ______
Elena shows **cleverness** when she ______		Elena shows she **wants her children to grow up "strong and full of hope"** when she ______
Elena shows **courage** when she ______		

Name ______________________________

Mapping the Story

Read the passage. Then complete the activity on page 327.

A Dangerous Journey

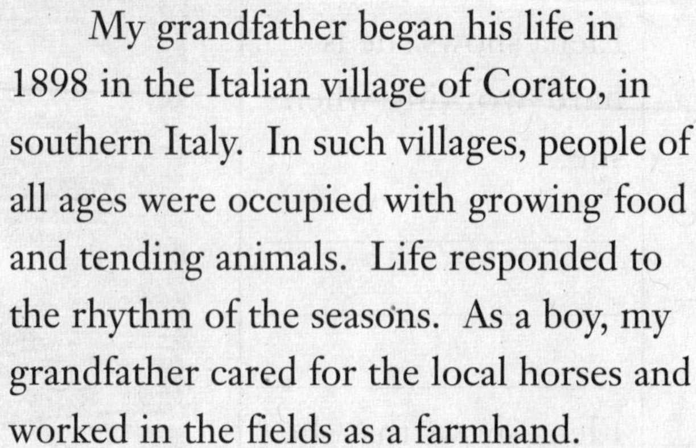

My grandfather began his life in 1898 in the Italian village of Corato, in southern Italy. In such villages, people of all ages were occupied with growing food and tending animals. Life responded to the rhythm of the seasons. As a boy, my grandfather cared for the local horses and worked in the fields as a farmhand.

By the time my grandfather was in his teens, World War I had broken out in Europe. One by one, the countries surrounding Italy entered the war. Italy managed to stay out of the fighting for nearly a year, but it was clearly only a matter of time before Italy, too, would be drawn into the conflict.

A powerful farm boy, my grandfather was a prime candidate for the Italian army. His mother, my great-grandmother, did not want to lose her son to war. She made what must have been one of the most difficult decisions of her life: she decided to send her son far away to America.

At that time, young men were being rounded up and forced to join the Italian army. My grandfather's family faced a daunting task—how to send my grandfather across Italy and onto a boat bound for America without the authorities finding out.

Very early one morning, well before dawn, a horse-drawn cart pulled up to my grandfather's house. The cart was filled with hay. To a casual observer, the cart was simply on its way from one farm to the next to deliver a load of hay. When the cart pulled away from the house, however, my grandfather lay hidden beneath the hay. In one hand he held a bundle that contained all his belongings. In the other, he held bread, fruit, and meat—enough food, his mother hoped, to last for at least part of the long journey that lay ahead.

The cart was bound for Bari, a seaport town on Italy's east coast. There my grandfather's family had arranged for a boat to take him on the first leg of the journey to America.

Elena

Comprehension Skill Story Structure

Name ______________________________

Mapping the Story continued

Answer these questions about the passage on page 326.

1. What is the setting in which the events described in the passage take place? (Include both the time and place.)

____

____

2. Who are the main characters in the passage?

____

____

3. What problem is described in the passage?

____

____

____

4. What is the solution to this problem?

____

____

____

____

5. Use the information above to write a brief summary of the passage.

____

____

____

____

____

____

____

Name ______________________________

I Spy the *Y*

Read the letter that Rosa might have written to a friend in Mexico. Circle words in which a *y* changed to *i* before an ending or suffix was added. On the lines below the letter, write the base word and the ending or suffix for each circled word.

Endings and Suffixes
- -ed
- -er
- -es
- -est
- -ful

Dear Maria,

I wish you could see California. It is beautiful! I will always love Mexico too, but I like it even better here. We live in the loveliest valley! And just think—there are no flies! We are so much luckier than the many families who were not able to escape the war in Mexico. I know Mother worried about how she could make a life for us here. But she has a good job, and we know the future is bright for all of us.

Love,
Rosa

1. ______________ + ______________
2. ______________ + ______________
3. ______________ + ______________
4. ______________ + ______________
5. ______________ + ______________
6. ______________ + ______________

Elena

Spelling Changing Final *y* to *i*

Name ______________________________

Changing Final *y* to *i*

Each Spelling Word has an ending or a suffix added to a base word. When a word ends with a consonant and *y*, change the *y* to *i* when adding *-es*, *-ed*, *-er*, *-est*, or *-ness*.

army + es = arm**ies** spy + ed = sp**ied**

dirty + er = dirt**ier** scary + est = scar**iest**

happy + ness = happ**iness**

Write each Spelling Word. Underline the letter that replaced the final *y* when the ending or the suffix was added.

Spelling Words

1. liberties
2. victories
3. countries
4. spied
5. enemies
6. armies
7. scariest
8. dirtier
9. happiness
10. abilities
11. pitied
12. ladies
13. busier
14. duties
15. lilies
16. worthiness
17. tiniest
18. emptiness
19. replies
20. dizziness

Final *y* changed to *i*

______________________ ______________________

______________________ ______________________

______________________ ______________________

______________________ ______________________

______________________ ______________________

______________________ ______________________

______________________ ______________________

______________________ ______________________

______________________ ______________________

______________________ ______________________

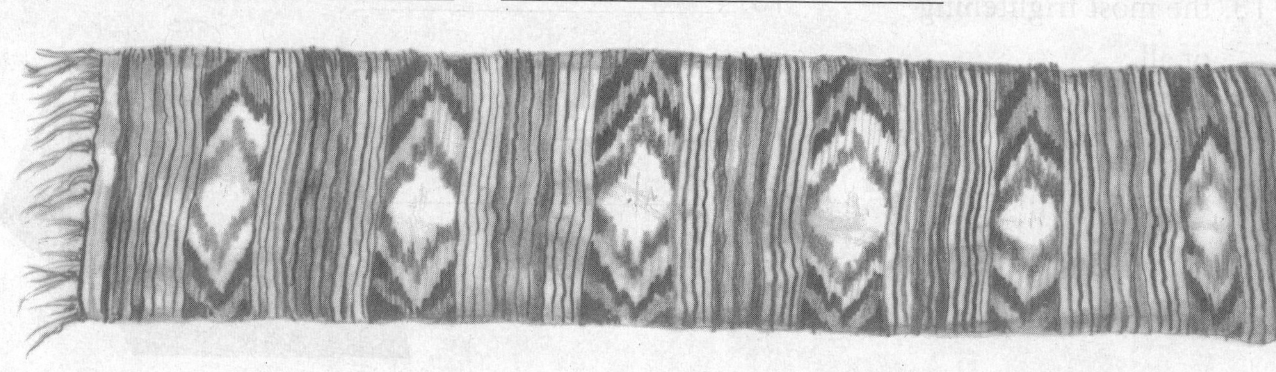

Name ______________________________

Spelling Spree

Adding Suffixes Write a Spelling Word by adding the correct suffix to the word part in each phrase below.

1. a trip through seven countr_____
2. dirt_____ than a pigsty
3. the dut_____ of the president
4. lad_____ and gentlemen
5. the empt_____ of a beach in winter
6. to send repl_____ to letters
7. a beautiful bouquet of lil_____

1. ______________
2. ______________
3. ______________
4. ______________
5. ______________
6. ______________
7. ______________

Word Clues Write a Spelling Word to fit each clue.

8. another word for *freedoms* 8. ______________
9. having more work to do than another 9. ______________
10. watched sneakily 10. ______________
11. felt sorry for 11. ______________
12. a synonym for *joy* 12. ______________
13. the most frightening of all 13. ______________
14. the opposite of *friends* 14. ______________
15. a result of spinning around 15. ______________

Spelling Words

1. liberties
2. victories
3. countries
4. spied
5. enemies
6. armies
7. scariest
8. dirtier
9. happiness
10. abilities
11. pitied
12. ladies
13. busier
14. duties
15. lilies
16. worthiness
17. tiniest
18. emptiness
19. replies
20. dizziness

Name ______________________________

Elena

Spelling Changing Final *y* to *i*

Proofreading and Writing

Proofreading Circle the five misspelled Spelling Words in this newspaper article. Then write each word correctly.

Guadalajara—The situation in Mexico continues to grow more serious. The government has no control over large areas of the country, and the rebel armys are increasing in strength. Each one of their victaries brings more support to the revolution. It is feared that by 1911 Mexico will be in even worse shape.

The rebels are hoping that the leaders of foreign countries will see the worthyness of their cause and send aid. Even the tieniest amount, they say, would be a great help. In the meantime, the Mexican people continue to suffer, while caring for their families to the best of their ablities.

1. ______________
2. ______________
3. ______________
4. ______________
5. ______________

Spelling Words

1. liberties
2. victories
3. countries
4. spied
5. enemies
6. armies
7. scariest
8. dirtier
9. happiness
10. abilities
11. pitied
12. ladies
13. busier
14. duties
15. lilies
16. worthiness
17. tiniest
18. emptiness
19. replies
20. dizziness

Write a Screenplay Suppose that *Elena* was being made into a movie. Think about the scene between Elena and Pablo just before Pablo dies. What do the characters say to each other during this scene? Are they sitting or standing while they talk? What tone of voice do they use? Do they look at each other while speaking?

On a separate piece of paper, write a screenplay for the scene between Elena and Pablo. Be sure to indicate when each new speaker begins. Use Spelling Words from the list.

Name ______________________________

Using Word Histories

Read the dictionary entries. Then read the sentences. For each underlined word, write the word origin and its meaning. Then use the clues to think of other common English words that have the same origin.

conquer 1. To defeat or subdue by force. 2. To gain control by overcoming difficulties. [Latin *com-*, intensive prefix + *quaerere*, to seek.]

expect To look forward to the probable occurrence or appearance of. [Latin *ex-*, off, away + *spectāre*, to look at.]

memory 1. The power or ability of remembering past experiences. 2. Something remembered. [Latin *memoria*, memory.]

1. Rosa had only a faint memory of her father.

   Word root: ______________

   Meaning: ______________

   a monument or holiday that serves as a remembrance of a person or event ______________

   to commit to memory; learn by heart ______________

2. Elena did not expect that Pancho Villa would ask for a sombrero.

   Word root: ______________

   Meaning: ______________

   an observer of an event ______________

   a pair of eyeglasses ______________

3. Elena had conquered mathematics and valued education.

   Word root: ______________

   Meaning: ______________

   to request information by asking questions ______________

   to get; gain; obtain ______________

Name ______________________________

How? When? Where?

Adverbs An adverb tells *how*, *when*, or *where.* Adverbs can describe verbs. Many adverbs end in *-ly*.

How	When	Where
fast	tomorrow	here
hard	later	inside
happily	again	north
quietly	first	forward
slowly	then	upstairs

Underline the adverb in each sentence below. Then on the line write *how, when,* or *where* to show what the adverb tells.

1. Elena and her family quickly left their home. ____________
2. They left early in the morning. ____________
3. The family traveled north. ____________
4. Everyone worked hard. ____________
5. The children greatly admired their mother. ____________
6. Did you suddenly leave? ____________
7. I stepped carefully over the ice. ____________
8. She went inside. ____________
9. Look closely at this picture. ____________
10. Do you see now? ____________

Name ______________________

Prepare to Compare

Comparing with Adverbs To compare two actions, add *-er* to most one-syllable adverbs; use *more* with adverbs of two or more syllables. To compare three or more actions, add *-est* to most one-syllable adverbs; use *most* with adverbs of two or more syllables.

My little sister runs **fast**.
My brother runs **faster** than she does.
My big sister runs **fastest** of all.

The weather here changes **quickly**.
It changes **more quickly** at the shore.
It changes **most quickly** in the mountains.

Write the correct form of the adverb to complete each sentence.

1. My alarm clock rings early.
2. My dad's alarm rings ______________ than mine.
3. My brother's alarm rings ______________ of all.
4. The retriever barks excitedly.
5. Our German shepherd barks ______________.
6. Of all the dogs, however, the chihuahua barks ______________.
7. Kim studies hard every evening.
8. Juan studies ______________ than Kim.
9. Sonya studies ______________ of all.
10. Jim scored high on the test.
11. His brother scored ______________ than Jim.
12. Of everyone in the class, Celia scored the ______________.
13. I painted carefully.
14. Mom painted ______________ than I did.
15. Dad painted the ______________ of all!

Name ______________________________

Expand Your Description

Expanding Sentences with Adverbs A good writer expands sentences with adverbs to describe action more clearly.

Camille bakes bread. Camille **cheerfully** bakes bread.

Anna wants her pen-pal in Mexico to imagine what life is like in her house, but she has not used any adverbs. On a separate sheet of paper rewrite her letter, adding adverbs from the list or those of your own choosing.

- slightly
- suddenly
- excitedly
- noisily
- happily
- loudly
- gracefully
- still
- carefully
- peacefully
- immediately
- heartily

Hi Pen-pal!

My family's dinner last night was unusual. We celebrated my good report card with a special dinner. Here is what happened: We all pulled out our chairs. My brother Todd remembered that the cat Clive was outside. Todd jumped up, and his chair fell to the floor. Everyone laughed. Mom carved the roast. Without warning, Clive lept into the middle of the table. Todd decided to put him back outside. We ate the rest of our dinner.

Your friend,
Anna

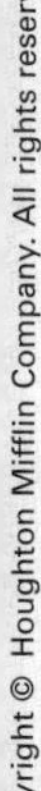

Name ______________________________

Writing a Compare/ Contrast Paragraph

In *Elena*, you read about how the lives of Elena and her children changed as a result of the Mexican Revolution in the early 1900s. One way to explore how things are alike and different is by writing a **compare/contrast paragraph.** Comparing shows how things are alike, and contrasting shows how they are different. A good compare/contrast paragraph describes both the ways things are alike and the ways they are different.

Use this Venn diagram to help you gather details about Elena's family's life in Mexico and about their life later in the United States.

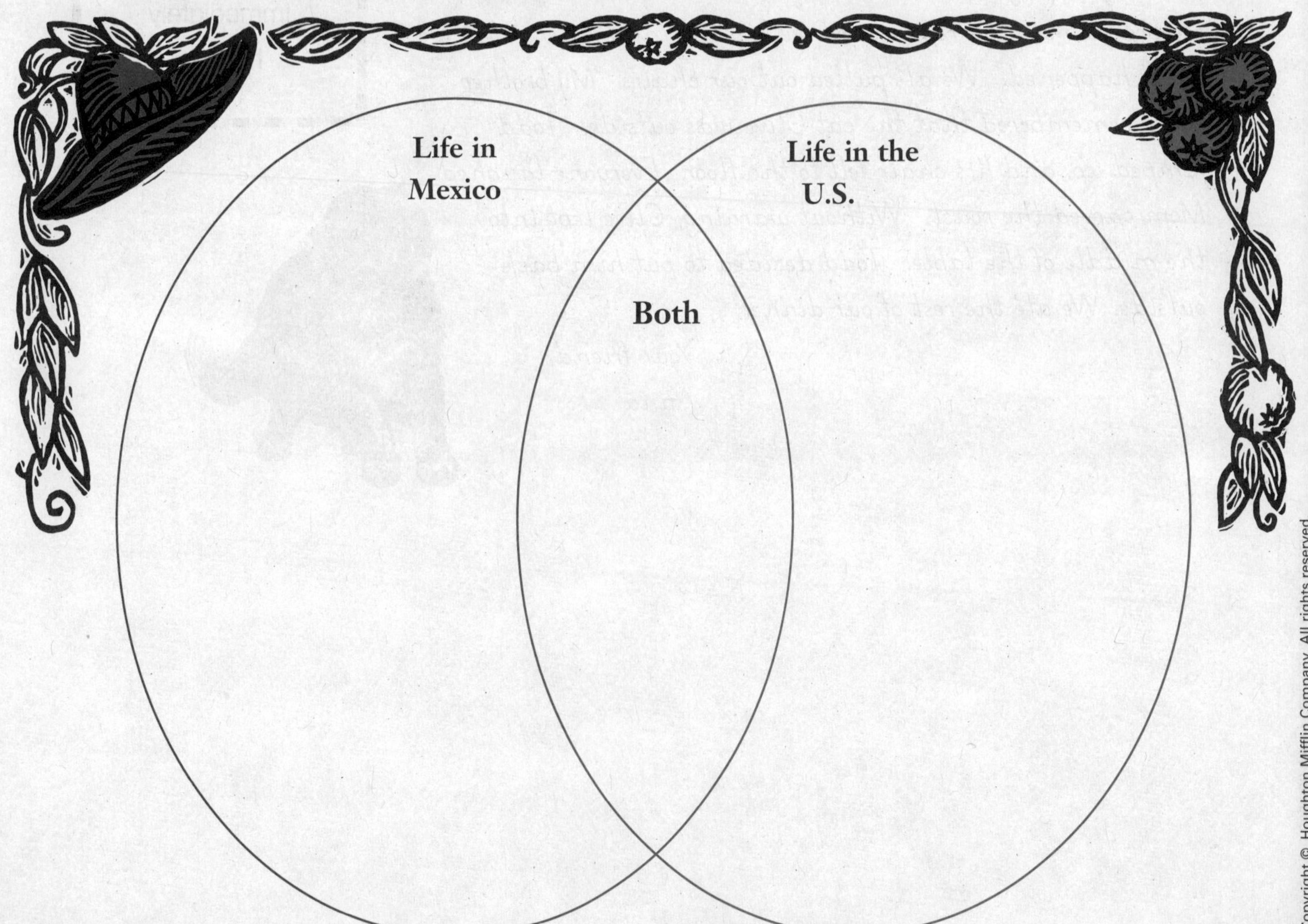

Name ____________________

Using Exact Adverbs

Adverbs such as *suddenly* and *wildly* clarify and enhance verbs or adjectives. A good writer uses exact adverbs to help sharpen the differences and similarities between things and to make details more vivid.

Suppose that Pablo made an advertisement for his sombreros. Read the ad and replace the inexact adverbs that have been underlined with more exact adverbs from the list. Write your revised ad on the lines.

Adverbs

- richly
- drably
- supremely
- handsomely
- exceptionally
- exquisitely

Why dress <u>plainly</u> when you can dress <u>well</u> instead? Buy a <u>very</u> well-made sombrero by Pablo. Unlike other hat makers, Pablo fashions his famous hats with velvety soft, smooth felt and then trims them <u>nicely</u> with gleaming silver. From the shaped crown to the detailed brim, Pablo's hats are <u>certainly</u> crafted. Pancho Villa says, "I'd never wear another. Pablo's sombreros are the finest in all of Mexico." You will be <u>very</u> happy wearing a one-of-a-kind sombrero by Pablo!

____

____

____

____

____

____

____

Name ______________________________

Writing an Answer to a Question

Use what you have learned about taking tests to help you write answers to questions about something you have read. This practice will help you when you take this kind of test.

Read these paragraphs from the story *A Boy Called Slow*.

As Slow grew up, he was not happy with his name. Few boys were given names they wanted to keep. No one wanted to be known as "Hungry Mouth" or "Curly" or "Runny Nose" or "Slow" all of his life. But until a child earned a new name by having a powerful dream or by doing some brave or special deed, it could not be changed.

Slow wished for this vision of bravery to come to him. He wished for a vision that would allow him to prove himself to his people.

Now write your answer to each question.

1. What kind of names were given to boys? How were these names different from the names they might get later?

____

____

____

____

____

____

____

Name ______________________________

Writing an Answer to a Question continued

2. Why didn't Slow like his name?

____
____
____
____
____
____
____

3. What are three ways that Slow could get his name changed?

____
____
____
____
____
____
____

Name ______________________

Spelling Review

Write Spelling Words from the list on this page to answer the questions.

1–8. Which eight words have the prefix *un*-, *dis*-, *in*-, or *re*-, or the suffix *-ion*?

1. ______ 5. ______
2. ______ 6. ______
3. ______ 7. ______
4. ______ 8. ______

9–15. Which seven words have the final /n/, /ən/, /chər/, or /zhər/ sounds?

9. ______ 13. ______
10. ______ 14. ______
11. ______ 15. ______
12. ______

16–22. In which seven words was the final *y* changed to *i* before an ending was added?

16. ______ 20. ______
17. ______ 21. ______
18. ______ 22. ______
19. ______

23–30. Which nine words are partly spelled below? Write each word. Then draw a line to divide each word into syllables.

23. sol— ______ 27. —tance ______
24. —age ______ 28. de— ______
25. spin— ______ 29. lan— ______
26. no— ______ 30. —tive ______

Spelling Words

1. adventure
2. treasure
3. solid
4. promotion
5. vulture
6. busier
7. voyage
8. unable
9. spinach
10. tension
11. curtain
12. pitied
13. furniture
14. notice
15. discover
16. react
17. mountain
18. countries
19. pleasure
20. spied
21. happiness
22. inspect
23. distance
24. correction
25. destroy
26. dirtier
27. language
28. native
29. respond
30. scariest

Name ____________________

Spelling Spree

Sentence Fillers Write the Spelling Word that best completes each sentence.

1. A person born in France is a __________ of France.
2. People in France speak the French __________.
3. You might see snow on a __________ peak.
4. Eating __________ will give you strong bones.
5. A cruise is a long sea __________.
6. Lower the __________ when the play is over.
7. A pirate buried his __________ in the sand.
8. Mom's __________ at work makes her a manager.
9. We did not mean to __________ your flowers.
10. There was great __________ between the two rivals.

Word Hunt Each word below is hidden in a Spelling Word. Write the Spelling Word.

11. cove __________
12. dirt __________
13. pine __________
14. plea __________
15. urn __________

Spelling Words

1. language
2. mountain
3. spinach
4. voyage
5. curtain
6. treasure
7. native
8. furniture
9. discover
10. promotion
11. destroy
12. tension
13. dirtier
14. happiness
15. pleasure

Name ______________________

Proofreading and Writing

Proofreading Circle the six misspelled Spelling Words in this letter. Then write each word correctly.

Our new neighbors just moved here from Mexico. Traveling such a long distence must be an aventure. They have two countrys to call home! I was unabel to meet their son until school started. We were editing a notise about tryouts for the school play, and we both started to make the same correcshun.

1. ______ 4. ______
2. ______ 5. ______
3. ______ 6. ______

Spelling Words

1. distance
2. scariest
3. adventure
4. countries
5. notice
6. unable
7. correction
8. inspect
9. react
10. busier
11. respond
12. spied
13. pitied
14. solid
15. vulture

Story Time Write a Spelling Word on each line to complete the story.

Before starting the trip, our leader took time to 7. ______ to our questions with expert advice. Then he had to carefully 8. ______ each wagon. He also tested each horse to see how it might 9. ______ to surprises on the trail. I 10. ______ the poor animals pulling the heavy wagons. As the departure neared, everybody was 11. ______ than ever. Even after two 12. ______ weeks of preparation, we still had plenty of work to do.

It was the leader's job to give a warning if he 13. ______ trouble. The first day out, a 14. ______ circled overhead and worried us. That, however, was not the 15. ______ moment of our trip.

7. ______ 10. ______ 13. ______
8. ______ 11. ______ 14. ______
9. ______ 12. ______ 15. ______

Write a Diary Entry On a separate sheet of paper, finish the story above by writing about the scariest moment on the trip. Use the Spelling Review Words.

Name ___________________________

Life Experiences

An autobiography helps you learn about other people's experiences. Complete the chart below by writing about an experience that was important to each author in *Focus on Autobiography.* What experience in your life has been important to you?

Author	Important Experience
Eloise Greenfield	
Jane Goodall	
Bill Peet	
Alex Rodriguez	
me	

Name ______________________________

How I Was Then . . .

It's the future, and you are famous. A children's magazine has asked you to tell its readers about what was important to you while you were growing up. Write a list of people, places, events, and interests that might be important in your life.

From My Childhood . . .

People: ______________________________

Places: ______________________________

Events: ______________________________

Interests: ______________________________

Name ___________________________

Animal Encounters

The selections in this theme explore some special relationships between people and wild creatures. After reading each selection, fill in this chart to show what you learned.

	What kind of writing is the selection an example of?	What creature or creatures does the selection describe?
Grizzly Bear Family Book		
The Golden Lion Tamarin Comes Home		
My Side of the Mountain		

Name ______________________________

Animal Encounters

	What is the purpose of the encounter between humans and animals?	What are the results of the encounter?
Grizzly Bear Family Book		
The Golden Lion Tamarin Comes Home		
My Side of the Mountain		

What are some ways in which people can help wild animals?

____

____

____

Name ______________________________

Creatures of the Far North

Answer each question with a word from the word box.

Vocabulary

- carcass
- caribou
- aggressive
- dominance
- subservience
- tundra
- wilderness
- abundant
- territory
- wariness

1. Which word names a grazing animal that lives in the Arctic?
____
2. Which word names the frozen land near the Arctic Ocean?
____
3. Which word names land that has not been developed?
____
4. Which word names the body of an animal that has died?
____
5. Which word is a synonym for *cautiousness*?
____
6. Which word names the region that a predator such as a bobcat or a grizzly bear ranges across to find food?
____
7. Which word is an adjective that means "likely to attack"?
____
8. Which word is an adjective that means "plentiful"?
____
9. Which word means "the state of controlling others"?
____
10. Which word means "the state of being willing to yield to others"? ______________________________

The Grizzly Bear Family Book

Graphic Organizer Generalizations Chart

Name ______________________________

Detective Work

What generalizations does the author make about bears, about people, and about the wilderness in this selection? As you read, look for generalizations on the pages listed below. Use the clues to help you recognize them. Write each generalization you find.

Page	Clue	Generalization
605	how people see bears	
607	what all living things do	
608	how grizzlies act toward each other during most of the year	
608	which bears command the best fishing spots	
609	the tolerance of mother bears	
610	bears selecting salmon	
612	bears and soapberries	
614	bears pursuing people	
615	how hunters kill bears	
616	how people treat nature	

Name ______________________________

Bear Facts

Write facts about bears in the web provided. Try to use each word in the creek at least once.

how bears act with each other

____

____

bears and humans

____

____

how bears survive the winter

____

____

how mother bears act

____

____

____

what bears eat

____

____

soapberries

carcass

sedges

subservience

nurse

salmon

tenderness

play

dominance

den

wariness

tolerant

Name ______________________________

Wolf Talk

Read the passage. Then complete the activity on page 351.

Saved From Extinction: The Story of the Gray Wolf

Long ago, the gray wolf roamed through most of North America, from Canada to Mexico. Today, gray wolves are still common in Alaska and parts of Canada. South of Canada, however, only a few gray wolves survive.

People in the United States have always considered wolves to be evil and dangerous. Settlers shot them to protect their families. Ranchers shot them to protect their livestock. For decades the federal government paid hunters cash bounties for shooting wolves.

In the late 1960s, when the gray wolf was nearly extinct in the United States, public opinion began to change. Most people came to regard wolves as a valuable part of the natural environment. All who cared about the wilderness believed that wolves should be allowed to thrive in America's northern forests.

In 1995 federal agencies began a program to return the gray wolf to parts of its former range. They airlifted wolves from Canada into Yellowstone National Park. From there, the wolves have begun to reinhabit parts of Wyoming, Montana, and Idaho. But not everyone is pleased by the program's success. The ranchers in these states fear that wolves will destroy their livestock and have demanded an end to the program.

What will the gray wolf's fate be? No one can be sure. But wherever wolves and people share the land, conflicts are likely to occur.

The Grizzly Bear Family Book

Comprehension Skill
Making Generalizations

Name ______________________________

Wolf Talk continued

Answer these questions about the passage on page 350.

1. What generalization does the author make in the second paragraph of the passage?

____

____

2. Is this generalization valid or invalid? Why?

____

____

3. What two generalizations does the author make in the third paragraph?

A. ____

____

B. ____

____

4. One of the generalizations in the third paragraph is invalid. Rewrite it to make it a valid statement.

____

____

5. What generalization does the author make in the fourth paragraph?

____

____

6. Rewrite the generalization in the fourth paragraph to make it a valid statement.

____

____

Name ______________________________

Prefix Prints

The words in the box begin with the prefix *com-*, *con-*, *en-*, *ex-*, *pre-*, or *pro-*. Find the word that matches each clue and write it in the letter spaces. Then read the tinted letters to find a word that means "to keep from harm, attack, or injury."

complete
continue
entrance
encourage
excited
predict
protest

1. bring to a finish ___ ___ ___ ___ ___ ___ ___ ___
2. a door, for example ___ ___ ___ ___ ___ ___ ___ ___
3. to fill with confidence ___ ___ ___ ___ ___ ___ ___ ___ ___
4. to keep on doing ___ ___ ___ ___ ___ ___ ___ ___
5. to tell what will happen ___ ___ ___ ___ ___ ___ ___
6. thrilled ___ ___ ___ ___ ___ ___ ___
7. to complain about ___ ___ ___ ___ ___ ___ ___

Write a sentence about grizzly bears, using a word from the box.

____

____

Name ______________________________

More Words with Prefixes

Com-, *con-*, *en-*, *ex-*, *pre-*, and *pro-* are prefixes. Because you know how to spell the prefix, pay special attention to the spelling of the base word or the word root. Spell the word by parts.

compare **con**vince **en**force
excite **pre**serve **pro**pose

Write each Spelling Word under its prefix.

com-, con-

________________ ________________
________________ ________________
________________ ________________
________________ ________________

en-, ex-

________________ ________________
________________ ________________
________________ ________________
____

pre-, pro-

________________ ________________
________________ ________________
____

Spelling Words

1. propose
2. convince
3. concern
4. enforce
5. compare
6. excuse
7. conduct
8. preserve
9. contain
10. excite
11. extend
12. prefix
13. engage
14. pronoun
15. consist
16. enclose
17. consent
18. proverb
19. complete
20. exchange

The Grizzly Bear Family Book

Spelling More Words with Prefixes

Name ______________________________

Spelling Spree

Alphabet Puzzler **Write the Spelling Word that fits alphabetically between the two words in each group.**

1. prong, _____, proof
2. company, _____, compass
3. enchant, _____, encore
4. contact, _____, contest
5. prefer, _____, preheat
6. convert, _____, convoy
7. consider, _____, consonant
8. express, _____, extinct

1. ______________________ 5. ______________________

2. ______________________ 6. ______________________

3. ______________________ 7. ______________________

4. ______________________ 8. ______________________

The Third Word **Write the Spelling Word that belongs in each group.**

9. trade, swap, _____
10. suggest, recommend, _____
11. agree, grant, _____
12. saying, phrase, _____
13. save, protect, _____
14. thrill, energize, _____
15. whole, total, _____

9. ______________________ 13. ______________________

10. ______________________ 14. ______________________

11. ______________________ 15. ______________________

12. ______________________

Spelling Words

1. propose
2. convince
3. concern
4. enforce
5. compare
6. excuse
7. conduct
8. preserve
9. contain
10. excite
11. extend
12. prefix
13. engage
14. pronoun
15. consist
16. enclose
17. consent
18. proverb
19. complete
20. exchange

Name ______________________________

Proofreading and Writing

Proofreading Circle the five misspelled words in these park rules. Then write each word correctly.

PARK RULES

While in the park, please condouct yourself as follows:

1. If you see a bear, do not try to ingage it. Instead, leave it in peace. Trust us! You don't want a bear to concirn itself with you.
2. If you come across a bear, *never* turn and run. It will excite the bear, who will then run after you. There is no way to outrun a bear!
3. Do not feed any park animals. There is no exscuse for breaking this rule. We will enforse it strictly.

Spelling Words

1. propose
2. convince
3. concern
4. enforce
5. compare
6. excuse
7. conduct
8. preserve
9. contain
10. excite
11. extend
12. prefix
13. engage
14. pronoun
15. consist
16. enclose
17. consent
18. proverb
19. complete
20. exchange

1. ______________ 4. ______________

2. ______________ 5. ______________

3. ______________

Write an Essay The author of this selection knew and respected grizzlies, but he was killed by one. Does this change your thinking about bears?

On a separate piece of paper, write a short essay stating your reaction to Michio Hoshino's fate. Use Spelling Words from the list.

The Grizzly Bear Family Book

Vocabulary Skill Using Context

Name ______________________________

A Search for Meaning

Read the passage. Then use context clues from the passage to figure out the underlined words. Write their meanings and the clues you used.

The Rivals

Bridget saw the fight through her binoculars. It was really just a brief quarrel between two bears who were fishing. The younger bear was smaller but more aggressive, and he soon proved to be the victor. The older bear turned around and retreated to the riverbank. The entire group of bears in the river then began to fish. The former rivals, now tolerant of one another, fished almost side by side. But Bridget's own feeling of wariness kept her from going any closer.

Word	Meaning	Clues from Context
victor		
retreated		
tolerant		
wariness		

Name ______________________________

Contraction Action

Contractions with *not* You can combine some verbs with the word *not* to make a **contraction**. An apostrophe takes the place of the letter or letters dropped to shorten the word.

In sentences 1–5, underline the word combination with *not* that can be written as a contraction. Then write the contraction on the line. For sentences 6–10, underline the contraction. On the line, write the words that make up the contraction.

Common Contractions with a Verb and *not*

do not	don't	have not	haven't
does not	doesn't	has not	hasn't
did not	didn't	had not	hadn't
is not	isn't	could not	couldn't
are not	aren't	would not	wouldn't
was not	wasn't	should not	shouldn't
were not	weren't	cannot	can't
will not	won't	must not	mustn't

1. Bears are not found around here. ______________________
2. I had not seen a bear until last year. ______________________
3. I could not visit Alaska. ______________________
4. A bear will not show up in my backyard. ______________________
5. I did not think I would ever see a bear. ______________________
6. "You haven't thought of going to the zoo!" said Dad. ______________________
7. "It isn't the same as seeing wild bears," I said. ______________________
8. He said, "The bears don't live in cages anymore." ______________________
9. The new habitat hasn't been at the zoo long. ______________________
10. You mustn't miss the bear cubs! ______________________

Name ______________________________

No! Not Negatives!

Negatives Words that mean "no" or "not" are **negatives.** Do not use **double negatives**, two negative words in the same sentence.

Negatives					
no	not	hardly	never	neither	none

There are often two ways to correct a double negative.

Incorrect: Fred **hasn't no** idea what Alaska is like.

Correct: Fred **hasn't any** idea what Alaska is like.

Correct: Fred **has no** idea what Alaska is like.

Rewrite each sentence to correct the double negative.

1. Fred had not read nothing about Alaska.

____

____

2. He didn't never plan to go there.

____

____

3. He hadn't no curiosity about our forty-ninth state.

____

____

4. Since reading Michio's story, he can't never read enough about Alaska!

____

____

5. Soon there won't be nobody who knows more about Alaska.

____

____

Name ______________________________

Is That an Adverb, Herb?

Adjective or Adverb? A good writer is careful to use **adverbs**, not **adjectives**, to tell *how much* or *to what extent* about adjectives.

Incorrect: The animal was **dreadful** hungry.

Correct: The animal was **dreadfully** hungry.

Sophie wrote to her friend June. In several places, Sophie used an adjective when she should have used an adverb. Proofread Sophie's letter, and make the corrections above the errors.

Dear June,

Last week, Mom and I saw a baby raccoon in our yard! It was real tiny. We knew that it should not be complete alone. After waiting for its mother for a terrible long time, Mom called the Wildlife Rescue Center. They sent an expert to help. She was awful kind. She said we should never touch a wild animal. She put it in a special cage so it wouldn't get hurt. The Rescue Center will take extreme good care of the baby. I wish you could have seen it.

Your friend,

Sophie

Name ______________________________

Writing an Opinion Composition

An **opinion** is a belief that may or may not be supported by facts. Some opinions, such as those offered by Michio Hoshino in *The Grizzly Bear Family Book,* are highly personal. For example, he says, "No matter how many books you read, no matter how much television you watch, there is no substitute for experiencing nature firsthand."

As you read *The Grizzly Bear Family Book,* consider the following question:

► ***Do you think grizzlies should be kept in zoos? Why or why not?***

Then use this diagram to record your opinion and to write facts and examples that support it.

Opinion

Facts and Examples	Facts and Examples	Facts and Examples

The Grizzly Bear Family Book

Writing Skill Improving Your Writing

Name ______________________________

Avoiding Double Negatives

The words *no, not, none,* and *nothing* are called **negatives.** A careful writer does not use two negatives within a single phrase. You can eliminate double negatives in your own writing by removing one of the negatives or by changing either one of the negatives to a positive.

Hunters do **not** have **no** right to shoot grizzlies in Alaska. (incorrect)

Hunters have **no** right to shoot grizzlies in Alaska. (corrected) or
Hunters do **not** have **any** right to shoot grizzlies in Alaska. (corrected)

Read the following letter to the editor of the *Alaskan Argus*. Use the proofreaders' delete mark ( ) to remove double negatives. You may replace some negatives with positive words such as *any* or *anything*. Write the positive word above the negative one you replace.

To the Editor:

I am concerned about a recent proposal to extend the hunting season in Alaska. In my opinion, the hunting season is long enough. Hunters from the lower United States and Europe do not need no more time to hunt.

Most wildlife cannot compete against no high-powered rifles. As a result of more opportunities for hunting animals, there might not be none left for the public to enjoy. Tourists will not come to the Alaskan wilderness if there is not nothing to observe there.

A longer hunting season increases the risk that people will be injured. I feel that if more trophy hunters are encouraged to come to Alaska, then we will not be able to do nothing to avoid the tragic consequences.

I strongly support keeping the hunting season the way it is now.

Sincerely,
Chris Morrow

Name ___________________________

Revising Your Persuasive Essay

Reread your persuasive essay. What do you need to do to make it better? Put a checkmark in each box that describes your essay.

Rings the Bell!

- ☐ My essay has a beginning that will capture my readers' attention.
- ☐ My goal is stated clearly at the beginning of the essay.
- ☐ I stated my reasons for my point of view and answered objections.
- ☐ I used facts and details to support my opinion.
- ☐ The essay is interesting to read and convincing.

Getting Stronger

- ☐ I could make the beginning more attention grabbing.
- ☐ I could state my goal more clearly.
- ☐ I could answer more objections people might raise.
- ☐ I need to add more facts and details to support my point of view.
- ☐ There are some run-on sentences I need to fix.
- ☐ There are a few other mistakes.

Try Harder

- ☐ I need a better beginning.
- ☐ I didn't state my goals or reasons for my opinion.
- ☐ I didn't answer any objections people might have.
- ☐ I need to add facts and details.
- ☐ This isn't very convincing.
- ☐ There are a lot of mistakes.

Name ____________________

Correcting Run-On Sentences

Correct each run-on sentence on the lines provided.

1. **Run-On:** Wolves are ranked in a pack it is called a hierarchy.

   Corrected: ____________________

2. **Run-On:** Lower-ranked wolves are submissive to higher-ranked wolves alpha wolves have dominance over the other wolves in the pack.

   Corrected: ____________________

3. **Run-On:** Wolves survive in different climates they are adaptable.

   Corrected: ____________________

4. **Run-On:** Wolves hunt in packs they catch larger prey such as moose or elk.

   Corrected: ____________________

5. **Run-On:** Wolves and dogs share many of the same traits they are both smart.

   Corrected: ____________________

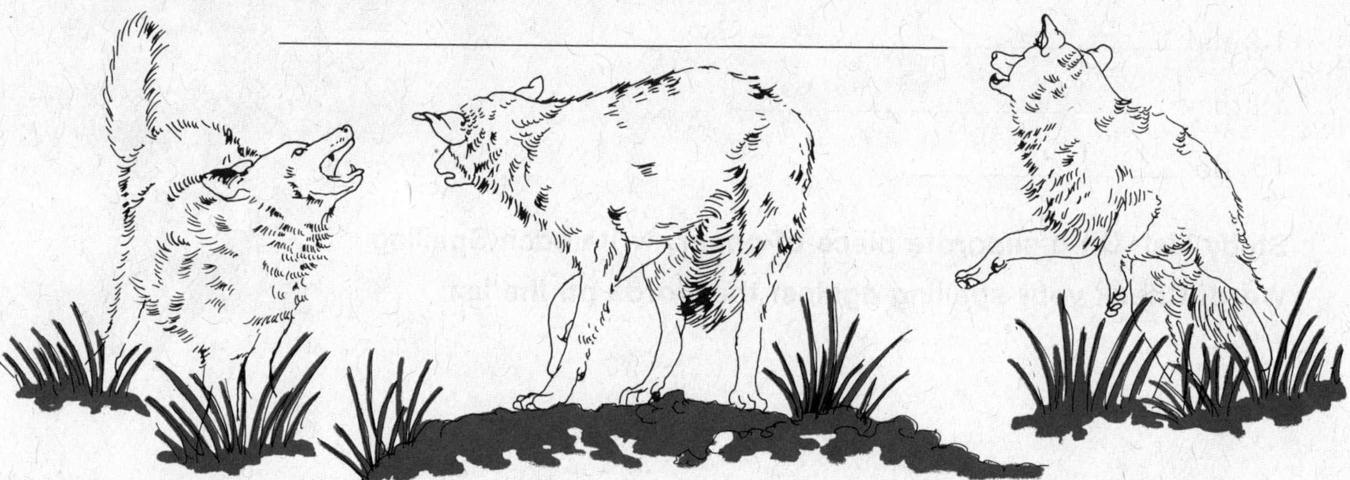

Name ______________________________

Spelling Words

Words Often Misspelled Look for familiar spelling patterns to help you remember how to spell the Spelling Words on this page. Think carefully about the parts that you find hard to spell in each word.

Write the missing letters and apostrophes in the Spelling Words below.

1. h ____ ____ d
2. y ____ ____ ____
3. you ____ ____ ____
4. f ____ ____ ____ d
5. b ____ y
6. fr ____ ____ nd
7. ____ ____ ess
8. c ____ ____ ____ ____ n
9. b ____ ____ ld
10. fam ____ ly
11. ca ____ ____ ____
12. ca ____ ____ ____ ____
13. did ____ ____ ____
14. hav ____ ____ ____ ____
15. do ____ ____ ____

Study List On a separate piece of paper, write each Spelling Word. Check your spelling against the words on the list.

Spelling Words

1. heard
2. your
3. you're
4. field
5. buy
6. friend
7. guess
8. cousin
9. build
10. family
11. can't
12. cannot
13. didn't
14. haven't
15. don't

Name ______________________

Reading-Writing Workshop

Frequently Misspelled Words

Spelling Spree

Alphabet Puzzler Write the Spelling Word that fits alphabetically between the two words in each group.

1. fried, ____, frighten
2. head, ____, heart
3. donation, ____, doom
4. familiar, ____, famous
5. guard, ____, guest
6. fiddle, ____, filed
7. button, ____, buzz
8. court, ____, cover

1. ______________
2. ______________
3. ______________
4. ______________
5. ______________
6. ______________
7. ______________
8. ______________

Spelling Words

1. heard
2. your
3. you're
4. field
5. buy
6. friend
7. guess
8. cousin
9. build
10. family
11. can't
12. cannot
13. didn't
14. haven't
15. don't

Letter Math Add and subtract letters from the words below to make Spelling Words. Write the new words.

9. carrot + nn – rr =
10. having – ing + en't =
11. sour – s + y =
12. want + ' – w + c =
13. guild – g + b =
14. they're + you – they =
15. hadn't + di –ha =

9. ______________
10. ______________
11. ______________
12. ______________
13. ______________
14. ______________
15. ______________

Name ______________________________

Proofreading and Writing

Proofreading **Circle the five misspelled Spelling Words in this wanted poster. Then write each word correctly.**

Spelling Words

1. heard
2. your
3. you're
4. field
5. buy
6. friend
7. guess
8. cousin
9. build
10. family
11. can't
12. cannot
13. didn't
14. haven't
15. don't

HAVE YOU SEEN THIS CAT?

You may have herd about the escape of this mountain lion from the county zoo. We have been searching for the past week, but we have'nt been able to track her down. Our best gess is that she is keeping to wooded areas, but we can't say for sure. As a result, we are asking that you be extremely careful when outdoors, and that you keep an eye on youre children and pets. Above all, if you see the cat, dont approach her. Instead, call the police, or call us at the zoo at 555-7372.

1. ______________________
2. ______________________
3. ______________________
4. ______________________
5. ______________________

Animal Riddles **On a separate piece of paper, write three riddles about animals. Include a Spelling Word in each riddle. Then trade riddles with a classmate and try to guess each other's answers.**

Name ______________________________

Saving a Species

Complete each statement with a word from the word box.

Vocabulary

- dilemma
- extinction
- predator
- observation
- canopy
- reintroduction
- habitat
- captive
- humid
- genes

1. If you are in the highest branches of the tallest trees in the rain forest, you are in the ______________________.
2. If the air has a lot of moisture in it, the weather is ______________________.
3. If you release animals into a wild area in which their ancestors once lived, you are helping with the ______________________ of a species.
4. If you study the region in which a wild creature lives, you study its ______________________.
5. If you are faced with a problem that seems to have no good solution, you are faced with a ______________________.
6. If you study the material that determines the characteristics of a plant or animal, you study its ______________________.
7. If no members of a species remain alive, that species has suffered ______________________.
8. If you are being held prisoner, you are a ______________________.
9. If an animal is being watched, it is under ______________________.
10. If an animal hunts other animals for food, it is a ______________________.

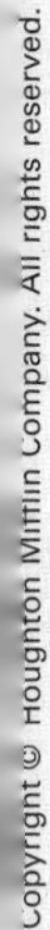

Name ______________________________

Get the Idea?

What are the main ideas of this selection? As you read, find the main ideas on the pages listed below. Then fill in the chart with the main idea and the details that support each main idea.

Topic: The conservation of golden lion tamarins.
(Page 630) Main Idea: ______________________________ ______________________________ **Details:** ______________________________ ______________________________
(Pages 632–633) Main Idea: ______________________________ ______________________________ **Details:** ______________________________ ______________________________
(Pages 634–637) Main Idea: ______________________________ ______________________________ **Details:** ______________________________ ______________________________
(Page 638) Main Idea: ______________________________ ______________________________ **Details:** ______________________________ ______________________________
(Pages 640–641) Main Idea: ______________________________ ______________________________ **Details:** ______________________________ ______________________________

Name ______________________________

The Lion Speaks

Fill in the blanks below with information from the story.

1. "I am a ______________________. My native home is in the rain forest of ______________."
2. "Unfortunately, humans have ____________ down many trees and ______________ much of the forest for their own use. Today I am in danger of ________________."
3. "That is why biologists have established a protected ______________ for us in the rain forest. Because many of us are bred in ______________, however, we must learn new ______________ before we go into the wild."
4. "We are trained at the ________________ Zoo in ________________________. Then we are shipped to our native country, ______________. There a team of ______________ first releases us into ______________ within the rain forest."
5. "When we are ready, they let us out. They ____________ us carefully and take detailed ______________ describing our behavior. They also give us ____________ and ____________ until we learn to find these things on our own."
6. "The ______________ among us adapt the fastest. Today only about ______ percent of us survive more than ______________ in the wild. The ____________________ Conservation Program hopes to have ____________ of us living in the wild by the year ____________."

Name ______________________________

Mind the Main Idea

Read the passage. Then complete the activity on page 371.

The Decline of the Tiger

Once, many different types of tigers roamed throughout Asia. These were the Indian, Indochinese, Chinese, Siberian, Sumatran, Caspian, Javan, and Balinese tigers. Today, three of these eight types are extinct and several of the others are rare. Wild tigers can still be found only in some parts of Southeast Asia and Siberia.

Two main factors have caused the decline of tiger populations. One factor is the destruction of tigers' habitats. In central Asia, for example, farmers burned wooded areas along waterways to clear the land for farming. Thousands of acres of forest were also set on fire. As a result, much of the tigers' natural prey disappeared. Without enough food to support their roughly four-hundred-pound bodies, the tigers have disappeared as well.

Hunting is the second factor that has caused the decline of tiger populations. With the loss of their habitats and natural prey, tigers began to hunt closer to people. Farmers shot them to protect their livestock. Others hunted them for sport or for their fur.

Today, efforts are being made in many regions to protect wild tigers. India and Nepal have set aside reserves for them. Many countries have outlawed the import or sale of tiger skins. Successful captive breeding programs in zoos are also helping to ensure that the survival of these great cats continues.

Name ______________________________

Mind the Main Idea continued

Answer the questions below. Use information from the passage on page 370.

1. What is the topic of the passage? ______________________________
2. Write the main idea or supporting details of the following paragraphs below.

First Paragraph	Main Idea:	Today, tiger populations are in decline.
	Supporting Details:	______________________________
Second and Third Paragraphs	Main Idea:	Two main factors caused the decline of tigers: destruction of their habitats and hunting.
	Supporting Details:	______________________________
Fourth Paragraph	Main Idea:	______________________________
	Supporting Details:	India and Nepal have set aside tiger reserves. Many countries outlawed importing or selling tiger fur. Zoos breed captive tigers to help more tigers survive.

Name ______________________

Syllable Sensations

Read the sentences. Then circle the correct way to divide the syllables of the underlined word. Check the syllable pattern that applies to the word.

1. In zoos, ropes are hung to simulate vines for the tamarins.

   si/mul/ate sim/u/late

2. Nesting boxes are made for the tamarins from modified picnic coolers.

   mod/if/ied mod/i/fied

3. After returning to the rain forest, the tamarins grow accustomed to their new surroundings.

   ac/cus/tomed acc/ust/omed

4. As immigrants, the newly arrived tamarins have a great deal to learn.

   imm/ig/rants im/mi/grants

5. Human observers watch and record everything the tamarins do.

   ob/ser/vers obs/erv/ers

6. Bit by bit, the tamarins become familiar with the rain forest.

   fa/mil/iar fam/i/liar

7. Older tamarins must unlearn behaviors that were adequate for zoo life but are useless in the forest.

   a/deq/uate ad/e/quate

VCV	VCCV

Name ______________________________

Three-Syllable Words

A three-syllable word has one stressed syllable and two syllables with less stress. To help you spell the word, divide it into its syllables. Note the spelling of the syllables that have less stress.

va | ca | tion /vā **kā**′ shən/
ed | u | cate /**ĕj**′ ə kāt′/

Write each Spelling Word under the heading that names its stressed syllable.

Stressed First Syllable

______________ ______________
______________ ______________
______________ ______________
______________ ______________
______________ ______________
______________ ______________
____

Stressed Second Syllable

______________ ______________
______________ ______________
______________ ______________
____

Spelling Words

1. dangerous
2. history
3. vacation
4. popular
5. favorite
6. memory
7. personal
8. educate
9. regular
10. continue
11. potato
12. natural
13. sensitive
14. energy
15. emotion
16. period
17. property
18. condition
19. imagine
20. attention

The Golden Lion Tamarin Comes Home

Spelling Three-Syllable Words

Name ______________________________

Spelling Spree

Syllable Scramble **Rearrange the syllables to write a Spelling Word. One syllable in each item is extra.**

1. ue con gel tin — 1. ____________
2. gy ro en er — 2. ____________
3. po to tion ta — 3. ____________
4. at tion men ten — 4. ____________
5. let vor fa ite — 5. ____________
6. sen ring tive si — 6. ____________
7. u ed gan cate — 7. ____________

Word Maze **Begin at the arrow and follow the Word Maze to find eight Spelling Words. Write the words in order.**

8. ____________ 12. ____________

9. ____________ 13. ____________

10. ____________ 14. ____________

11. ____________ 15. ____________

Spelling Words

1. dangerous
2. history
3. vacation
4. popular
5. favorite
6. memory
7. personal
8. educate
9. regular
10. continue
11. potato
12. natural
13. sensitive
14. energy
15. emotion
16. period
17. property
18. condition
19. imagine
20. attention

Name ______________________________

Proofreading and Writing

Proofreading Circle the five misspelled Spelling Words in this brochure. Then write each word correctly.

The golden lion tamarin has a sad histrey. Over a perriod of years, much of Brazil's rain forest was cut down. The tamarin, therefore, was driven out of its naturel habitat. Most of the forest was turned into private propety. Brazil's government has now set aside some of the remaining forest as a wildlife refuge. Since then, the tamarins' condishun has improved. There is still much to be done, however. Won't you help us continue our work?

Spelling Words

1. dangerous
2. history
3. vacation
4. popular
5. favorite
6. memory
7. personal
8. educate
9. regular
10. continue
11. potato
12. natural
13. sensitive
14. energy
15. emotion
16. period
17. property
18. condition
19. imagine
20. attention

1. ______________________
2. ______________________
3. ______________________
4. ______________________
5. ______________________

Write an Opinion Only three out of every ten reintroduced tamarins survive for more than two years in the wild. Do you think the time and money spent in this effort is worth it? Why or why not?

On a separate piece of paper, write your opinion of the Golden Lion Tamarin Conservation Program. Use Spelling Words from the list.

The Golden Lion Tamarin Comes Home

Vocabulary Skill Dictionary: Variations in Pronunciation

Name ____________________

A Pronounced Difference!

Read the dictionary entries, paying special attention to the pronunciations. Then answer the questions below.

gum
jam
pie
seen
sheen
sit

different /dĭf/ər/ənt/ or /dĭf/rənt/ *adj.* Unlike in form, quality, or nature.

diversity /dĭv/ûr/sĭ/tē/ or /dī/vûr/sĭ/tē/ *n.* 1. Difference. 2. Variety.

program /prō/grăm/ or /prō/grəm/ *n.* A public performance or presentation.

species /spē/shēz/ or /spē/sēz/ *n.* A group of similar animals or plants that are of the same kind and are able to produce fertile offspring.

water /wô/tər/ or /wŏt/ər/ *n.* A compound of hydrogen and oxygen occurring as a liquid.

1. How does the number of syllables change in the two pronunciations of *different*?

____

2. *Diversity* differs in pronunciation only in the ____________ two syllables. Which two words from the box have the same vowel sounds as the pronunciations of the first syllable in *diversity*? ____________

3. *Program* differs in pronunciation in the ____________ syllable. Which two words from the box have the same vowel sounds as the pronunciations of that syllable? ____________

4. Which word from the box has the same consonant and vowel sounds as the second syllable in the first pronunciation of *species*? ____________

5. If you use the first pronunciation of *water*, are you saying WAHtur or WAWtur? (Circle the correct answer.)

Name ______________________________

Prepositions Give Positions

Prepositions A **preposition** relates the noun or pronoun that follows it to another word in the sentence. The **object of the proposition** is the noun or pronoun that follows the **preposition**.

Common Prepositions

about	around	beside	for	near	outside	under
above	at	by	from	of	over	until
across	before	down	in	off	past	up
after	behind	during	inside	on	through	with
along	below	except	into	out	to	without

Underline each preposition and circle the object of each preposition.

1. Sandy visited the rain forest with other tourists.
2. Moisture dripped from the leaves.
3. The tourists heard bird squawks in the distance.
4. Sandy took pictures of exotic orchids.
5. The world would be a poorer place without these forests.
6. Above our heads, we saw howler monkeys.
7. Jaguars roam the forest during the night.
8. We traveled up a river to a small village.
9. The people there made fantastic animal carvings in wood.
10. I bought a toucan carving from one artist.

Name ______________________________

Prepositional Phrases Don't Faze Us

Prepositional Phrases A **prepositional phrase** is made up of a preposition, the object of the preposition, and all the words in between.

Write each prepositional phrase on the line.

1. My friend Molly watches birds in her backyard.

____

2. Molly's family lives far from town.

____

3. In the field wildflowers grow.

____

4. Animals leave tracks by the pond.

____

5. The hoots of an owl fill the air.

____

6. Sometimes we camp out in the yard.

____

7. At night stars twinkle in the sky.

____

8. We make out constellations above our heads.

____

9. We tell ghost stories inside the tent.

____

10. We can hardly sleep during the night.

____

The Golden Lion Tamarin Comes Home

Grammar Skill Prepositional Phrases

Name ______________________________

Expanding Isn't Demanding

Expanding Sentences with Prepositional Phrases A good writer can make sentences say more by adding prepositional phrases.

I took a walk.

Expanded: I took a walk along the path through the woods.

Read Charlie's paragraph. Add details to his description by adding prepositional phrases in the blanks. Ask yourself, Where? When? How? What? Use your imagination!

I walked through the woods ______________________. As I walked, I looked ______________. I hoped to see birds, but they must have been hiding ______________________. I continued my walk ______________________. I saw tracks ______________________. I followed them ______________________. ______________________ I found the owner of the tracks. It stared ______________________. Not wanting to frighten it, I stood quietly ______________________. Then it disappeared. Was it a dream, or did I really see a unicorn ______________________?

Name ______________________________

Writing a Compare/ Contrast Essay

In *The Golden Lion Tamarin Comes Home*, you read about similarities and differences between captive-born golden lion tamarins and those born in the wild. Both eat fruit, for example, but golden lion tamarins born in zoos do not know how to hunt or forage for food. One way to explain similarities and differences is by writing a **compare/contrast essay**. Comparing shows how things are alike, and contrasting shows how they are different.

Using the Venn diagram, gather and organize details that compare and contrast grizzly bears with golden lion tamarins. Jot down facts about the two species, including their habitats, their diets, and threats to their survival.

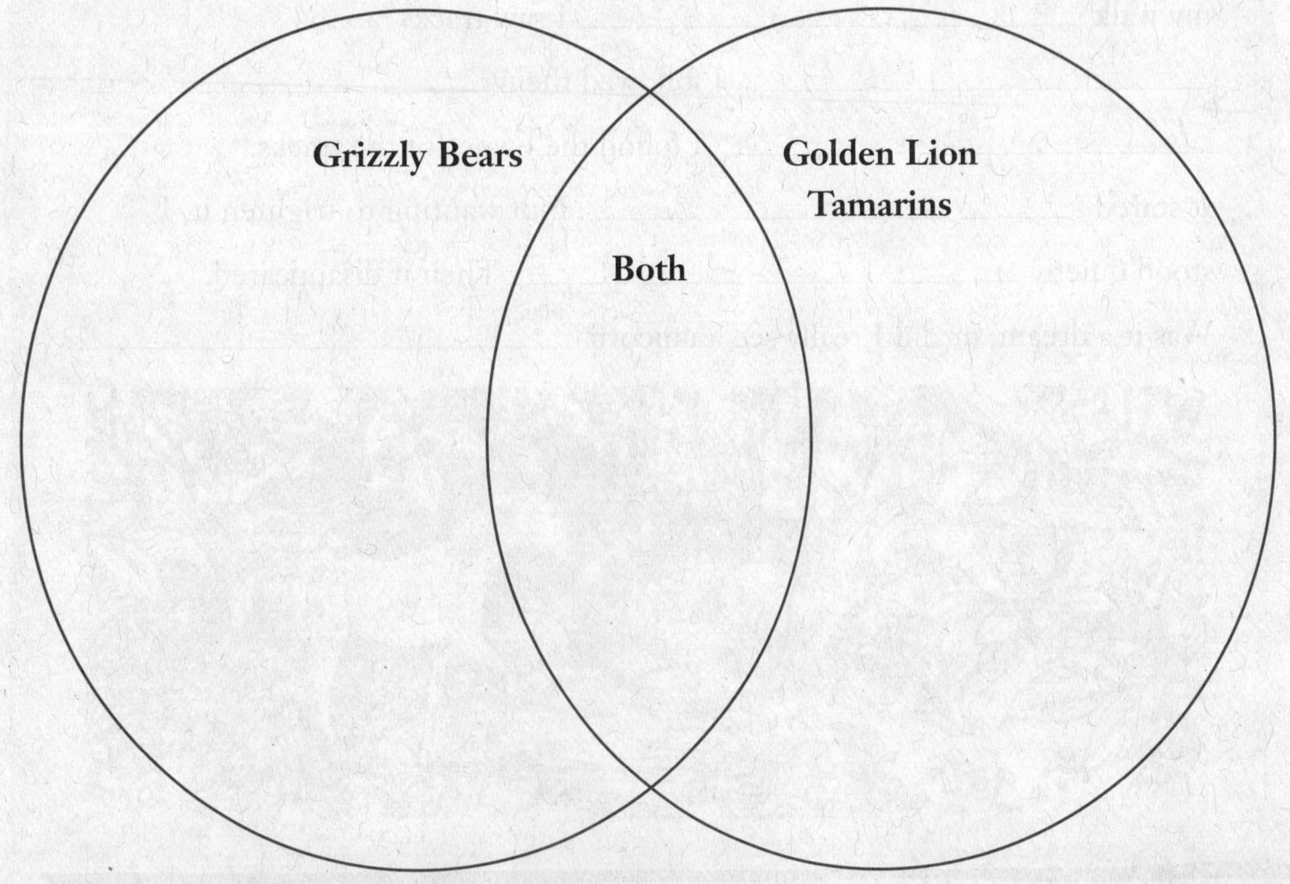

Name ______________________________

Combining Sentences

Good writers are always looking for ways to improve their writing. One method to streamline your writing is to combine short sentences that have a repeated subject but differing prepositional phrases into a single sentence with consecutive prepositional phrases.

The biologist was **in a tropical rain forest.** He stood **beneath some tall trees.** He peered **into the green vines.** He spotted a few golden lion tamarins **above him.**

Standing **beneath some tall trees in a tropical rain forest,** the biologist peered **into the green vines above him** and spotted a few golden lion tamarins.

Revise these field notes. Combine short sentences that have a repeated subject but differing prepositional phrases into a single sentence. Write the revised notes on the lines.

Thursday, 10:20 A.M.

My tamarin family, which I call the green team, peeks out. The monkeys look out from a hole. The hole is in the top chamber. The chamber is part of a nesting box. One by one, the tamarins leave the box. Hungrily, the adults poke into the feeder. They probe the feeder with their long fingers and nails. The golden lion tamarins also eat some partly peeled bananas. The bananas are left on the branches. The branches hang near the nesting box.

____

____

____

____

____

Name ______________________________

Late Autumn in the Woods

Complete the paragraph below with words from the word box.

Vocabulary

- storehouse
- harsh
- survival
- cache
- harvesting
- fashion
- migration

The leaves have turned colors and fallen from the trees. Most birds have made their ______________ south to warmer lands. Farmers have finished ______________ the last of the wheat and rye, and they have filled crates with apples and have placed them in a cool ______________. Each squirrel is busy adding a few more nuts to its ______________ of food for winter. Bears gorge themselves on one last meal of berries, for they need to have a thick layer of fat to ensure ______________ through the long winter. The few settlers who have come to the wild lands late in the season hurry to ______________ shelter that will protect them from the ______________ weather soon to arrive.

Write three more sentences using words from the box to continue the paragraph.

____

____

____

____

____

____

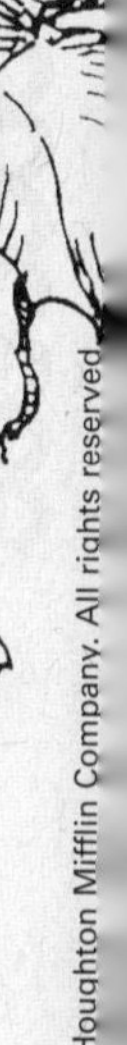

My Side of the Mountain

Graphic Organizer
Conclusions Chart

Name ______________________________

Use the Clues

Read the story clues and conclusions provided in the boxes below. Fill in the missing information with text from the selection.

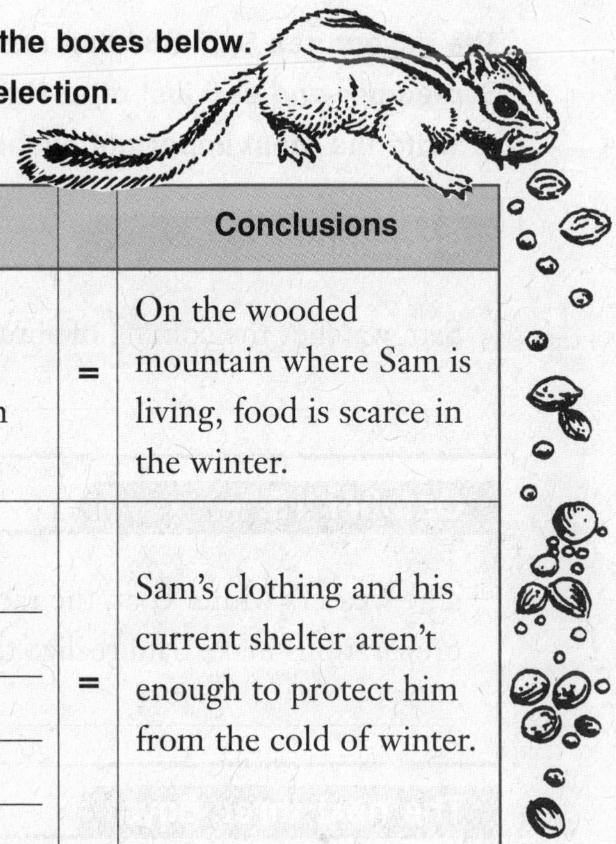

Story Clues				Conclusions
pages 652–653 Mice, squirrels, and chipmunks collected seeds and nuts.	+	Sam gathers various roots and smokes fish and rabbit.	=	On the wooded mountain where Sam is living, food is scarce in the winter.
pages 654–655 ______	+	______	=	Sam's clothing and his current shelter aren't enough to protect him from the cold of winter.
pages 656–658 Sam playfully chases the Baron Weasel up the mountain.	+	Sam runs after Frightful because he is warned the falcon has left him.	=	______
pages 660–665 ______	+	______	=	Even though Sam enjoys the animals' company, he must remain alert around these wild creatures.

Name ______________________________

Autumn Adventures

The adventures Sam has that are recounted in this story begin in September and end just after Halloween. Use the sequence chart below to write the most important events in the order in which they occurred.

September

Sam watches the coming of autumn. He

____

October 15

The weasel's winter coat, the raccoon's rolls of fat, and the other animals' winter preparations make Sam realize that

____

The next three days

Sam brings clay back to his tree and fashions a chimney. He then

____

October 31

After the Baron visits, Sam realizes that it is Halloween. He decides

____

November 1

The animals finally show up and there is a wild party in which Sam learns that he

____

Name ______________________________

My Side of the Mountain

Comprehension Skill Drawing Conclusions

Gather the Clues

Read the passage. Then answer the questions on page 386.

Taking Stock

It was nearing dusk when I got back to camp. The crickets were just launching into their evening serenade. I set my backpack down on the slab of granite I used as my table and began to unpack the treasures of the day.

I pulled out the sack of miner's lettuce that I'd gathered near the waterfall. Next, I lifted out a pouch of wild blackberries packed in a soft cushion of moss. From the bottom of the pack I drew handfuls of walnuts. The berries I'd expected to find, but the walnuts were an unexpected luxury, from a walnut tree I'd discovered in a grove of tan oaks. I carefully laid the food out on the stone. I had smoked two small trout the day before; these I had wrapped in paper and stored in a tree, away from hungry bears. The trout, nuts, and lettuce, with the berries as dessert, would make a feast indeed.

I then turned my attention to building a fire. The day had been a hot one, but I knew how fast the temperature would drop when the sun went down. After I had the campfire crackling cheerfully, I sat down to take stock.

Some things had gone better than I'd expected. Staying warm and dry had been easy. Even the rainstorm on the second night didn't soak any of my belongings. Other things, like finding enough to eat, had proved harder than I'd expected. An hour of picking lettuce resulted in a very small pile of greens. Overall, though, I couldn't complain. I thought about my two-way radio inside the tent. I hadn't had to use it yet. With luck, I wouldn't need to unpack it at all.

Name ______________________________

Gather the Clues

Answer these questions about the passage on page 385.

1. Where is the narrator? How do you know?

____

____

____

2. Is the narrator stranded or did she choose to be there? How can you tell?

____

____

____

3. What time of year do you think it is? Why?

____

____

____

4. What do you think the two-way radio might be used for? Why do you think this?

____

____

____

5. Do you think the narrator has had other experiences in the wilderness? Why or why not?

____

____

____

Name ______________________________

Significant Suffixes

-able, -ible	*-ant, -ent*
edible	defiant
irresistible	hesitant
climbable	observant
indestructible	tolerant

You are writing a description of *My Side of the Mountain* for your school's Book Week. You need to liven up your description. Use the words from the box above to complete the sentences.

Even when he's angry at them, Sam finds the animals on the mountain ______________________ for the funny things they do. Except for Frightful, he is ______________________ to get too close to them. Sam tries to be ______________________ of their bad behavior. But when the Baron Weasel gets that ______________________ look in his eye, watch out!

Sam must prepare a winter shelter that is ______________________, even in the worst storm. When out walking, Sam must always be ______________________ in order to find ______________________ food. He looks for trees that are ______________________ so that he can pick the fruit from their high branches.

My Side of the Mountain

Spelling Words with *-ent, -ant; -able, -ible*

Name ______________________

Words with *-ent, -ant; -able, -ible*

The suffixes *-ent* and *-ant* and the suffixes *-able* and *-ible* sound alike but are spelled differently. You have to remember the spellings of these suffixes because they begin with a schwa sound.

/ənt/ stud**ent**, merch**ant**

/əbəl/ suit**able**, poss**ible**

Write each Spelling Word under its suffix.

-ent

____

____

____

____

____

-ant

____

____

____

-able

____

____

____

____

____

____

____

____

____

-ible

____

____

____

Spelling Words

1. fashionable
2. comfortable
3. different
4. suitable
5. merchant
6. profitable
7. student
8. possible
9. resident
10. terrible
11. absent
12. vacant
13. servant
14. valuable
15. accident
16. horrible
17. honorable
18. reasonable
19. remarkable
20. laughable

My Side of the Mountain

Spelling Words with *-ent, -ant; -able, -ible*

Name ______________________________

Spelling Spree

Finding Words Each word below is hidden in a Spelling Word. Write the Spelling Word.

1. chant ______________________
2. sent ______________________
3. fit ______________________
4. side ______________________
5. rent ______________________
6. suit ______________________
7. fort ______________________

Crack the Code Some Spelling Words have been written in the code below. Use the code to figure out each word. Then write the words correctly.

8. DHAKHIAP	8. ______________
9. URLLSIAP	9. ______________
10. BHMUSRFHIAP	10. ______________
11. WPLLSIAP	11. ______________
12. MWKOPFW	12. ______________
13. MPLDHFW	13. ______________
14. URFRLHIAP	14. ______________
15. YRMMSIAP	15. ______________

Spelling Words

1. fashionable
2. comfortable
3. different
4. suitable
5. merchant
6. profitable
7. student
8. possible
9. resident
10. terrible
11. absent
12. vacant
13. servant
14. valuable
15. accident
16. horrible
17. honorable
18. reasonable
19. remarkable
20. laughable

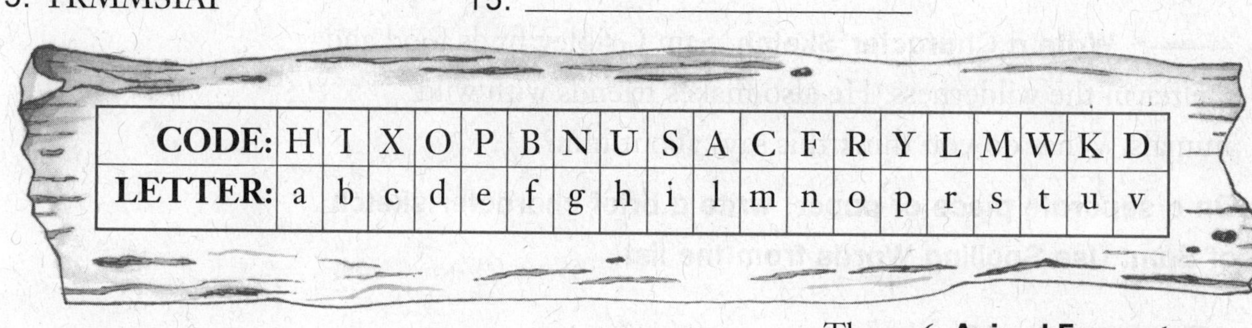

CODE:	H	I	X	O	P	B	N	U	S	A	C	F	R	Y	L	M	W	K	D
LETTER:	a	b	c	d	e	f	g	h	i	l	m	n	o	p	r	s	t	u	v

Name ______________________

Proofreading and Writing

Proofreading Circle the five misspelled Spelling Words in this news report. Then write each word correctly.

Finally tonight, remarkabel stories continue to filter in. We have learned of a wild boy living on a nearby mountain. Most of the sightings have been near a vaccant farm lot. Town leaders are dismissing the claims as laughible. Still, as one resident put it, "I don't think it's an accidant that these sightings keep coming in. If that many people say they've seen him, there's a reasenable chance he's out there."

1. ______________
2. ______________
3. ______________
4. ______________
5. ______________

Spelling Words

1. fashionable
2. comfortable
3. different
4. suitable
5. merchant
6. profitable
7. student
8. possible
9. resident
10. terrible
11. absent
12. vacant
13. servant
14. valuable
15. accident
16. horrible
17. honorable
18. reasonable
19. remarkable
20. laughable

Write a Character Sketch Sam Gribley finds food and shelter in the wilderness. He also makes friends with wild animals. What do you think this says about him?

On a separate piece of paper, write a brief character sketch of Sam. Use Spelling Words from the list.

Name ______________________________

Dictionary Division

Read the dictionary entries and sentences. On the line after each sentence, write if the underlined part of the sentence is an idiom or run-on entry. If it is an idiom, also write what it means. If it is a run-on entry, also write its part of speech and the main entry word it belongs with.

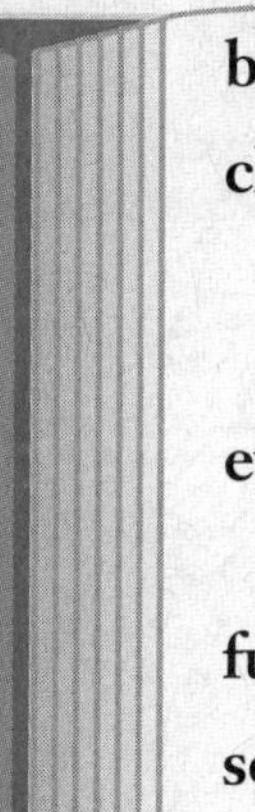

bold *adj.* Having no fear; brave. –boldly *adv.* –boldness *n.*

clear *adj.* Free from anything that obscures; transparent. *–idioms.* **clear out.** To leave a place, often quickly. **in the clear.** Free from dangers. –clearly *adv.* –clearness *n.*

eye *n.* An organ of the body through which an animal sees. *–idioms.* **eye to eye.** In agreement. **lay (one's) eyes on.** To see.

furious *adj.* 1. Raging. 2. Fierce; violent. –furiously *adv.* –furiousness *n.*

soft *adj.* Smooth or fine to the touch. –softly *adv.* –softness *n.*

take *v.* To carry to another place. *–idioms.* **take care.** To be careful. **take off.** To rise in flight.

1. Sam was sure that Frightful had taken off on a fall migration.

   ____

2. In the clearness of the stream Sam could see fish flashing by.

   ____

3. As soon as the skunk laid its eyes on Sam, it sprayed.

   ____

4. The squirrels were furiously harvesting nuts.

   ____

5. When Sam shouted, the animals cleared out of his house.

   ____

6. Sam kneaded and rubbed the rabbit hides to softness.

   ____

Name ______________________________

I Don't Object to Objects

Object Pronouns in Prepositional Phrases Use **object pronouns** as objects in prepositional phrases.

Object Pronouns

Singular	**Plural**
me	us
you	you
him, her, it	them

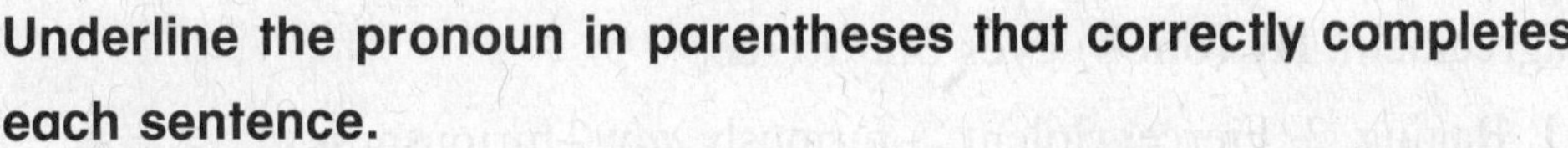

Underline the pronoun in parentheses that correctly completes each sentence.

1. Randy and his dog Maggie came with (I/me) on my walk up Mt. Hunter.
2. It seemed to (he/him) that we had found an old farmhouse.
3. We imagined the people who once lived here and told stories about (they/them).
4. For (we/us), the old farm was a window into the past.
5. Maggie barked, and we walked toward (she/her).
6. A squirrel in a tree chittered, and Maggie barked at (him/he).
7. More squirrels chittered, and we looked up at (them/they).
8. I guess to (they/them), we were enemies.
9. To (I/me), however, the squirrels were a surprise.
10. We went home. The day had been a success for (we/us).

Name ______________________________

My Side of the Mountain

Grammar Skill Pronouns in Prepositional Phrases with Compound Objects

Pronoun Pronouncements

Pronouns in Prepositional Phrases with Compound Objects Use an object pronoun in a compound object of a preposition. To see whether a pronoun is correct, say the sentence aloud without the other part of the compound.

Underline the pronoun in parentheses that correctly completes each sentence.

1. Lois gave a book about bats to Marjorie and (I/me).
2. We called for Todd and then looked for (he/him) and Adam.
3. Todd stood behind Adam and (I/me) as we looked for bats under the eaves.
4. Lois gave a flashlight to Adam and (we/us).
5. Suddenly, a bat flew in the direction of Adam and (she/her)!
6. Would it fly near Todd and (we/us) too?
7. Marjorie wasn't afraid since she had read the book Lois gave to (she/her) and me.
8. I knew that the bat did not care about Todd or (we/us).
9. Lois did not know that the bat would not fly at the boys or (she/her).
10. The bat flew away, and I gave the book to Todd and (she/her).

Name ______________________________

Pronouns in Compounds

Using the Correct Pronoun in a Compound Structure Good writers are careful to use subject pronouns in compound subjects. They are also careful to use object pronouns in compound objects of a preposition.

Underline incorrect compound subjects and objects in the record below. Then on the lines, write each underlined compound correctly.

June 3, Monday, 4:30 P.M.

Elizabeth and I walked Princess and Sherlock. Ann arrived to help us. Her and Elizabeth took Sherlock, while I took Princess. Then we met Rick. Him and Ann threw a ball for the dogs.

We also took care of Lanford the parrot. Elizabeth asked about he and Jackie the parakeet. Elizabeth and me are the bird experts. The birds always have something to say to Elizabeth and I. Today they squawked, "Feathers not fur! Feathers not fur!"

1. ______________________
2. ______________________
3. ______________________
4. ______________________
5. ______________________

Name ______________________________

Responding to a Prompt

Prompt:

Fall is coming and Sam has mixed feelings about it. Review the part of *My Side of the Mountain* that begins on page 652 and ends with the first paragraph on page 655. In your own words, write a summary of this part of the story.

Characters	Setting

Plot Events

Name ___________________________________

Placing Prepositional Phrases Correctly

Careful writers check the placement of prepositional phrases in their writing. If prepositional phrases appear in the wrong places in a sentence, they can make a sentence unclear. To avoid confusion, place prepositional phrases as close as possible to the words or phrases that they describe.

> **On a boulder** Sam Gribley dried apple slices **in the sun.**
>
> Sam Gribley dried apple slices **on a boulder in the sun.**

Revise the sentences from notes that Sam Gribley might have written. Make the meaning of each sentence clearer by moving one prepositional phrase as close as possible to the word that it describes. Circle the misplaced prepositional phrase, and then draw an arrow to show where it should go.

1. I steered my raft down the creek with a long stick to deep pools.
2. In the icy water I drifted with my line for an hour.
3. Suddenly the line jerked from my hand behind the raft. Dinner!
4. I pulled a fish onto the dry logs from the blue water of my raft.
5. Then I pushed near my home the raft to the muddy banks.
6. I sprinkled dried herbs on the fresh fish from a leather pouch.
7. Over a fire I grilled the fish outside my tree for a delicious meal.

Name ______________________________

Writing an Opinion Essay

Use what you have learned about taking tests to write an essay that gives your opinion about a topic. This practice will help you when you take this kind of test.

Many animals in the world are endangered. In *The Golden Lion Tamarin Comes Home*, you learned about the Golden Lion Tamarin Conservation Program and how this animal has been reintroduced to its natural habitat. Write an essay explaining what you think of the efforts of human beings to save endangered animals. Are these efforts important? Is it our responsibility to help these animals?

ENDANGERED

Name ____________________

Writing an Opinion Essay

continued

Read your essay. Check to be sure that

- each paragraph has a topic sentence that tells the main idea
- your reasons are strong and are supported with details
- your writing sounds like you
- the end of your essay sums up the important points
- there are few mistakes in capitalization, punctuation, grammar, or spelling

Now pick one way to improve your essay. Make your changes below.

Name ______________________________

Spelling Review

Write Spelling Words from the list on this page to answer the questions.

1–12. Which twelve words have the prefix *com-*, *con-*, *en-*, *ex-*, *pre-*, or *pro-*?

1. ______________ 7. ______________
2. ______________ 8. ______________
3. ______________ 9. ______________
4. ______________ 10. ______________
5. ______________ 11. ______________
6. ______________ 12. ______________

13–22. Which ten words have the suffixes *-ent*, *-ant*, *-able*, or *-ible*?

13. ______________ 18. ______________
14. ______________ 19. ______________
15. ______________ 20. ______________
16. ______________ 21. ______________
17. ______________ 22. ______________

23–30. Which eight words have letters missing below? Write each word.

23. emo—— ______________ 27. ima—— ______________
24. sensi—— ______________ 28. ——ous ______________
25. pota—— ______________ 29. ——ation ______________
26. ——ural ______________ 30. reg—— ______________

Spelling Words

1. remarkable
2. emotion
3. accident
4. sensitive
5. enforce
6. potato
7. suitable
8. prefix
9. vacant
10. condition
11. excite
12. consist
13. fashionable
14. enclose
15. natural
16. proverb
17. resident
18. possible
19. imagine
20. preserve
21. complete
22. merchant
23. dangerous
24. concern
25. terrible
26. propose
27. laughable
28. vacation
29. regular
30. continue

Name ______________________________

Spelling Spree

Hint and Hunt **Write the Spelling Word that best answers each question.**

1. What word could describe lions and mountain climbing?
   ____
2. What word refers to nature? ______________
3. What vegetable grows in the ground? ______________
4. What is a short saying that states an idea or truth?
   ____
5. What do you call a person who dresses in the latest styles?
   ____
6. What do police officers and principals do with rules?
   ______________ them
7. What word means "strong feeling"?
   ____
8. What is the word for a person who buys and sells things?
   ____

Spelling Words

1. enforce
2. continue
3. emotion
4. prefix
5. merchant
6. remarkable
7. natural
8. dangerous
9. potato
10. fashionable
11. excite
12. preserve
13. possible
14. terrible
15. proverb

Contrast Clues **Write the Spelling Word that means the opposite of the following words.**

9. not *to bore*, but to ______________
10. not *to destroy*, but to ______________
11. not a *suffix*, but a ______________
12. not *impossible*, but ______________
13. not *ordinary*, but ______________
14. not *wonderful*, but ______________
15. not *to stop*, but to ______________

Name ______________________

Proofreading and Writing

Proofreading Circle the six misspelled Spelling Words in this paragraph. Then write each word correctly.

Before we went on vacashion, I tried to imajine what animals we might see. First we saw a small bird who was a residunt of the rain forest. It lived in a vakant hollow tree trunk. We thought it might be sensative to noise, so we watched quietly. It was laffable how it tried to catch a fly.

1. ______________ 4. ______________
2. ______________ 5. ______________
3. ______________ 6. ______________

Spelling Words

1. imagine
2. vacation
3. resident
4. vacant
5. sensitive
6. laughable
7. consist
8. complete
9. enclose
10. concern
11. propose
12. regular
13. suitable
14. accident
15. condition

Half Notes Write Spelling Words to complete these notes.

What does a spider web ______________ of?

If I write down everything I see, my notes will be ______________.

Should it ______________ me that a snake is sleeping in my tent?

I ______________ that we wake at dawn each day.

At home my ______________ breakfast is cereal, but here I eat powdered eggs. Yuck!

A cold northern region is a ______________ habitat for a polar bear.

I can't follow the tracks because the ______________ of the footprints is poor.

I squashed a bug by ______________!

If I can ______________ these insects in a cage, I can study them.

Write Ideas On a separate sheet of paper, write about an animal you would like to study in the wild. Use the Spelling Review Words.

Student
Handbook

Contents

How to Study a Word

1. LOOK at the word.

- ► What does the word mean?
- ► What letters are in the word?
- ► Name and touch each letter.

2. SAY the word.

- ► Listen for the consonant sounds.
- ► Listen for the vowel sounds.

3. THINK about the word.

- ► How is each sound spelled?
- ► Close your eyes and picture the word.
- ► What familiar spelling patterns do you see?
- ► Did you see any prefixes, suffixes, or other word parts?

4. WRITE the word.

- ► Think about the sounds and the letters.
- ► Form the letters correctly.

5. CHECK the spelling.

- ► Did you spell the word the same way it is spelled in your word list?
- ► If you did not spell the word correctly, write the word again.

Words Often Misspelled

accept	buy	friend		
ache	by	goes		
again	calendar	going	ninth	tried
all right	cannot	grammar	often	tries
almost	can't	guard	once	truly
already	careful	guess	other	two
although	catch	guide	people	unknown
always	caught	half	principal	until
angel	chief	haven't	quiet	unusual
angle	children	hear	quit	wasn't
answer	choose	heard	quite	wear
argue	chose	heavy	really	weather
asked	color	height	receive	Wednesday
aunt	cough	here	rhythm	weird
author	cousin	hers	right	we'll
awful	decide	hole	Saturday	we're
babies	divide	hoping	stretch	weren't
been	does	hour	surely	we've
believe	don't	its	their	where
bother	early	it's	theirs	which
bought	enough	January	there	whole
break	every	let's	they're	witch
breakfast	exact	listen	they've	won't
breathe	except	loose	those	wouldn't
broken	excite	lose	though	write
brother	expect	minute	thought	writing
brought	February	muscle	through	written
bruise	finally	neighbor	tied	you're
build	forty	nickel	tired	yours
business	fourth	ninety	to	
busy	Friday	ninety-nine	too	

Take-Home Word List

Eye of the Storm

The /ā/, /ē/, and /ī/ Sounds
/ā/ → **male**, cl**ai**m, str**ay**
/ē/ → l**ea**f, fl**ee**t
/ī/ → str**i**k**e**, th**igh**, s**ig**n

Spelling Words

1. speech
2. claim
3. strike
4. stray
5. fade
6. sign
7. leaf
8. thigh
9. thief
10. height
11. mild
12. waist
13. sway
14. beast
15. stain
16. fleet
17. stride
18. praise
19. slight
20. niece

Challenge Words

1. campaign
2. describe
3. cease
4. sacrifice
5. plight

My Study List
Add your own spelling words on the back. →

Take-Home Word List

Nature's Fury Reading-Writing Workshop

Look for familiar spelling patterns in these words to help you remember their spellings.

Spelling Words

1. enough
2. caught
3. brought
4. thought
5. every
6. ninety
7. their
8. they're
9. there
10. there's
11. know
12. knew
13. o'clock
14. we're
15. people

Challenge Words

1. decent
2. stationery
3. stationary
4. correspond
5. reversible

My Study List
Add your own spelling words on the back. →

Take-Home Word List

Earthquake Terror

Short Vowels
/ă/ → staff
/ĕ/ → slept
/ĭ/ → mist
/ŏ/ → dock
/ŭ/ → bunk

Spelling Words

1. bunk
2. staff
3. dock
4. slept
5. mist
6. bunch
7. swift
8. stuck
9. breath
10. tough
11. fond
12. crush
13. grasp
14. dwell
15. fund
16. ditch
17. split
18. swept
19. deaf
20. rough

Challenge Words

1. trek
2. frantic
3. summit
4. rustic
5. mascot

My Study List
Add your own spelling words on the back. →

Take-Home Word List

Name ______________________

My Study List

1. ______________________
2. ______________________
3. ______________________
4. ______________________
5. ______________________
6. ______________________
7. ______________________
8. ______________________
9. ______________________
10. ______________________

Review Words

1. trunk
2. skill
3. track
4. fresh
5. odd

How to Study a Word

Look at the word.
Say the word.
Think about the word.
Write the word.
Check the spelling.

Take-Home Word List

Name ______________________

My Study List

1. ______________________
2. ______________________
3. ______________________
4. ______________________
5. ______________________
6. ______________________
7. ______________________
8. ______________________
9. ______________________
10. ______________________

How to Study a Word

Look at the word.
Say the word.
Think about the word.
Write the word.
Check the spelling.

Take-Home Word List

Name ______________________

My Study List

1. ______________________
2. ______________________
3. ______________________
4. ______________________
5. ______________________
6. ______________________
7. ______________________
8. ______________________
9. ______________________
10. ______________________

Review Words

1. free
2. twice
3. gray
4. least
5. safe

How to Study a Word

Look at the word.
Say the word.
Think about the word.
Write the word.
Check the spelling.

Take-Home Word List

Michelle Kwan: Heart of a Champion

Compound Words
wheel + chair = wheelchair
up + to + date = up-to-date
first + aid = first aid

Spelling Words

1. basketball
2. wheelchair
3. cheerleader
4. newscast
5. weekend
6. everybody
7. up-to-date
8. grandparent
9. first aid
10. wildlife
11. highway
12. daytime
13. whoever
14. test tube
15. turnpike
16. shipyard
17. homemade
18. household
19. salesperson
20. brother-in-law

Challenge Words

1. extraordinary
2. self-assured
3. quick-witted
4. limelight
5. junior high school

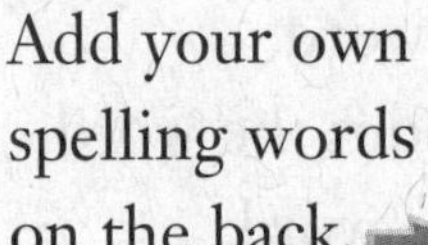

My Study List
Add your own spelling words on the back.

Take-Home Word List

Nature's Fury Spelling Review

Spelling Words

1. slept
2. split
3. staff
4. fade
5. praise
6. slope
7. claim
8. stroll
9. mood
10. beast
11. crush
12. fond
13. dwell
14. strike
15. clue
16. boast
17. flute
18. sway
19. cruise
20. mild
21. grasp
22. swift
23. bunk
24. slight
25. thrown
26. stole
27. fleet
28. dew
29. youth
30. thigh

See the back for Challenge Words.

My Study List
Add your own spelling words on the back.

Take-Home Word List

Volcanoes

The /ō/, /o͞o/, and /yo͞o/ Sounds
/ō/ → stole, boast, thrown, stroll
/o͞o/ or /yo͞o/ → rule, clue, dew, mood, cruise, route

Spelling Words

1. thrown
2. stole
3. clue
4. dew
5. choose
6. rule
7. boast
8. cruise
9. stroll
10. route
11. mood
12. loaf
13. growth
14. youth
15. slope
16. bruise
17. loose
18. rude
19. flow
20. flute

Challenge Words

1. subdue
2. pursuit
3. molten
4. reproach
5. presume

My Study List
Add your own spelling words on the back.

Take-Home Word List

Name ______________

My Study List

1. ______________
2. ______________
3. ______________
4. ______________
5. ______________
6. ______________
7. ______________
8. ______________
9. ______________
10. ______________

Review Words

1. group
2. goal
3. fruit
4. blew
5. broke

How to Study a Word

Look at the word.
Say the word.
Think about the word.
Write the word.
Check the spelling.

Take-Home Word List

Name ______________

My Study List

1. ______________
2. ______________
3. ______________
4. ______________
5. ______________
6. ______________
7. ______________
8. ______________
9. ______________
10. ______________

Challenge Words

1. frantic
2. trek
3. cease
4. molten
5. pursuit
6. rustic
7. describe
8. campaign
9. subdue
10. reproach

How to Study a Word

Look at the word.
Say the word.
Think about the word.
Write the word.
Check the spelling.

Take-Home Word List

Name ______________

My Study List

1. ______________
2. ______________
3. ______________
4. ______________
5. ______________
6. ______________
7. ______________
8. ______________
9. ______________
10. ______________

Review Words

1. afternoon
2. ninety-nine
3. everywhere
4. all right
5. breakfast

How to Study a Word

Look at the word.
Say the word.
Think about the word.
Write the word.
Check the spelling.

Take-Home Word List

The Fear Place

The /ôr/, /âr/, and /är/ Sounds
/ôr/ → torch, soar, sore
/âr/ → hare, flair
/är/ → scar

Spelling Words

1. hare
2. scar
3. torch
4. soar
5. harsh
6. sore
7. lord
8. flair
9. warn
10. floor
11. tore
12. lair
13. snare
14. carve
15. bore
16. fare
17. gorge
18. barge
19. flare
20. rare

Challenge Words

1. folklore
2. unicorn
3. ordinary
4. marvelous
5. hoard

My Study List
Add your own spelling words on the back. →

Take-Home Word List

La Bamba

The /ou/, /ô/, and /oi/ Sounds
/ou/ → ounce, tower
/ô/ → claw, pause, bald
/oi/ → moist, loyal

Spelling Words

1. hawk
2. claw
3. bald
4. tower
5. halt
6. prowl
7. loyal
8. pause
9. moist
10. ounce
11. launch
12. royal
13. scowl
14. haunt
15. noisy
16. coward
17. fawn
18. thousand
19. drown
20. fault

Challenge Words

1. announce
2. poise
3. loiter
4. somersault
5. awkward

My Study List
Add your own spelling words on the back. →

Take-Home Word List

Give It All You've Got! Reading-Writing Workshop

Look for familiar spelling patterns in these words to help you remember their spellings.

Spelling Words

1. would
2. wouldn't
3. clothes
4. happened
5. someone
6. sometimes
7. different
8. another
9. weird
10. eighth
11. coming
12. getting
13. going
14. stopped
15. here

Challenge Words

1. irresponsible
2. affectionate
3. brilliance
4. audible
5. menace

My Study List
Add your own spelling words on the back. →

Take-Home Word List

Name ____________

My Study List

1. ____________
2. ____________
3. ____________
4. ____________
5. ____________
6. ____________
7. ____________
8. ____________
9. ____________
10. ____________

How to Study a Word

Look at the word.
Say the word.
Think about the word.
Write the word.
Check the spelling.

Take-Home Word List

Name ____________

My Study List

1. ____________
2. ____________
3. ____________
4. ____________
5. ____________
6. ____________
7. ____________
8. ____________
9. ____________
10. ____________

Review Words

1. proud
2. dawn
3. false
4. cause
5. howl

How to Study a Word

Look at the word.
Say the word.
Think about the word.
Write the word.
Check the spelling.

Take-Home Word List

Name ____________

My Study List

1. ____________
2. ____________
3. ____________
4. ____________
5. ____________
6. ____________
7. ____________
8. ____________
9. ____________
10. ____________

Review Words

1. horse
2. sharp
3. square
4. stairs
5. board

How to Study a Word

Look at the word.
Say the word.
Think about the word.
Write the word.
Check the spelling.

Take-Home Word List

And Then What Happened, Paul Revere?

Final /ər/
/ər/ → anger, actor pillar

Spelling Words

1. theater
2. actor
3. mirror
4. powder
5. humor
6. anger
7. banner
8. pillar
9. major
10. thunder
11. flavor
12. finger
13. mayor
14. polar
15. clover
16. burglar
17. tractor
18. matter
19. lunar
20. quarter

Challenge Words

1. oyster
2. clamor
3. tremor
4. scholar
5. chamber

My Study List
Add your own spelling words on the back. →

Take-Home Word List

Give It All You've Got! Spelling Review

Spelling Words

1. weekend
2. hawk
3. flair
4. stir
5. first aid
6. halt
7. royal
8. carve
9. worth
10. hurl
11. up-to-date
12. noisy
13. soar
14. barge
15. steer
16. wildlife
17. coward
18. gorge
19. return
20. smear
21. brother-in-law
22. thousand
23. tore
24. early
25. pearl
26. test tube
27. launch
28. snare
29. perch
30. wheelchair

See the back for Challenge Words.

My Study List
Add your own spelling words on the back. →

Take-Home Word List

Mae Jemison

The /ûr/ and /îr/ Sounds
/ûr/ → germ, stir, return, early, worth
/îr/ → peer, smear

Spelling Words

1. smear
2. germ
3. return
4. peer
5. stir
6. squirm
7. nerve
8. early
9. worth
10. pier
11. thirst
12. burnt
13. rear
14. term
15. steer
16. pearl
17. squirt
18. perch
19. hurl
20. worse

Challenge Words

1. interpret
2. yearn
3. emergency
4. dreary
5. career

My Study List
Add your own spelling words on the back. →

Take-Home Word List

Name

My Study List

1.
2.
3.
4.
5.
6.
7.
8.
9.
10.

Review Words

1. learn
2. curve
3. world
4. firm
5. year

How to Study a Word

Look at the word.
Say the word.
Think about the word.
Write the word.
Check the spelling.

Take-Home Word List

Name

My Study List

1.
2.
3.
4.
5.
6.
7.
8.
9.
10.

Challenge Words

1. extra-ordinary
2. announce
3. loiter
4. marvelous
5. yearn
6. self-assured
7. somersault
8. ordinary
9. emergency
10. dreary

How to Study a Word

Look at the word.
Say the word.
Think about the word.
Write the word.
Check the spelling.

Take-Home Word List

Name

My Study List

1.
2.
3.
4.
5.
6.
7.
8.
9.
10.

Review Words

1. enter
2. honor
3. answer
4. collar
5. doctor

How to Study a Word

Look at the word.
Say the word.
Think about the word.
Write the word.
Check the spelling.

Take-Home Word List

James Forten

Final /l/ or /əl/

/l/ or /əl/ → sparkle, jewel, legal

Spelling Words

1. jewel
2. sparkle
3. angle
4. shovel
5. single
6. normal
7. angel
8. legal
9. whistle
10. fossil
11. puzzle
12. bushel
13. mortal
14. gentle
15. level
16. label
17. pedal
18. ankle
19. needle
20. devil

Challenge Words

1. mineral
2. influential
3. vital
4. neutral
5. kernel

My Study List
Add your own spelling words on the back. →

Take-Home Word List

Katie's Trunk

VCCV and VCV Patterns

VC|CV	VC|V	V|CV
ar|rive	val|ue	tu|lip
par|lor	clos|et	a|ware
		be|have

Spelling Words

1. equal
2. parlor
3. collect
4. closet
5. perhaps
6. wedding
7. rapid
8. value
9. arrive
10. behave
11. shoulder
12. novel
13. tulip
14. sorrow
15. vanish
16. essay
17. publish
18. aware
19. subject
20. prefer

Challenge Words

1. device
2. skittish
3. logic
4. sincere
5. nuisance

My Study List
Add your own spelling words on the back. →

Take-Home Word List

Voices of the Revolution Reading-Writing Workshop

Look for familiar spelling patterns in these words to help you remember their spellings.

Spelling Words

1. happily
2. minute
3. beautiful
4. usually
5. instead
6. stretch
7. lying
8. excite
9. millimeter
10. divide
11. until
12. writing
13. tried
14. before
15. Saturday

Challenge Words

1. fatigue
2. antique
3. accumulate
4. camouflage
5. tongue

My Study List
Add your own spelling words on the back. →

Take-Home Word List

Name ____________

My Study List

1. ____________
2. ____________
3. ____________
4. ____________
5. ____________
6. ____________
7. ____________
8. ____________
9. ____________
10. ____________

How to Study a Word

Look at the word.
Say the word.
Think about the word.
Write the word.
Check the spelling.

Take-Home Word List

Name ____________

My Study List

1. ____________
2. ____________
3. ____________
4. ____________
5. ____________
6. ____________
7. ____________
8. ____________
9. ____________
10. ____________

Review Words

1. person
2. mistake
3. human
4. bottom
5. stomach

How to Study a Word

Look at the word.
Say the word.
Think about the word.
Write the word.
Check the spelling.

Take-Home Word List

Name ____________

My Study List

1. ____________
2. ____________
3. ____________
4. ____________
5. ____________
6. ____________
7. ____________
8. ____________
9. ____________
10. ____________

Review Words

1. simple
2. special
3. metal
4. nickel
5. double

How to Study a Word

Look at the word.
Say the word.
Think about the word.
Write the word.
Check the spelling.

Take-Home Word List

Person to Person Reading-Writing Workshop

Look for familiar spelling patterns in these words to help you remember their spellings.

Spelling Words

1. a lot
2. because
3. school
4. its
5. it's
6. tonight
7. might
8. right
9. write
10. again
11. to
12. too
13. two
14. they
15. that's

Challenge Words

1. opposite
2. scenery
3. questionnaire
4. excellence
5. pennant

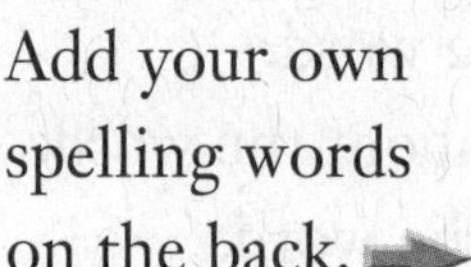

My Study List
Add your own spelling words on the back.

Take-Home Word List

Mariah Keeps Cool

VCCCV Pattern
VCC|CV: **laugh|ter**
VC|CCV: **com|plain**

Spelling Words

1. district
2. address
3. complain
4. explain
5. improve
6. farther
7. simply
8. hundred
9. although
10. laughter
11. mischief
12. complex
13. partner
14. orphan
15. constant
16. dolphin
17. employ
18. sandwich
19. monster
20. orchard

Challenge Words

1. control
2. abstain
3. conscience
4. function
5. extreme

My Study List
Add your own spelling words on the back.

Take-Home Word List

Voices of the Revolution Spelling Review

Spelling Words

1. powder
2. burglar
3. rapid
4. value
5. bushel
6. actor
7. equal
8. publish
9. tractor
10. pedal
11. polar
12. aware
13. matter
14. single
15. sparkle
16. humor
17. behave
18. quarter
19. whistle
20. needle
21. mayor
22. sorrow
23. parlor
24. mortal
25. gentle
26. lunar
27. shoulder
28. jewel
29. legal
30. wedding

See the back for Challenge Words.

My Study List
Add your own spelling words on the back.

Take-Home Word List

Name ______________

My Study List

1. ______________
2. ______________
3. ______________
4. ______________
5. ______________
6. ______________
7. ______________
8. ______________
9. ______________
10. ______________

Challenge Words

1. oyster
2. skittish
3. influential
4. kernel
5. clamor
6. device
7. mineral
8. vital
9. sincere
10. scholar

How to Study a Word

Look at the word.
Say the word.
Think about the word.
Write the word.
Check the spelling.

Take-Home Word List

Name ______________

My Study List

1. ______________
2. ______________
3. ______________
4. ______________
5. ______________
6. ______________
7. ______________
8. ______________
9. ______________
10. ______________

Review Words

1. empty
2. hungry
3. handsome
4. quickly
5. illness

How to Study a Word

Look at the word.
Say the word.
Think about the word.
Write the word.
Check the spelling.

Take-Home Word List

Name ______________

My Study List

1. ______________
2. ______________
3. ______________
4. ______________
5. ______________
6. ______________
7. ______________
8. ______________
9. ______________
10. ______________

How to Study a Word

Look at the word.
Say the word.
Think about the word.
Write the word.
Check the spelling.

Take-Home Word List

Dear Mr. Henshaw

Words with Suffixes

safe + ly = safe**ly**
pale + ness = pale**ness**
enjoy + ment = enjoy**ment**
cheer + ful = cheer**ful**
speech + less = speech**less**

Spelling Words

1. dreadful
2. enjoyment
3. safely
4. watchful
5. speechless
6. paleness
7. breathless
8. government
9. cheerful
10. actively
11. closeness
12. lately
13. goodness
14. retirement
15. forgetful
16. basement
17. softness
18. delightful
19. settlement
20. countless

Challenge Words

1. suspenseful
2. suspiciously
3. defenseless
4. seriousness
5. contentment

My Study List
Add your own spelling words on the back.

Take-Home Word List

Yang the Second and Her Secret Admirers

Words with *-ed* or *-ing*

deserve + ed = deserv**ed**
offer + ed = offer**ed**
rise + ing = ris**ing**
direct + ing = direct**ing**

Spelling Words

1. covered
2. directing
3. bragging
4. amusing
5. offered
6. planned
7. rising
8. deserved
9. visiting
10. mixed
11. swimming
12. sheltered
13. resulting
14. spotted
15. suffering
16. arrested
17. squeezing
18. ordered
19. decided
20. hitting

Challenge Words

1. rehearsing
2. shredded
3. anticipated
4. scalloped
5. entertaining

My Study List
Add your own spelling words on the back.

Take-Home Word List

Mom's Best Friend

VV Pattern

V | V
po | em
cre | ate

Spelling Words

1. poem
2. idea
3. create
4. diary
5. area
6. giant
7. usual
8. radio
9. cruel
10. quiet
11. diet
12. liar
13. fuel
14. riot
15. actual
16. lion
17. ruin
18. trial
19. rodeo
20. science

Challenge Words

1. appreciate
2. variety
3. enthusiastic
4. realize
5. eventually

My Study List
Add your own spelling words on the back.

Take-Home Word List

Name ______________

My Study List

1. ______________
2. ______________
3. ______________
4. ______________
5. ______________
6. ______________
7. ______________
8. ______________
9. ______________
10. ______________

Review Words

1. title
2. listen
3. wrote
4. finish
5. music

How to Study a Word

Look at the word.
Say the word.
Think about the word.
Write the word.
Check the spelling.

Take-Home Word List

Name ______________

My Study List

1. ______________
2. ______________
3. ______________
4. ______________
5. ______________
6. ______________
7. ______________
8. ______________
9. ______________
10. ______________

Review Words

1. dancing
2. flipped
3. dared
4. checking
5. rubbing

How to Study a Word

Look at the word.
Say the word.
Think about the word.
Write the word.
Check the spelling.

Take-Home Word List

Name ______________

My Study List

1. ______________
2. ______________
3. ______________
4. ______________
5. ______________
6. ______________
7. ______________
8. ______________
9. ______________
10. ______________

Review Words

1. fearful
2. movement
3. careless
4. lonely
5. powerful

How to Study a Word

Look at the word.
Say the word.
Think about the word.
Write the word.
Check the spelling.

Take-Home Word List

One Land, Many Trails Reading-Writing Workshop

Look for familiar spelling patterns in these words to help you remember their spellings.

Spelling Words

1. while
2. whole
3. anyway
4. anyone
5. anything
6. favorite
7. once
8. suppose
9. everybody
10. everyone
11. really
12. morning
13. also
14. always
15. first

Challenge Words

1. embarrass
2. recommend
3. confidence
4. regretted
5. laboratory

My Study List
Add your own spelling words on the back.

Take-Home Word List

A Boy Called Slow

Words with a Prefix or a Suffix

PREFIX + BASE WORD:
unable, **dis**cover

PREFIX + WORD ROOT:
inspect, **re**port

VERB + *-ion* = NOUN:
react, reac**tion**
promot**e**, promot**ion**
express, express**ion**

Spelling Words

1. unable
2. discover
3. report
4. disaster
5. unaware
6. remind
7. televise
8. television
9. inspect
10. inspection
11. react
12. reaction
13. tense
14. tension
15. correct
16. correction
17. promote
18. promotion
19. express
20. expression

Challenge Words

1. inquiry
2. unnecessary
3. responsible
4. except
5. exception

My Study List
Add your own spelling words on the back.

Take-Home Word List

Person to Person Spelling Review

Spelling Words

1. laughter
2. sandwich
3. mischief
4. actual
5. offered
6. watchful
7. cruel
8. planned
9. lately
10. countless
11. complain
12. address
13. usual
14. riot
15. amusing
16. ordered
17. diary
18. covered
19. visiting
20. govern-ment
21. improve
22. farther
23. radio
24. fuel
25. hitting
26. goodness
27. decided
28. actively
29. delightful
30. rodeo

See the back for Challenge Words.

My Study List
Add your own spelling words on the back.

Take-Home Word List

Name ______________

My Study List

1. ______________
2. ______________
3. ______________
4. ______________
5. ______________
6. ______________
7. ______________
8. ______________
9. ______________
10. ______________

Challenge Words

1. control
2. extreme
3. rehearsing
4. anticipated
5. defenseless
6. conscience
7. enthusiastic
8. suspenseful
9. entertaining
10. realize

How to Study a Word

Look at the word.
Say the word.
Think about the word.
Write the word.
Check the spelling.

Take-Home Word List

Name ______________

My Study List

1. ______________
2. ______________
3. ______________
4. ______________
5. ______________
6. ______________
7. ______________
8. ______________
9. ______________
10. ______________

Review Words

1. unsure
2. dislike
3. repaint
4. disorder
5. uneven

How to Study a Word

Look at the word.
Say the word.
Think about the word.
Write the word.
Check the spelling.

Take-Home Word List

Name ______________

My Study List

1. ______________
2. ______________
3. ______________
4. ______________
5. ______________
6. ______________
7. ______________
8. ______________
9. ______________
10. ______________

How to Study a Word

Look at the word.
Say the word.
Think about the word.
Write the word.
Check the spelling.

Take-Home Word List

Elena

Changing Final *y* to *i*

army + es = arm**ies**
dirty + er = dirt**ier**
scary + est = scar**iest**
happy + ness = happ**iness**

Spelling Words

1. liberties
2. victories
3. countries
4. spied
5. enemies
6. armies
7. scariest
8. dirtier
9. happiness
10. abilities
11. pitied
12. ladies
13. busier
14. duties
15. lilies
16. worthiness
17. tiniest
18. emptiness
19. replies
20. dizziness

Challenge Words

1. unified
2. levied
3. colonies
4. loveliest
5. strategies

My Study List
Add your own spelling words on the back.

Take-Home Word List

Black Cowboy, Wild Horses

Final /n/ or /ən/, /chər/, /zhər/

/n/ or /ən/ → capt**ain**
/chər/ → cul**ture**
/zhər/ → trea**sure**

Spelling Words

1. mountain
2. treasure
3. culture
4. fountain
5. creature
6. captain
7. future
8. adventure
9. moisture
10. surgeon
11. lecture
12. curtain
13. pasture
14. measure
15. vulture
16. feature
17. furniture
18. pleasure
19. mixture
20. luncheon

Challenge Words

1. departure
2. leisure
3. architecture
4. texture
5. villain

My Study List
Add your own spelling words on the back.

Take-Home Word List

Pioneer Girl

Unstressed Syllables

voy | age /**voi**ʹ ĭj/
na | tive /**nā**ʹ tĭv/
no | tice /**nō**ʹ tĭs/
dis | tance /**dĭs**ʹ təns/
for | bid /fər **bĭd**ʹ/
de | stroy /dĭ **stroi**ʹ/

Spelling Words

1. dozen
2. voyage
3. forbid
4. native
5. language
6. destroy
7. notice
8. distance
9. carrot
10. knowledge
11. captive
12. spinach
13. solid
14. justice
15. ashamed
16. program
17. message
18. respond
19. service
20. relative

Challenge Words

1. adapt
2. discourage
3. cooperative
4. apprentice
5. somber

My Study List
Add your own spelling words on the back.

Take-Home Word List

Name ____________

My Study List

1. ____________
2. ____________
3. ____________
4. ____________
5. ____________
6. ____________
7. ____________
8. ____________
9. ____________
10. ____________

Review Words

1. marriage
2. harvest
3. allow
4. package
5. middle

How to Study a Word

Look at the word.
Say the word.
Think about the word.
Write the word.
Check the spelling.

Take-Home Word List

Name ____________

My Study List

1. ____________
2. ____________
3. ____________
4. ____________
5. ____________
6. ____________
7. ____________
8. ____________
9. ____________
10. ____________

Review Words

1. nature
2. picture
3. capture
4. certain

How to Study a Word

Look at the word.
Say the word.
Think about the word.
Write the word.
Check the spelling.

Take-Home Word List

Name ____________

My Study List

1. ____________
2. ____________
3. ____________
4. ____________
5. ____________
6. ____________
7. ____________
8. ____________
9. ____________
10. ____________

Review Words

1. cities
2. easier
3. families
4. studied
5. angriest

How to Study a Word

Look at the word.
Say the word.
Think about the word.
Write the word.
Check the spelling.

Take-Home Word List

Animal Encounters Reading-Writing Workshop

Look for familiar spelling patterns in these words to help you remember their spellings.

Spelling Words

1. heard
2. your
3. you're
4. field
5. buy
6. friend
7. guess
8. cousin
9. build
10. family
11. can't
12. cannot
13. didn't
14. haven't
15. don't

Challenge Words

1. truly
2. benefited
3. height
4. believe
5. received

My Study List
Add your own spelling words on the back.

Take-Home Word List

Grizzly Bear Family Book

More Words with Prefixes

compare	**con**vince
excite	**en**force
preserve	**pro**pose

Spelling Words

1. propose
2. convince
3. concern
4. enforce
5. compare
6. excuse
7. conduct
8. preserve
9. contain
10. excite
11. extend
12. prefix
13. engage
14. pronoun
15. consist
16. enclose
17. consent
18. proverb
19. complete
20. exchange

Challenge Words

1. enactment
2. procedure
3. confront
4. preamble
5. concise

My Study List
Add your own spelling words on the back.

Take-Home Word List

One Land, Many Trails Spelling Review

Spelling Words

1. unable
2. correction
3. native
4. distance
5. spinach
6. vulture
7. curtain
8. dirtier
9. spied
10. treasure
11. discover
12. inspect
13. tension
14. language
15. respond
16. voyage
17. pleasure
18. countries
19. happiness
20. furniture
21. promotion
22. react
23. solid
24. notice
25. destroy
26. mountain
27. adventure
28. busier
29. pitied
30. scariest

See the back for Challenge Words.

My Study List
Add your own spelling words on the back.

Take-Home Word List

Name ______________

My Study List

1. ______________
2. ______________
3. ______________
4. ______________
5. ______________
6. ______________
7. ______________
8. ______________
9. ______________
10. ______________

Challenge Words

1. except
2. apprentice
3. loveliest
4. strategies
5. inquiry
6. architecture
7. colonies
8. unified
9. villain
10. discourage

How to Study a Word

Look at the word.
Say the word.
Think about the word.
Write the word.
Check the spelling.

Take-Home Word List

Name ______________

My Study List

1. ______________
2. ______________
3. ______________
4. ______________
5. ______________
6. ______________
7. ______________
8. ______________
9. ______________
10. ______________

Review Words

1. compose
2. exact
3. enjoy
4. common
5. expert

How to Study a Word

Look at the word.
Say the word.
Think about the word.
Write the word.
Check the spelling.

Take-Home Word List

Name ______________

My Study List

1. ______________
2. ______________
3. ______________
4. ______________
5. ______________
6. ______________
7. ______________
8. ______________
9. ______________
10. ______________

How to Study a Word

Look at the word.
Say the word.
Think about the word.
Write the word.
Check the spelling.

Take-Home Word List

Animal Encounters Spelling Review

Spelling Words

1. excite
2. concern
3. imagine
4. continue
5. enforce
6. propose
7. condition
8. resident
9. possible
10. fashionable
11. consist
12. prefix
13. sensitive
14. suitable
15. vacant
16. preserve
17. dangerous
18. vacation
19. terrible
20. accident
21. complete
22. regular
23. potato
24. laughable
25. remarkable
26. proverb
27. natural
28. emotion
29. merchant
30. enclose

See the back for Challenge Words.

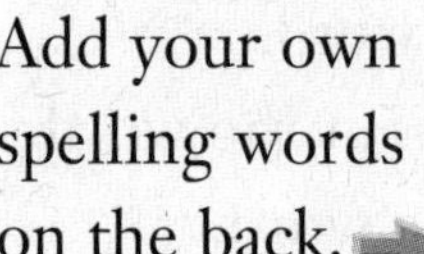

My Study List
Add your own spelling words on the back.

Take-Home Word List

My Side of the Mountain

Words with *-ent, -ant; -able, -ible*

/ənt/ → stud**ent**, merch**ant**
/ə bəl/ → suit**able**, poss**ible**

Spelling Words

1. fashionable
2. comfortable
3. different
4. suitable
5. merchant
6. profitable
7. student
8. possible
9. resident
10. terrible
11. absent
12. vacant
13. servant
14. valuable
15. accident
16. horrible
17. honorable
18. reasonable
19. remarkable
20. laughable

Challenge Words

1. excellent
2. prominent
3. extravagant
4. durable
5. reversible

My Study List
Add your own spelling words on the back.

Take-Home Word List

The Golden Lion Tamarin Comes Home

Three-Syllable Words

va | ca | tion → /vā **kā′** shən/
ed | u | cate → /**ĕj′** ə kāt′/
dan | ger | ous → /**dān′** jər əs/
e | mo | tion → /ĭ **mō′** shən/

Spelling Words

1. dangerous
2. history
3. vacation
4. popular
5. favorite
6. memory
7. personal
8. educate
9. regular
10. continue
11. potato
12. natural
13. sensitive
14. energy
15. emotion
16. period
17. property
18. condition
19. imagine
20. attention

Challenge Words

1. juvenile
2. astonish
3. ovation
4. amateur
5. obvious

My Study List
Add your own spelling words on the back.

Take-Home Word List

Name ______

My Study List

1. ______
2. ______
3. ______
4. ______
5. ______
6. ______
7. ______
8. ______
9. ______
10. ______

Review Words

1. together
2. beautiful
3. library
4. hospital
5. another

How to Study a Word

Look at the word.
Say the word.
Think about the word.
Write the word.
Check the spelling.

Take-Home Word List

Name ______

My Study List

1. ______
2. ______
3. ______
4. ______
5. ______
6. ______
7. ______
8. ______
9. ______
10. ______

Review Words

1. current
2. important
3. moment
4. silent
5. parent

How to Study a Word

Look at the word.
Say the word.
Think about the word.
Write the word.
Check the spelling.

Take-Home Word List

Name ______

My Study List

1. ______
2. ______
3. ______
4. ______
5. ______
6. ______
7. ______
8. ______
9. ______
10. ______

Challenge Words

1. confront
2. preamble
3. astonish
4. excellent
5. reversible
6. enactment
7. juvenile
8. amateur
9. extravagant
10. durable

How to Study a Word

Look at the word.
Say the word.
Think about the word.
Write the word.
Check the spelling.

Problem Words

Words	Rules	Examples
bad badly	*Bad* is an adjective. It can be used after linking verbs like *look* and *feel.* *Badly* is an adverb.	This was a bad day. I feel bad. I play badly.
borrow lend	*Borrow* means "to take." *Lend* means "to give."	You may borrow my pen. I will lend it to you for the day.
can may	*Can* means "to be able to do something." *May* means "to be allowed or permitted."	Nellie can read quickly. May I borrow your book?
good well	*Good* is an adjective. *Well* is usually an adverb. It is an adjective only when it refers to health.	The weather looks good. She sings well. Do you feel well?
in into	*In* means "located within." *Into* means "movement from the outside to the inside."	Your lunch is in that bag. He jumped into the pool.
its it's	*Its* is a possessive pronoun. *It's* is a contraction of *it is.*	The dog wagged its tail. It's cold today.
let leave	*Let* means "to permit or allow." *Leave* means "to go away from" or "to let remain in place."	Please let me go swimming. I will leave soon. Leave it on my desk.
lie lay	*Lie* means "to rest or recline." *Lay* means "to put or place something."	The dog lies in its bed. Please lay the books there.

Problem Words continued

Words	Rules	Examples
sit set	*Sit* means "to rest in one place." *Set* means "to place or put."	Please sit in this chair. Set the vase on the table.
teach learn	*Teach* means "to give instruction." *Learn* means "to receive instruction."	He teaches us how to dance. I learned about history.
their there they're	*Their* is a possessive pronoun. *There* is an adverb. It may also begin a sentence. *They're* is a contraction of *they are.*	Their coats are on the bed. Is Carlos there? There is my book. They're going to the store.
two to too	*Two* is a number. *To* means "in the direction of." *Too* means "more than enough" and "also."	I bought two shirts. A squirrel ran to the tree. May we go too?
whose who's	*Whose* is a possessive pronoun. *Who's* is a contraction for *who is.*	Whose tickets are these? Who's that woman?
your you're	*Your* is a possessive pronoun. *You're* is a contraction for *you are.*	Are these your glasses? You're late again!

Proofreading Checklist

Read each question below. Then check your paper. Correct any mistakes you find. After you have corrected them, put a check mark in the box next to the question.

- ☐ 1. Did I spell all the words correctly?
- ☐ 2. Did I indent each paragraph?
- ☐ 3. Does each sentence state a complete thought?
- ☐ 4. Are there any run-on sentences or fragments?
- ☐ 5. Did I begin each sentence with a capital letter?
- ☐ 6. Did I capitalize all proper nouns?
- ☐ 7. Did I end each sentence with the correct end mark?
- ☐ 8. Did I use commas, apostrophes, and quotation marks correctly?

Are there other problem areas you should watch for? Make your own proofreading checklist.

- ☐ ______________________________
- ☐ ______________________________
- ☐ ______________________________
- ☐ ______________________________
- ☐ ______________________________
- ☐ ______________________________
- ☐ ______________________________

Proofreading Marks

Mark	Explanation	Examples
¶	Begin a new paragraph. Indent the paragraph.	¶The space shuttle landed safely after its five-day voyage. It glided to a smooth, perfect halt.
^	Add letters, words, or sentences.	My ^best friend eats lunch with me ev^ery day.
^,	Add a comma.	Carlton^, my Siamese cat^, has a mind of his own.
“ ”	Add quotation marks.	“Where do you want us to put the piano?” asked the gasping movers.
⊙	Add a period.	Don't forget to put a period at the end of every statement⊙
ℓ	Take out words, sentences, and punctuation marks. Correct spelling.	We ~~looked at and~~ admired the model air~~a~~planes.
/	Change a capital letter to a small letter.	We are studying about the Louisiana Purchase in History class.
≡	Change a small letter to a capital letter.	The Nile river in africa is the longest river in the world.
∽	Reverse letters or words.	To complete the task successfully, you must follow carefully the steps.

Writing Conference

In a writing conference, a writer reads a draft to a partner or a small group. The listeners tell what they like, ask questions, and make suggestions.

When you're the listener...

► Listen carefully as the writer reads. Don't let your thoughts wander.

► Say two things you like about the paper.

► Ask questions about anything you didn't understand.

► Share any ideas you have that might make the paper clearer or more interesting.

► Express your suggestions in a positive way so that you don't discourage the writer.

When you're the writer...

► Read your paper aloud, slowly and clearly.

► Listen carefully to your partner's comments and suggestions. Keep an open mind.

► Take notes to remember any compliments, questions, or suggestions.

► Afterwards, reread your paper and your notes.

► Decide what changes you want to make in your paper.

Guidelines for Writing an Article

- Write about an interesting or unusual event.
- Write facts, not opinions.
- Use the facts to answer the questions *Who? What? When? Where? Why? How?*
- Write the most important facts at the beginning of the article.
- Write your beginning in a way that captures the reader's attention.
- Use details to help explain or clarify the facts.
- Use quotations to make the article come alive. Make sure the quotations are exactly what people said.

Writing Traits Rubric
Article

Use this rubric to evaluate your draft. Circle a number to rate your writing, trait by trait. Then revise to improve your score.

Writing Traits	Score 4	Score 3	Score 2	Score 1
✔ **Ideas** Does my article answer these questions: *Who? What? When? Where? Why?* and *How?*	**4** My article answers all of these questions.	**3** My article answers most of these questions.	**2** My article answers some of these questions.	**1** My article answers one of these questions.
✔ **Organization** Did I begin the article with the most important facts?	**4** I began with all of the most important facts.	**3** I began with some of the most important facts.	**2** I began with one important fact and some less important ones.	**1** I did not begin with any of the most important facts.
✔ **Sentence Fluency** Did I often combine sentences to make my writing flow smoothly?	**4** I often combined sentences to make my writing flow smoothly.	**3** I sometimes combined sentences to make my writing flow smoothly.	**2** I once combined sentences to make my writing flow smoothly.	**1** I did not combined sentences to make my writing flow smoothly.
✔ **Word Choice** Did I add details that clearly and accurately explain the facts?	**4** I added many clear, accurate details.	**3** I added some clear, accurate details.	**2** I added some details, but not all were clear or accurate.	**1** I did not add details to explain the facts.
✔ **Voice** Did I avoid stating personal opinions in the article?	**4** I did not include my personal opinions at all.	**3** I included my personal opinion once.	**2** I included my personal opinions a few times.	**1** I included my personal opinions throughout the article.
✔ **Conventions** Did I use correct spelling, grammar, and punctuation?	**4** There are no errors.	**3** There are few errors.	**2** There are some errors.	**1** There are many errors.

Guidelines for Writing on Demand

- Read the prompt, or question, carefully.
- Look for key words, or clues, in the prompt that tell you what to focus on. Are you summarizing or expressing an opinion? Are you writing about a character?
- Be aware of how much time you have to answer the prompt. Divide the time: time to think about and organize your response quickly, and time to write and edit your work.
- Before you write, think back to the passage or reread it with the question in mind.
- Make notes in an organized way. Draw a chart if you need to.
- Look at your notes. Which details or thoughts are most important? Be sure to include those first.
- Begin your answer or response by restating the question.
- As you write, use clear, exact language. Stay on the topic.
- When you finish, look back over your work and correct an mistakes.

Writing Traits Rubric
Response to Literature

Use this rubric to evaluate your draft. Circle a number to rate your writing, trait by trait. Then revise to improve your score.

Writing Traits	Score 4	Score 3	Score 2	Score 1
✔ **Ideas** Did I answer all parts of the prompt?	4 I answered all parts of the prompt.	3 I answered some parts of the prompt.	2 I answered one part of the prompt.	1 I did not answer any part of the prompt.
✔ **Organization** Did I put each main idea in a separate paragraph?	4 I put all main ideas in separate paragraphs.	3 I put most main ideas in separate paragraphs.	2 I put few main ideas in separate paragraphs.	1 I put all main ideas in one paragraph.
✔ **Sentence Fluency** Did I avoid writing run-on sentences?	4 There are no run-on sentences in my writing.	3 There are few run-on sentences in my writing.	2 There are some run-on sentences in my writing.	1 There are many run-on sentences in my writing.
✔ **Word Choice** Did I use key words from the prompt?	4 I used all of the key words from the prompt.	3 I used some of the key words from the prompt.	2 I used one of the key words from the prompt.	1 I did not use any key words from the prompt.
✔ **Voice** Is my response clear and informative?	4 All of my response is clear and informative.	3 Most of my response is clear and informative.	2 Some of my response is clear and informative.	1 None of my response is clear and informative.
✔ **Conventions** Did I use correct spelling, grammar, and punctuation?	4 There are no errors.	3 There are few errors.	2 There are some errors.	1 There are many errors.

Name ______________________________

Response to Literature

Prompt: The following article is about the dangers of lightning. What advice would you give for staying safe during a thunderstorm? Explain what to do and what not to do, using details from the article.

Danger — Lightning!

It's a warm summer afternoon. Over a lake, dark clouds slowly cover the sky. After a rumble of thunder, the lifeguard whistles all the swimmers in. The danger isn't rain; it's lightning.

Every year, about a thousand people in the United States are struck by lightning. Between the clouds and the ground, a negative and positive charge meet, creating a spark hotter than the surface of the sun! Often the charge from above is attracted to a tall structure, like a telephone pole or a tall tree.

Being outside anywhere is dangerous during a thunderstorm. Even blades of grass can attract the charge from the sky. Water attracts electricity especially well. The current zips over the surface of water in all directions. If you can't avoid being out on land, it is safer to drop to the ground in a crouch than it is to lie down flat.

Being inside an enclosed car or a large building offers much better protection, but there are still risks indoors. Using a telephone, electronic devices (TV, computer, CD player), or appliances can be dangerous—or running water!

Guidelines for Writing a Report

- Select an interesting topic that you know something about.
- Include a topic sentence that tells what the paragraph is about. The topic sentence is usually the first sentence in the paragraph.
- Include several supporting sentences that give more information about the topic. Make sure your sentences are in a logical order.
- Leave out any sentences that don't give more information about your topic.
- Include facts only—don't include your opinions.
- Remember to indent the first sentence of each paragraph.
- Conclude with a sentence that restates the topic.

Writing Traits Rubric Report

Use this rubric to evaluate your draft. Circle a number to rate your writing, trait by trait. Then revise to improve your score.

Writing Traits	Score 4	Score 3	Score 2	Score 1
✔ **Ideas** Does my first paragraph introduce the topic in an interesting way?	**4** My first paragraph introduces the topic in an interesting way.	**3** My first paragraph introduces the topic in a somewhat interesting way.	**2** My first paragraph introduces the topic in an uninteresting way.	**1** My first paragraph does not introduce the topic at all.
✔ **Organization** Did I write at least one paragraph for each main idea?	**4** All of my main ideas have at least one paragraph.	**3** Most of my main ideas have at least one paragraph.	**2** Some of my main ideas have at least one paragraph.	**1** None of my main ideas has at least one paragraph.
✔ **Sentence Fluency** Did I avoid sentence fragments in my report?	**4** My report has no sentence fragments.	**3** My report has one sentence fragment.	**2** My report has some sentence fragments.	**1** My report has many sentence fragments.
✔ **Word Choice** Did I use my own words in my report?	**4** All of the words in my report are my own.	**3** Most of the words in my report are my own.	**2** Some of the words in my report are my own.	**1** Few or none of the words in my report are my own.
✔ **Voice** Did I keep my personal opinions out of the report?	**4** I did not include my personal opinions at all.	**3** I included my personal opinion once.	**2** I included my personal opinions a few times.	**1** I included my personal opinions throughout the article.
✔ **Conventions** Did I use correct spelling, grammar, and punctuation?	**4** There are no errors.	**3** There are few errors.	**2** There are some errors.	**1** There are many errors.

Guidelines for Writing an Autobiography

- Choose a time period. Will your episode be about one event in your life or a longer period of time?
- Choose your topic and purpose. What is the most important idea or message you want to convey to your audience?
- Decide how to describe the setting and the important people involved.
- Select details to include that clearly explain what happened and how you felt about the events.
- Write in the first person, using *I* and *me*.
- Write about real events in your life in the order they happened.
- Share your thoughts and feelings, in your own voice, about this part of your life.

Writing Traits Rubric Autobiography

Use this rubric to evaluate your draft. Circle a number to rate your writing, trait by trait. Then revise to improve your score.

Writing Traits	Score 4	Score 3	Score 2	Score 1
✔ **Ideas** Did I include important details of events as well as my thoughts and feelings about those events?	4 I included many important details of events as well as my thoughts and feelings about those events.	3 I included many important details of events but not my thoughts and feelings about those events.	2 I included a few important details of events but not my thoughts and feelings about those events.	1 I did not include important details of events or thoughts and feelings about those events.
✔ **Organization** Did I put the events in chronological order?	4 I put all events in chronological order.	3 I put most events in chronological order.	2 I put some events in chronological order.	1 I did not put events in chronological order.
✔ **Sentence Fluency** Did I vary my sentence types and lengths?	4 There is excellent variety in my sentence types and lengths.	3 There is good variety in my sentence types and lengths.	2 There is little variety in my sentence types and lengths.	1 There is no variety in my sentence types and lengths.
✔ **Word Choice** Did I use transition words to show chronological order?	4 I included many transition words.	3 I included some transition words.	2 I included one transition word.	1 I did not include any transition words.
✔ **Voice** Did I write in the first person?	4 I wrote in the first person most of the time.	3 I wrote in the first person some of the time.	2 I wrote in the first person a few times.	1 I did not write in the first person.
✔ **Conventions** Did I use correct spelling, grammar, and punctuation?	4 There are no errors.	3 There are few errors.	2 There are some errors.	1 There are many errors.

Guidelines for Writing a Summary

- Briefly describe the setting and the important characters.
- Retell the key events of the plot, including the problem and the solution, in sequence.
- Include only events or ideas that are important to understanding the story.
- Leave out the unimportant details and minor events or characters.
- Use your own words.
- Make your summary brief.

Writing Traits Rubric Writing a Summary

Use this rubric to evaluate your draft. Circle a number to rate your writing, trait by trait. Then revise to improve your score.

Writing Traits	Score 4	Score 3	Score 2	Score 1
✔ **Ideas** Did I include the important story events and characters?	4 I included all the important story events and characters.	3 I included most of the important story events and characters.	2 I included some important and some unimportant story events and characters.	1 I included few important and many unimportant story events and characters.
✔ **Organization** Did I keep the order of events the same as in the story?	4 I put all events in the same order as in the story.	3 I put many events in the same order as in the story.	2 I put a few events in the same order as in the story.	1 I put no events in the same order as in the story.
✔ **Sentence Fluency** Did I avoid sentence fragments when I paraphrased?	4 My writing contains no sentence fragments.	3 My writing contains one sentence fragment.	2 My writing contains few sentence fragments.	1 My writing contains many sentence fragments.
✔ **Word Choice** Did I use synonyms when I paraphrased?	4 I used many synonyms while paraphrasing.	3 I used some synonyms while paraphrasing.	2 I used few synonyms while paraphrasing.	1 I used no synonyms while paraphrasing.
✔ **Voice** Did I restate the author's ideas in my own words?	4 Every sentence is in my own words.	3 Almost every sentence is in my own words.	2 I copied a few sentences.	1 I copied many sentences.
✔ **Conventions** Did I use correct spelling, grammar, and punctuation?	4 There are no errors.	3 There are few errors.	2 There are some errors.	1 There are many errors.

Guidelines for Writing a Clarification Composition

- Include the quotation you will clarify in the first paragraph. Also tell the source of the quotation—who said or wrote it.
- Write your interpretation of the quotation. Restate it in your own words, telling what you think the quotation means.
- In the paragraph or paragraphs that follow, write supporting examples and details. Clearly explain your interpretation of the quotation.
- In the final paragraph, write a concluding statement that summarizes your interpretation.
- Write three to five paragraphs in all.

Writing Traits Rubric Clarification Composition

Use this rubric to evaluate your draft. Circle a number to rate your writing, trait by trait. Then revise to improve your score.

Writing Traits	Score 4	Score 3	Score 2	Score 1
✔ **Ideas** How well did I support my interpretation with details and examples?	**4** I included many details and examples that support my interpretation.	**3** I included some details and examples that support my interpretation.	**2** I included few details and examples that support my interpretation.	**1** I included no details and examples that support my interpretation.
✔ **Organization** Did I include an interpretation, supporting details, and a summary?	**4** I included an interpretation, many supporting details, and a summary.	**3** I included an interpretation, some supporting details, and a summary.	**2** I included an interpretation and a few supporting details.	**1** I included only an interpretation.
✔ **Sentence Fluency** Did I combine sentences to make my writing flow smoothly?	**4** I combined many sentences to make my writing flow smoothly.	**3** I combined some sentences to make my writing flow smoothly.	**2** I combined few sentences to make my writing flow smoothly.	**1** I did not combine sentences and my writing does not flow smoothly.
✔ **Word Choice** Did I use exact nouns and verbs?	**4** I used plenty of exact nouns and verbs.	**3** I used some exact nouns and verbs.	**2** I used few exact nouns and verbs.	**1** I did not use exact nouns and verbs.
✔ **Voice** Did I show my interest in the topic?	**4** My interest in the topic is clear.	**3** My interest in the topic is mostly clear.	**2** My interest in the topic is somewhat clear.	**1** My interest in the topic is not clear.
✔ **Conventions** Did I use correct spelling, grammar, and punctuation?	**4** There are no errors.	**3** There are few errors.	**2** There are some errors.	**1** There are many errors.

Guidelines for Writing a Persuasive Business Letter

- Include a heading that gives your address and the date.
- Include an inside address. This should show the name and address of the business or organization that is to receive the letter. It can also give the name and title of a specific person.
- Include a greeting, followed by a title of respect, such as *Ms.* or *Mr.*, and a last name. If you do not know whose name to write, use *Dear Sir or Madam.* Add a colon after the greeting.
- Write the body of the letter. State your purpose, or goal, for writing. Then provide specific examples or reasons that explain why you think or believe as you do. Address any concerns the reader might have.
- In writing the body of the letter, come right to the point. Present all necessary details clearly and briefly. Use a formal, polite tone.
- Restate your purpose for writing in the closing paragraph.
- Include a closing to finish the letter. Write a polite expression such as *Cordially*, *Sincerely*, or *Yours truly.* Add a comma after the closing.
- Sign your first and last name. Type your full name below your signature.

Writing Traits Rubric
Persuasive Business Letter

Use this rubric to evaluate your draft. Circle a number to rate your writing, trait by trait. Then revise to improve your score.

Writing Traits	Score 4	Score 3	Score 2	Score 1
✔ **Ideas** Do my reasons support the persuasive purpose of my letter?	**4** All of my reasons support my purpose.	**3** Most of my reasons support my purpose.	**2** Few of my reasons support my purpose.	**1** None of my reasons support my purpose.
✔ **Organization** Did I include all six parts of a business letter?	**4** I included all of the parts of a business letter.	**3** I included most of the parts of a business letter.	**2** I included some of the parts of a business letter.	**1** I included none of the parts of a business letter.
✔ **Sentence Fluency** Did I vary my sentence types and lengths?	**4** There is excellent variety in my sentence types and lengths.	**3** There is good variety in my sentence types and lengths.	**2** There is little variety in my sentence types and lengths.	**1** There is no variety in my sentence types and lengths.
✔ **Word Choice** Did I use exact nouns?	**4** I used plenty of exact nouns.	**3** I used some exact nouns.	**2** I used few exact nouns.	**1** I used no exact nouns.
✔ **Voice** Did I express myself in a polite, formal tone?	**4** My entire letter has a polite, formal tone.	**3** Most of my letter has a polite, formal tone.	**2** Some of my letter has a polite, formal tone.	**1** My letter does not have a polite, formal tone.
✔ **Conventions** Did I use correct spelling, grammar, and punctuation?	**4** There are no errors.	**3** There are few errors.	**2** There are some errors.	**1** There are many errors.

Guidelines for Writing a Description of a Character

- Write about a person in history or a story character who interests you.
- Begin with a quotation about the character or an example of something that he or she does.
- In the first paragraph, write a sentence of two that sums up the character's most important traits.
- In the paragraphs that follow, include details that support your summary of the character's traits.
- Include details about the character's appearance, if you know what the person looked or looks like.
- Include interesting details about what the character does.
- Include details about what he or she thinks.
- End with a conclusion that tells what you think of the character or something that you especially want the reader to remember about the character.

Writing Traits Rubric Description

Use this rubric to evaluate your draft. Circle a number to rate your writing, trait by trait. Then revise to improve your score.

Writing Traits	Score 4	Score 3	Score 2	Score 1
✔ **Ideas** Did I include details about the character's traits, actions, and thoughts?	**4** I wrote plenty of details about the character's traits, actions, and thoughts.	**3** I wrote some details about the character's traits, actions, and thoughts.	**2** I wrote few details about the character's traits, actions, and thoughts.	**1** I wrote no details about the character's traits, actions, and thoughts.
✔ **Organization** Did I sum up the character's traits first and then support this with details?	**4** I summed up the character's traits first and then supported this with details.	**3** I provided details and then summed up the character's traits.	**2** I summed up the character's traits but provided few details.	**1** I didn't sum up the character's traits and I provided few details.
✔ **Sentence Fluency** Did I combine sentences for better flow?	**4** All my sentences flow smoothly.	**3** Most of my sentences flow smoothly.	**2** Some of my sentences flow smoothly.	**1** Few of my sentences flow smoothly.
✔ **Word Choice** Did I use exact nouns and verbs to describe my character?	**4** I used plenty of exact nouns and verbs to describe my character.	**3** I used some exact nouns and verbs to describe my character.	**2** I used few exact nouns and verbs to describe my character.	**1** I used no exact nouns and verbs to describe my character.
✔ **Voice** Did I reveal my feelings about my character?	**4** Many details reveal my feelings about my character.	**3** Some details reveal my feelings about my character.	**2** Few details reveal my feelings about my character.	**1** No details reveal my feelings about my character.
✔ **Conventions** Did I use correct spelling, grammar, and punctuation?	**4** There are no errors.	**3** There are few errors.	**2** There are some errors.	**1** There are many errors.

Guidelines for Writing a Friendly Letter

- Include the five parts of a letter: a heading, a greeting, a body, a closing, and a signature.
- Use a friendly tone and informal language. Write as if you were talking to the person.
- Tell events or other information. Keep to the point.
- Include exact words that will interest your reader.
- End with a question or comment that encourages your reader to write back soon.

Writing Traits Rubric
Friendly Letter

Use this rubric to evaluate your draft. Circle a number to rate your writing, trait by trait. Then revise to improve your score.

Writing Traits	Score 4	Score 3	Score 2	Score 1
✔ **Ideas** Do all of the details in my letter fit my purpose?	4 All of my details fit my purpose.	3 Most of my details fit my purpose.	2 Few of my details fit my purpose.	1 None of my details fits my purpose.
✔ **Organization** Did I use the correct format for a friendly letter?	4 I included all of the parts of a friendly letter.	3 I included most of the parts of a friendly letter.	2 I included some of the parts of a friendly letter.	1 I included none of the parts of a friendly letter.
✔ **Sentence Fluency** Did I vary my sentence types and lengths?	4 There is excellent variety in my sentence types and lengths.	3 There is good variety in my sentence types and lengths.	2 There is little variety in my sentence types and lengths.	1 There is no variety in my sentence types and lengths.
✔ **Word Choice** Did I use informal words and expressions?	4 I used plenty of informal words and expressions.	3 I used some informal words and expressions.	2 I used few informal words and expressions.	1 I used no informal words or expressions.
✔ **Voice** Do my feelings and personality come through?	4 My feelings and personality come through very well.	3 My feelings and personality come through well.	2 My feelings and personality come through somewhat.	1 My feelings and personality do not come through.
✔ **Conventions** Did I use correct spelling, grammar, and punctuation?	4 There are no errors.	3 There are few errors.	2 There are some errors.	1 There are many errors.

Guidelines for Writing a Biography

- ► Research the person's life. Use at least two sources.
- ► Take notes about important facts, dates, places, events, and accomplishments in the person's life.
- ► Use your notes to organize important events in the person's life in sequence on a time line.
- ► Write an interesting beginning for your biography. You may want to tell an anecdote or repeat a famous quotation about the person.
- ► Write about the events in chronological order. Include important dates and time-order words.
- ► Focus on telling about events that best reveal the person's character or lifetime achievements.
- ► Leave out minor events or details that don't greatly affect the person's life.
- ► End by summarizing why the person is remembered.

Writing Traits Rubric
Biography

Use this rubric to evaluate your draft. Circle a number to rate your writing, trait by trait. Then revise to improve your score.

Writing Traits	Score 4	Score 3	Score 2	Score 1
✔ **Ideas** Did I choose important and interesting events from the person's life?	**4** I chose many important and interesting events.	**3** I chose some important and interesting events.	**2** I chose few important and interesting events.	**1** I chose no important and interesting events.
✔ **Organization** Did I put events in the right sequence?	**4** All events are in the right sequence.	**3** Most events are in the right sequence.	**2** Some events are in the right sequence.	**1** Few or no events are in the right sequence.
✔ **Sentence Fluency** Did I keep my verbs in the same tense?	**4** My verb tenses never change.	**3** My verb tenses rarely change.	**2** My verb tenses sometimes change.	**1** My verb tenses often change.
✔ **Word Choice** Did I use dates or time-order words to show the sequence of events?	**4** I used many dates or time-order words to show sequence.	**3** I used some dates or time-order words to show sequence.	**2** I used few dates or time-order words to show sequence.	**1** I used no dates or time-order words to show sequence.
✔ **Voice** Is my writing clear and informative?	**4** My writing is always clear and informative.	**3** My writing is usually clear and informative.	**2** My writing is sometimes clear and informative.	**1** My writing is very unclear.
✔ **Conventions** Did I use correct spelling, grammar, and punctuation?	**4** There are no errors.	**3** There are few errors.	**2** There are some errors.	**1** There are many errors.

Guidelines for Writing a Fictional Narrative

- Tell the events in order, with a clear beginning, middle, and end.
- Write an opening that introduces the setting and characters.
- Describe the setting by telling where and when the story takes place.
- Create interesting, believable characters.
- Include sensory details to describe the setting and characters.
- Develop an engaging plot that includes a conflict, a climax, and a resolution.
- Include details and dialogue to bring characters, setting, and events to life.
- Write an ending that resolves the conflict and wraps up the story.

Writing Traits Rubric
Fictional Narrative

Use this rubric to evaluate your draft. Circle a number to rate your writing, trait by trait. Then revise to improve your score.

Writing Traits	Score 4	Score 3	Score 2	Score 1
✔ **Ideas** Does my narrative have characters, a setting, and a plot with a conflict, climax, and resolution?	**4** My narrative has characters, a setting, and a plot with a conflict, climax, and resolution.	**3** My narrative has characters and a plot with a conflict and resolution.	**2** My narrative has characters and a plot with a conflict.	**1** My narrative has a plot.
✔ **Organization** Is the order of events in my narrative clear?	**4** The order of all events is clear.	**3** The order of most events is clear.	**2** The order of some events is clear.	**1** The order of events is not clear.
✔ **Sentence Fluency** Did I vary the position of adjectives in my sentences?	**4** There is great variety in the position of adjectives in my sentences.	**3** There is some variety in the position of adjectives in my sentences.	**2** There is little variety in the position of adjectives in my sentences.	**1** There is no variety in the position of adjectives in my sentences.
✔ **Word Choice** Did I include exact, descriptive words?	**4** I used plenty of exact, descriptive words.	**3** I used some exact, descriptive words.	**2** I used few exact, descriptive words.	**1** I used no exact, descriptive words.
✔ **Voice** Did I show a strong interest in my characters and events?	**4** I showed a strong interest in my characters and events.	**3** I showed some interest in my characters and events.	**2** I showed little interest in my characters and events.	**1** I showed no interest in my characters and events.
✔ **Conventions** Did I use correct spelling, grammar, and punctuation?	**4** There are no errors.	**3** There are few errors.	**2** There are some errors.	**1** There are many errors.

Guidelines for Writing a Summary

- Use your own words.
- Briefly sum up the important ideas and important events.
- Organize the ideas and events in a logical order.
- Include main ideas and key names, dates, and places that are important to understanding the selection.
- Leave out the unimportant details and minor events.
- Make your summary brief.

Writing Traits Rubric Writing a Summary

Use this rubric to evaluate your draft. Circle a number to rate your writing, trait by trait. Then revise to improve your score.

Writing Traits	Score 4	Score 3	Score 2	Score 1
✔ **Ideas** Did I include the important ideas or events?	**4** I included all the important ideas or events.	**3** I included most of the important ideas or events.	**2** I included some important and some unimportant ideas or events.	**1** I included few important and many unimportant ideas or events.
✔ **Organization** Did I summarize ideas or events in a logical order?	**4** All the information in my summary is in a logical order.	**3** Most of the information in my summary is in a logical order.	**2** Some of the information in my summary is in a logical order.	**1** The information in my summary is not in a logical order.
✔ **Sentence Fluency** Did I avoid writing choppy or repetitious sentences?	**4** My writing includes no choppy or repetitious sentences.	**3** My writing contains one choppy or repetitious sentence.	**2** My writing contains few choppy or repetitious sentences.	**1** My writing contains many choppy or repetitious sentences.
✔ **Word Choice** Did I use exact nouns and verbs?	**4** I used many exact nouns and verbs.	**3** I used some exact nouns and verbs.	**2** I used few exact nouns and verbs.	**1** I used no exact nouns and verbs.
✔ **Voice** Did I restate the author's ideas in my own words?	**4** Every sentence is in my own words.	**3** Almost every sentence is in my own words.	**2** I copied a few sentences.	**1** I copied many sentences.
✔ **Conventions** Did I use correct spelling, grammar, and punctuation?	**4** There are no errors.	**3** There are few errors.	**2** There are some errors.	**1** There are many errors.

Guidelines for Writing Instructions

- Before writing, review each step by doing the activity yourself, if possible. Make notes about each step.
- Write a title that describes what the instructions are for.
- List any materials that are needed.
- Explain each step clearly and in order.
- Use order words such as *first*, *next*, *then*, *before*, *after*, and *finally* to help readers follow the sequence.
- Include diagrams or pictures if they help to make the steps clearer.

Writing Traits Rubric Instructions

Use this rubric to evaluate your draft. Circle a number to rate your writing, trait by trait. Then revise to improve your score.

Writing Traits	Score 4	Score 3	Score 2	Score 1
✔ **Ideas** Did I include a title, list the materials that are needed, and explain every step?	**4** I included a title, listed all the materials needed, and explained every step.	**3** I listed some materials needed and explained every step.	**2** I explained most steps.	**1** I explained some but not all steps.
✔ **Organization** Did I put all the steps of the activity in order?	**4** I put all the steps of the activity in order.	**3** I put most of the steps of the activity in order.	**2** I put some of the steps of the activity in order.	**1** I put few or none of the steps of the activity in order.
✔ **Sentence Fluency** Did I vary the way I start my sentences?	**4** There is good variety in the way I start my sentences.	**3** There is some variety in the way I start my sentences.	**2** There is little variety in the way I start my sentences.	**1** There is no variety in the way I start my sentences.
✔ **Word Choice** Did I use order words to clarify the order of steps?	**4** I used order words in all steps of the activity.	**3** I used order words in most steps of the activity.	**2** I used order words in some steps of the activity.	**1** I did not use any order words.
✔ **Voice** Did I use clear, simple language that my readers will understand?	**4** My language is very clear and simple.	**3** My language is mostly clear and simple.	**2** My language is somewhat clear and simple.	**1** My language is not clear and simple.
✔ **Conventions** Did I use correct spelling, grammar, and punctuation?	**4** There are no errors.	**3** There are few errors.	**2** There are some errors.	**1** There are many errors.

Guidelines for Writing a Journal Entry

- Write the date at the beginning. Include the time if you will be writing more than one entry on the same day. Remember to use a colon to separate the hours and minutes.
- If you are traveling, you might also include the location.
- Write in the first person, using the pronouns *I*, *me*, *my*, *mine*, *we*, and *our*.
- Narrate or describe the day's events or experiences.
- Include personal thoughts, feelings, reactions, questions, and ideas.
- Use details to describe what you saw or experienced.

Writing Traits Rubric Journal Entry

Use this rubric to evaluate your draft. Circle a number to rate your writing, trait by trait. Then revise to improve your score.

Writing Traits	Score 4	Score 3	Score 2	Score 1
✔ **Ideas** Did I record thoughts and feelings that were part of my experience?	**4** I recorded many of my thoughts and feelings.	**3** I recorded some of my thoughts and feelings.	**2** I recorded a few of my thoughts and feelings.	**1** I didn't record any of my thoughts and feelings.
✔ **Organization** Did I include a date and information in a logical order?	**4** I included a date and information in a logical order.	**3** I included a date and some information in a logical order.	**2** I included some information in a logical order.	**1** I did not include a date or information in a logical order.
✔ **Sentence Fluency** Did I vary my sentence types and lengths?	**4** There is excellent variety in my sentence types and lengths.	**3** There is good variety in my sentence types and lengths.	**2** There is little variety in my sentence types and lengths.	**1** There is no variety in my sentence types and lengths.
✔ **Word Choice** Did I create vivid details by using many adjectives?	**4** I included many adjectives in my details.	**3** I included some adjectives in my details.	**2** I included few adjectives in my details.	**1** I included no adjectives in my details.
✔ **Voice** Did I write in the first person?	**4** I wrote in the first person all of the time.	**3** I wrote in the first person most of the time.	**2** I wrote in the first person a few times.	**1** I did not write in the first person.
✔ **Conventions** Did I use correct spelling, grammar, and punctuation?	**4** There are no errors.	**3** There are few errors.	**2** There are some errors.	**1** There are many errors.

Guidelines for Writing a Persuasive Speech

- Decide who your audience will be.
- Write an introduction that gets your audience's attention. Identify your audience, and explain your purpose or goal in speaking to them.
- Develop support for your position in the body of your speech. Give your reasons and include evidence to explain them.
- Order your reasons from least to most important, from most to least important, or in another logical order.
- Include a variety of sentence types and lengths in your speech. Doing so will help hold your audience's attention.
- Write a conclusion that sums or restates your purpose and your main points.

Delivering Your Speech

- Try to not read your speech word for word. Write an outline on note cards or highlight your important points in your paper so that they will stand out when you glance down.
- Speak loudly enough for your audience to hear.
- Let the pitch and tone of your voice reflect your message.
- Emphasize your most important points, to help your audience follow your main idea.
- Use visuals, whether physical or electronic, if they will make your speech more convincing.
- Use a minimum of gestures, using them to explain visuals or to stress your important points.

Writing Traits Rubric
Persuasive Speech

Use this rubric to evaluate your draft. Circle a number to rate your writing, trait by trait. Then revise to improve your score.

Writing Traits	Score 4	Score 3	Score 2	Score 1
✔ **Ideas** Did I include convincing reasons in my persuasive speech?	**4** I included plenty of convincing reasons.	**3** I included some convincing reasons.	**2** I included one convincing reason.	**1** I included no convincing reasons.
✔ **Organization** Did I state my purpose or goal at the beginning and the end of the speech?	**4** I stated my purpose or goal at the beginning and the end of the speech.	**3** I stated my purpose or goal at the beginning of the speech.	**2** I stated my purpose or goal at the end of the speech.	**1** I did not state my purpose or goal at all.
✔ **Sentence Fluency** Did I vary my sentence types and lengths?	**4** There is excellent variety in my sentence types and lengths.	**3** There is good variety in my sentence types and lengths.	**2** There is little variety in my sentence types and lengths.	**1** There is no variety in my sentence types and lengths.
✔ **Word Choice** Did I use powerful, emotional words to make my point?	**4** I used many powerful, emotional words.	**3** I used some powerful, emotional words.	**2** I used few powerful, emotional words.	**1** I used no powerful, emotional words.
✔ **Voice** Is my personality strongly expressed in my speech?	**4** My personality is strongly expressed in my speech.	**3** My personality is somewhat expressed in my speech.	**2** My personality is weakly expressed in my speech.	**1** My personality is not expressed in my speech.
✔ **Conventions** Did I use correct spelling, grammar, and punctuation?	**4** There are no errors.	**3** There are few errors.	**2** There are some errors.	**1** There are many errors.

Guidelines for Writing Problem-Solution Essay

- Write an introductory sentence that tells who or what you are writing about.
- Include two or three paragraphs.
- Clearly explain the problem in the first paragraph.
- Describe the solution in the following paragraphs. Include details that explain more about the solution and how to reach it.
- End your essay with a strong concluding sentence about the outcome.

Writing Traits Rubric
Problem-Solution Essay

Use this rubric to evaluate your draft. Circle a number to rate your writing, trait by trait. Then revise to improve your score.

Writing Traits	Score 4	Score 3	Score 2	Score 1
✔ **Ideas** Did I include clear details to explain the problem and the solution?	**4** I used plenty of clear details to fully explain the problem and the solution.	**3** I used almost enough clear details to explain the problem and the solution.	**2** I used few details to explain the problem and the solution.	**1** I used no details to explain the problem and the solution.
✔ **Organization** Did I present information in the correct order: problem, solution, and conclusion?	**4** I presented all information in the correct order.	**3** I presented most information in the correct order.	**2** I presented some information in the correct order.	**1** I did not present information in the correct order.
✔ **Sentence Fluency** Did I combine sentences to make my writing flow smoothly?	**4** I combined many sentences to make my writing flow smoothly.	**3** I combined some sentences to make my writing flow smoothly.	**2** I combined few sentences to make my writing flow smoothly.	**1** I did not combine sentences and my writing does not flow smoothly.
✔ **Word Choice** Did I use precise nouns and verbs?	**4** I used many precise nouns and verbs.	**3** I used some precise nouns and verbs.	**2** I used few precise nouns and verbs.	**1** I did not use precise nouns and verbs.
✔ **Voice** Does my writing show how I feel about my subject?	**4** My writing frequently shows how I feel about my subject.	**3** My writing sometimes shows how I feel about my subject.	**2** My writing rarely shows how I feel about my subject.	**1** My writing does not show how I feel about my subject.
✔ **Conventions** Did I use correct spelling, grammar, and punctuation?	**4** There are no errors.	**3** There are few errors.	**2** There are some errors.	**1** There are many errors.

Guidelines for Writing an Explanation

- Pick a topic you know well or would like to know about.
- If you have chosen an unfamiliar topic, do any necessary research before you begin your draft.
- Begin with a topic sentence that tells what you will explain.
- Provide specific examples or steps that explain your topic.
- Include details that give more information about each example or step.
- Organize the information in a logical order. Group details with the examples or steps they support.
- Keep your language simple and clear. Define terms likely to be unfamiliar and all technical terms the first time you use them.

Writing Traits Rubric Explanation

Use this rubric to evaluate your draft. Circle a number to rate your writing, trait by trait. Then revise to improve your score.

Writing Traits	Score 4	Score 3	Score 2	Score 1
✔ **Ideas** Did I include detailed steps or examples?	4 I included plenty of detailed steps or examples.	3 I included some detailed steps or examples.	2 I included few steps or examples.	1 I did not include steps or examples.
✔ **Organization** Did I put the information in a logical order?	4 All of my information is in a logical order.	3 Most of my information is in a logical order.	2 Some of my information is in a logical order.	1 None of my information is in a logical order.
✔ **Sentence Fluency** Do my sentences flow smoothly?	4 All of my sentences flow smoothly.	3 Most of my sentences flow smoothly.	2 Some of my sentences flow smoothly.	1 Few or none of my sentences flow smoothly.
✔ **Word Choice** Did I use transition words or phrases to help organize the information?	4 I used many transitions words or phrases.	3 I used some transitions words or phrases.	2 I used few transitions words or phrases.	1 I used no transitions words or phrases.
✔ **Voice** Did I use clear, simple language that my readers will understand?	4 My language is very clear and simple.	3 My language is mostly clear and simple.	2 My language is somewhat clear and simple.	1 My language is not clear and simple.
✔ **Conventions** Did I use correct spelling, grammar, and punctuation?	4 There are no errors.	3 There are few errors.	2 There are some errors.	1 There are many errors.

Guidelines for Writing a Compare-Contrast Paragraph

- Choose a subject that can be compared and contrasted.
- Create a Venn diagram to list likenesses and differences.
- In the opening sentence, clearly state the subject to be compared and contrasted.
- In the supporting sentences, compare and contrast similar kinds of details in a clear manner.
- Explain similarities and differences in an order that makes sense.

Writing Traits Rubric
Compare-Contrast Paragraph

Use this rubric to evaluate your draft. Circle a number to rate your writing, trait by trait. Then revise to improve your score.

Writing Traits	Score 4	Score 3	Score 2	Score 1
✔ **Ideas** Did I give examples of similarities and differences?	**4** I gave several examples of similarities and differences.	**3** I gave a couple of examples of similarities and differences.	**2** I gave one example of a similarity and a difference.	**1** I gave no examples of similarities and differences.
✔ **Organization** Did I compare and contrast similar details in an order that makes sense?	**4** I compared and contrasted all similar details in an order that makes sense.	**3** I compared and contrasted some similar details in an order that makes sense.	**2** I compared and contrasted a few similar details in an order that makes sense.	**1** I did not compare and contrast similar details in an order that makes sense.
✔ **Sentence Fluency** Do my sentences flow smoothly?	**4** All of my sentences flow smoothly.	**3** Most of my sentences flow smoothly.	**2** Some of my sentences flow smoothly.	**1** Few or none of my sentences flow smoothly.
✔ **Word Choice** Did I use exact adverbs to make details more vivid?	**4** I used many exact adverbs.	**3** I used some exact adverbs.	**2** I used few exact adverbs.	**1** I used no exact adverbs.
✔ **Voice** Did I show my interest in the topic?	**4** My interest in the topic is very clear.	**3** My interest in the topic is mostly clear.	**2** My interest in the topic is somewhat clear.	**1** My interest in the topic is not clear.
✔ **Conventions** Did I use correct spelling, grammar, and punctuation?	**4** There are no errors.	**3** There are few errors.	**2** There are some errors.	**1** There are many errors.

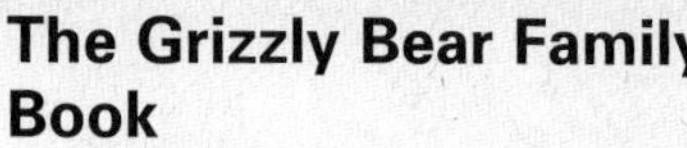

Guidelines for Writing an Opinion Composition

- Begin by expressing a strong statement of your opinion.
- Give several strong reasons for your opinion in the paragraphs that follow.
- Include facts, examples, and other supporting evidence to support and explain the reasons for your opinion.
- Organize your reasons from most to least important, from least to most important, or in another logical order.
- Include a strong conclusion that restates your opinion.

Writing Traits Rubric Opinion Composition

Use this rubric to evaluate your draft. Circle a number to rate your writing, trait by trait. Then revise to improve your score.

Writing Traits	Score 4	Score 3	Score 2	Score 1
✔ **Ideas** Did I include strong reasons for my opinion?	4 I included plenty of strong reasons for my opinion.	3 I included almost enough strong reasons for my opinion.	2 I included few strong reasons for my opinion.	1 I did not include any strong reasons for my opinion.
✔ **Organization** Did I put my opinion statement at the beginning and at the end?	4 I put my opinion statement at the beginning and at the end.	3 I put my opinion statement at the beginning but not at the end.	2 I put my opinion statement at the end but not at the beginning.	1 I did not write an opinion statement at all.
✔ **Sentence Fluency** Do my sentences flow smoothly?	4 All of my sentences flow smoothly.	3 Most of my sentences flow smoothly.	2 Some of my sentences flow smoothly.	1 Few or none of my sentences flow smoothly.
✔ **Word Choice** Did I avoid the use of double negatives?	4 I did not use double negatives.	3 I used a double negative.	2 I used a few double negatives.	1 I used several double negatives.
✔ **Voice** Is my personality strongly expressed in my opinion?	4 My personality is strongly expressed in my opinion.	3 My personality is somewhat expressed in my opinion.	2 My personality is weakly expressed in my opinion.	1 My personality is not expressed in my opinion.
✔ **Conventions** Did I use correct spelling, grammar, and punctuation?	4 There are no errors.	3 There are few errors.	2 There are some errors.	1 There are many errors.

Guidelines for Writing a Compare/Contrast Essay

- Choose two subjects that have likenesses and differences that you can compare.
- Create a Venn diagram to list likenesses and differences.
- In the opening paragraph, clearly state the subjects that are being compared and contrasted.
- In the paragraphs that follow, compare and contrast similar kinds of features in a clear manner.
- Organize ideas by grouping details that describe the similarities and details that describe the differences in separate paragraphs.
- Include clue words to help the reader identify likenesses and differences.

Writing Traits Rubric
Compare/Contrast Essay

Use this rubric to evaluate your draft. Circle a number to rate your writing, trait by trait. Then revise to improve your score.

Writing Traits	Score 4	Score 3	Score 2	Score 1
✔ **Ideas** Did I give many examples of similarities and differences?	**4** I gave many examples of similarities and differences.	**3** I gave a few examples of similarities and differences.	**2** I gave one example of a similarity and a difference.	**1** I gave no examples of similarities and differences.
✔ **Organization** Did I put details that compare and details that contrast into separate paragraphs?	**4** I put all details into separate paragraphs.	**3** I put some details into separate paragraphs.	**2** I put a few details into separate paragraphs.	**1** I did not put details into separate paragraphs.
✔ **Sentence Fluency** Did I combine sentences to make my writing flow smoothly?	**4** I combined many sentences to make my writing flow smoothly.	**3** I combined some sentences to make my writing flow smoothly.	**2** I combined few sentences to make my writing flow smoothly.	**1** I did not combine sentences and my writing does not flow smoothly.
✔ **Word Choice** Did I use clue words that signal similarities and differences?	**4** I used many clue words that signal similarities and differences.	**3** I used some clue words that signal similarities and differences.	**2** I used few clue words that signal similarities and differences.	**1** I used no clue words that signal similarities and differences.
✔ **Voice** Is my writing clear and informative?	**4** My writing is always clear and informative.	**3** My writing is usually clear and informative.	**2** My writing is sometimes clear and informative.	**1** My writing is very unclear.
✔ **Conventions** Did I use correct spelling, grammar, and punctuation?	**4** There are no errors.	**3** There are few errors.	**2** There are some errors.	**1** There are many errors.

Guidelines for Writing on Demand

- Read the prompt, or question, carefully.
- Look for key words, or clues, in the prompt that tell you what to focus on. Are you summarizing or expressing an opinion? Are you writing about a character?
- Be aware of how much time you have to answer the prompt. Divide the time: time to think about and organize your response quickly, and time to write and edit your work.
- Before you write, think back to the passage or reread it with the question in mind.
- Make notes in an organized way. Draw a chart if you need to.
- Look at your notes. Which details or thoughts are most important? Be sure to include those first.
- Begin your answer or response by restating the question.
- As you write, use clear, exact language. Stay on the topic.
- When you finish, look back over your work and correct any mistakes.

Writing Traits Rubric
Persuasive Letter

Write a letter persuading a family member to let you take a course sponsored by a local nature club. The course involves spending a week in the forest, learning how to live off the land. Include reasons and supporting details and address any objections you think will be raised.

Writing Traits	Score 4	Score 3	Score 2	Score 1
✔ **Ideas** Did I include convincing reasons in my persuasive letter?	**4** I included plenty of convincing reasons.	**3** I included some convincing reasons.	**2** I included one convincing reason.	**1** I included no convincing reasons.
✔ **Organization** Did I respond to all parts of the prompt?	**4** I responded to all parts of the prompt.	**3** I responded to some parts of the prompt.	**2** I responded to one part of the prompt.	**1** I did not respond to any part of the prompt.
✔ **Sentence Fluency** Did I vary my sentence types and lengths?	**4** There is excellent variety in my sentence types and lengths.	**3** There is good variety in my sentence types and lengths.	**2** There is little variety in my sentence types and lengths.	**1** There is no variety in my sentence types and lengths.
✔ **Word Choice** Did I use key words from the prompt?	**4** I used all key words from the prompt.	**3** I used some key words from the prompt.	**2** I used few key words from the prompt.	**1** I used no key words from the prompt.
✔ **Voice** Did I write in a tone that fits my readers?	**4** My entire letter has a tone that fits my readers.	**3** Most of my letter has a tone that fits my readers.	**2** Some of my letter has a tone that fits my readers.	**1** The tone of my letter does not fit my readers.
✔ **Conventions** Did I use correct spelling, grammar, and punctuation?	**4** There are no errors.	**3** There are few errors.	**2** There are some errors.	**1** There are many errors.

Writing Traits Rubric
Fictional Narrative

Imagine that you have spent a week in the wilderness. Like Sam Gribley, you encountered different kinds of animals and learned things by observing them. Write a narrative about your week in the wilderness and the lessons you learned.

Writing Traits	Score 4	Score 3	Score 2	Score 1
✔ **Ideas** Does my narrative include key words from the prompt?	**4** My narrative includes all the key words from the prompt.	**3** My narrative includes some of the key words from the prompt.	**2** My narrative includes one key word from the prompt.	**1** My narrative includes none of the key words from the prompt.
✔ **Organization** Did I respond to all parts of the prompt?	**4** I responded to all parts of the prompt.	**3** I responded to some parts of the prompt.	**2** I responded to one part of the prompt.	**1** I did not respond to any part of the prompt.
✔ **Sentence Fluency** Did I avoid sentence fragments in my writing?	**4** There are no sentence fragments in my writing.	**3** There are few sentence fragments in my writing.	**2** There are some sentence fragments in my writing.	**1** There are many sentence fragments in my writing.
✔ **Word Choice** Did I use exact, descriptive words in my narrative?	**4** I used many exact, descriptive words in my narrative.	**3** I used some exact, descriptive words in my narrative.	**2** I used few exact, descriptive words in my narrative.	**1** I used no exact, descriptive words in my narrative.
✔ **Voice** Does my writing show my feelings and personality?	**4** My writing shows my feelings and personality very well.	**3** My writing shows my feelings and personality well.	**2** My writing shows my feelings and personality somewhat.	**1** My writing does not show my feelings and personality.
✔ **Conventions** Did I use correct spelling, grammar, and punctuation?	**4** There are no errors.	**3** There are few errors.	**2** There are some errors.	**1** There are many errors.